THE BEDFORD SERIES IN HISTORY AND CULTURE

Defending Slavery

Proslavery Thought in the Old South

A BRIEF HISTORY WITH DOCUMENTS

Related Titles in
THE BEDFORD SERIES IN HISTORY AND CULTURE
Advisory Editors: Lynn Hunt, *University of California, Los Angeles*
David W. Blight, *Yale University*
Bonnie G. Smith, *Rutgers University*
Natalie Zemon Davis, *Princeton University*
Ernest R. May, *Harvard University*

THE BEDFORD SERIES IN HISTORY AND CULTURE

Defending Slavery

Proslavery Thought in the Old South

A BRIEF HISTORY WITH DOCUMENTS

Paul Finkelman

University of Tulsa College of Law

BEDFORD/ST. MARTIN'S   Boston ♦ New York

Dedicated to Florence and Julius Finkelman, with much love.

For Bedford/St. Martin's

Publisher for History: Patricia A. Rossi
Director of Development for History: Jane Knetzger
Developmental Editor: Michael Weber
Associate Editor, Publishing Services: Maria Teresa Burwell
Production Supervisor: Jennifer Wetzel
Marketing Manager: Jenna Bookin Barry
Project Management: Books By Design, Inc.
Text Design: Claire Seng-Niemoeller
Photo Research: Alice Lundoff
Indexer: Books By Design, Inc.
Cover Design: Billy Boardman
Cover Photos: (left to right) *James Henry Hammond,* from the original in the South Carolina Library, University of South Carolina; *John C. Calhoun,* Culver Pictures; *Roger B. Taney,* Culver Pictures.
Composition: Stratford Publishing Services, Inc.
Printing and Binding: Haddon Craftsmen, an RR Donnelley & Sons Company

President: Joan E. Feinberg
Editorial Director: Denise B. Wydra
Director of Marketing: Karen R. Melton
Director of Editing, Design, and Production: Marcia Cohen
Manager, Publishing Services: Emily Berleth

Library of Congress Control Number: 2002111605

Manufactured in the United States of America.

8   7   6
f   e

For information, write: Bedford/St. Martin's, 75 Arlington Street, Boston, MA 02116 (617-399-4000)

ISBN-10: 0-312-13327-8
ISBN-13: 978-0-312-13327-6

Foreword

The Bedford Series in History and Culture is designed so that readers can study the past as historians do.

The historian's first task is finding the evidence. Documents, letters, memoirs, interviews, pictures, movies, novels, or poems can provide facts and clues. Then the historian questions and compares the sources. There is more to do than in a courtroom, for hearsay evidence is welcome, and the historian is usually looking for answers beyond act and motive. Different views of an event may be as important as a single verdict. How a story is told may yield as much information as what it says.

Along the way the historian seeks help from other historians and perhaps from specialists in other disciplines. Finally, it is time to write, to decide on an interpretation and how to arrange the evidence for readers.

Each book in this series contains an important historical document or group of documents, each document a witness from the past and open to interpretation in different ways. The documents are combined with some element of historical narrative—an introduction or a biographical essay, for example—that provides students with an analysis of the primary source material and important background information about the world in which it was produced.

Each book in the series focuses on a specific topic within a specific historical period. Each provides a basis for lively thought and discussion about several aspects of the topic and the historian's role. Each is short enough (and inexpensive enough) to be a reasonable one-week assignment in a college course. Whether as classroom or personal reading, each book in the series provides firsthand experience of the challenge—and fun—of discovering, recreating, and interpreting the past.

Lynn Hunt
David W. Blight
Bonnie G. Smith
Natalie Zemon Davis
Ernest R. May

Preface

American slavery was destroyed nearly a century and a half ago by a combination of presidential order, military success, legislative action, constitutional enactment, and the individual and collective acts of tens of thousands of people held in bondage. But the end of slavery did not bring an end to the pain it caused, nor did emancipation eliminate slavery's cultural and intellectual legacy. To this day Americans argue about the impact of slavery on our culture, our economy, our political structure, and our history. Throughout the nation there are new museums dedicated wholly or in part to telling the story of slavery, antislavery, and the Underground Railroad. Movies, popular novels, and television often focus on slavery. In recent years American icons—most notably Thomas Jefferson—have been reevaluated in light of their involvement with slavery. As this book goes to press, Americans are being asked to consider whether the nation should pay reparations or in some other way compensate the descendants of slaves. Whatever the outcome of these conversations, the issue of slavery will remain vital to the essence of who we are as a people and what we stand for as a nation.

There will be, however, few monuments or museums dedicated to most of the writers in this book, those who defended slavery. These authors differed in many ways. Some were devoutly religious, while others rejected the Bible and organized religion itself. Some were skeptical even about the existence of God. Some were, for their day, cutting-edge scientists, while others had little regard for science or what it might teach. Some authors were antagonistic to democracy and equality, and defended slavery from an aristocratic perspective. Others, like Senator James Henry Hammond, argued that democracy was only possible if slavery was present to provide a natural "mudsill" on which the rest of society could be built.

Although their defenses and ideologies varied, all these authors agreed that American slavery was an essential form of race control. Most argued that slavery was a positive good and that it was a necessary, even essential, institution for a successful society. They were certain that whites constituted a superior race and that blacks were members of an inferior race. This was a central theme of their proslavery arguments.

The goal of this volume is to enable students to read the best and most interesting Southern defenses of slavery. With a few exceptions, these were written in the last decade or so before the Civil War, when the Southern defense of slavery had reached its most mature and sophisticated form. They were written mainly by elite, or at least well-educated, men. This should not be surprising. Less well-educated, poorer Southerners were unlikely to write and publish their views on slavery. Similarly, in a highly patriarchal culture, few women wrote about public issues in public forums. As is often the case, elite leaders articulated the ideas of the society and published them. Thus, for better or worse, the majority of the authors in this volume were lawyers, politicians, physicians, and other well-educated Old South leaders. From our perspective, we may think of these proslavery theorists as somewhat monstrous and out of touch with the reality of human equality. But, in fact, they were men of their times—and often well meaning within the constraints of their culture, their social goals, and, always, their racial assumptions.

An understanding of the defense of slavery is necessary to place America's greatest social and military conflict—the Civil War—in some perspective. Why did the Confederate states fight so hard, and so long, in such a losing struggle against such overwhelming odds? One answer is that white Southerners could not conceive of a world in which slavery did not exist. As Alexander Stephens, the Confederate vice president noted, slavery was the "cornerstone" of the would-be Southern nation. The war was, from the beginning, about slavery, and by the end it was only about slavery. White Confederates fought so hard to preserve slavery because they had so deeply internalized the proslavery ideology that they could not conceive of a world in which there was no slavery and in which African Americans were free, and perhaps enfranchised, citizens.

We must understand these defenses of slavery to understand fully American slavery, American race relations, American history, and modern American culture. Race relations remain the great social and cultural issue of American society. The struggle for equality remains the great American dilemma. The solution to that dilemma is complicated by the heritage of slavery and of proslavery thought, which, in odd and sometimes surprising ways, remains with us long after the last slaves and the last masters have died. Perhaps only when we fully understand the nature of proslavery thought can we finally come to terms with its legacy.

THE STRUCTURE OF THIS VOLUME

The introduction to this book sets the stage for a fuller understanding of the proslavery argument. First, I discuss *why* Southerners felt they had to defend slavery. While self-evident to today's students, the need for a defense was not self-evident to many people before the mid- or late eighteenth century. Up to that time slavery had been accepted as part of the human condition. Southerners were compelled to begin their defense of slavery only when large numbers of free people in America, Britain, and Western Europe reached the conclusion that slavery was fundamentally wrong on moral, political, or economic grounds—or all of these. Then I set out the overall nature and complexity of proslavery thought and place it in the context of the founding of America and the subsequent antebellum crisis.

The documents themselves are arranged topically, and chronologically within each topic. They come from a variety of sources, including writings and addresses by eminent thinkers and political leaders (among them an excerpt from Thomas Jefferson's *Notes on the State of Virginia,* two speeches delivered on the floor of the U.S. Senate, and the address by Confederate Vice President Stephens noted above); judicial decisions; articles from scientific and medical journals; biblical and theological disquisitions; and a poem by a proslavery South Carolina Unionist.

Each document is introduced with a headnote, and questions for consideration appear near the end of the volume. The headnotes and questions are designed to guide students to and through the material without spoon-feeding it to them. Illustrations of some of the proslavery theorists and their books—as well as of Dred Scott and his wife, Harriet—will, I hope, humanize those who took part in the debate. The slavery chronology, which precedes the questions for consideration, helps place the proslavery arguments in the context of the relevant larger political issues of the period. Finally, I include a selected bibliography of secondary material to guide students to more elaborate discussions of proslavery thought.

ACKNOWLEDGMENTS

I have been working on this book for far longer than I would have liked. The University of Tulsa College of Law and Dean Martin H. Belsky provided me with research time and support for the completion of this book. My administrative assistant at Tulsa Law School, Rita Langford, cheerfully helped with many of the technical aspects of putting this book together. Our fabulous Law Library staff, especially Faye Hadley, Kathy Kane, and Melanie Nelson, and our interlibrary loan guru, Carol Arnold, found all sorts of obscure books and pamphlets for me. Over the years I have had productive conversations with numerous colleagues about the nature of proslavery thought. I owe special thanks to Douglas Ambrose, Richard Aynes, David Cobin, Robert Cottrol, David Brion Davis, Rob Forbes, John Hope Franklin, Peter Onuf, Judy Schafer, Ricki Shine, Peter Wallenstein, and Cary Wintz. I also benefited from the comments of the readers Bedford/ St. Martin's engaged to review the manuscript: W. Fitzhugh Brundage, University of North Carolina at Chapel Hill; Stanley Engerman, University of Rochester; Matthew Guterl, Washington State University; and Clyde N. Wilson, University of South Carolina; as well as Professors Wallenstein (Virginia Tech) and Wintz (Texas Southern University). Gillian Berchowitz read the introduction with a sharp eye and a sharper mind. My editors at Bedford/St. Martin's, Patricia Rossi and Michael Weber, did what good editors always do: they pushed and prodded me and helped make the book much better than it would have been without their advice and counsel.

Paul Finkelman

Contents

PART ONE

Introduction:
Defending Slavery

At first glance, the very presence of slavery in the early United States seems jarring. It is like a relic of an earlier age that somehow survived the American Revolution, despite the new nation's emphasis on natural rights and its assertion in the Declaration of Independence that "all Men are created equal." Slavery was an oddity that surely was in conflict with the professed political ideals of the nation. Slavery seemed to run counter to the evangelical Protestant faith that most white Americans shared before the Civil War. How could Americans believe in doing unto others as they would have done unto themselves, and still hold slaves? By the mid-nineteenth century, slavery appeared to contradict the notion of free labor pervading America at that time.

Slavery was also at odds with America's legal structures. It undermined the "more perfect Union"[1] created by the Constitution, and it seemed to be contrary to the nation's common-law traditions. The place of slavery in our political and constitutional structure was a significant issue at the Philadelphia convention in 1787.[2] The presence of slaves in the nation caused sharp debates over the nature of representation, and the demand of the Deep South for special protection of the African slave trade led to vitriolic arguments among the delegates.

1

The importance of slavery at the Constitutional Convention illustrated the cleavage between the slave South and what was emerging as the free North. The final document, the Constitution itself, supported slavery in a number of ways, as slavery was both protected by the Constitution and woven into the nation's constitutional fabric.[3]

By 1804, all of the states north of Virginia, Maryland, and Delaware had either ended slavery outright or had passed legislation to gradually abolish the institution. Thus, after 1804, slavery was peculiar to the South.[4] But despite its geographic isolation within the United States, the influence of slavery was felt nationally and internationally. It was recognized and protected by national laws and the Constitution and was not considered illegal under nineteenth-century notions of international law.[5] In the decades before the Civil War, the Supreme Court gave unambiguous support for slavery, although usually with sharp dissents from one or two justices who could not accept the majority view that slavery was imbedded in the Constitution.[6]

Slavery was in fact integral to American culture and politics. In part because of proslavery compromises at the Constitutional Convention, slaveowners were able to dominate all three branches of the national government from the inauguration of Thomas Jefferson in 1801 until the inauguration of Abraham Lincoln in 1861. During this sixty-year period, slaveowners held the presidency for forty-two years. Even when Northerners held high office, they were almost always open supporters of slavery, like Presidents Martin Van Buren, Franklin Pierce, and James Buchanan. Indeed, between 1801 and 1861, only one opponent of slavery—John Quincy Adams—served as president, and in his single term he had neither the clout nor the time to challenge the institution.

Despite the Southern dominance of the national government and the reluctance of most Northerners to support the abolitionist movement, slaveowners were constantly worried about slavery. Calling it "our peculiar institution," Southerners were fully aware of the contradictions and the inherent challenges slavery posed to American culture. They understood that many Americans were hostile to slavery. Moreover, the growth of the antislavery movement in Great Britain further unsettled them. Thus, as early as the Revolution, Southerners began to offer defenses of slavery. After the debates leading to the Missouri Compromise, these defenses intensified. By the eve of the Civil War, Southerners had developed a variety of defenses of their special institution.

NORTHERNERS, SOUTHERNERS, AND SLAVERY

Only a few Northerners defended slavery. The most common Northern discussion of slavery is what we might call "abstention." Northerners, especially Northern politicians, asserted that slavery was a "Southern problem" and that Northerners should leave the South alone. For example, at the Constitutional Convention, Roger Sherman rather naively declared that "the abolition of slavery seemed to be going on in the U.S." and if left alone, the "good sense of the several States" would soon put an end to all slavery in the country.[7] From the Constitutional Convention until the eve of the Civil War, other Northern politicians would make similar arguments, urging that the free states simply leave the South alone. This was not much of a defense of slavery, and it actually implied that slavery ought to be abolished some day. Nevertheless, most Southerners, at least until the late 1850s, appreciated the political value of such a position. Such attitudes kept the Democratic party together until 1860, when demands from most Southerners for affirmative protection of slavery in the territories tore that party apart.

Other Northerners argued that slavery was vital to the Northern economy. The Northern textile mill owners—the "Lords of the Loom," as their critics called them—also offered some support for slavery, on a purely practical level. They needed cotton for their mills, and they argued that Southern slavery was the best way to produce it. Some other Northerners argued that slave-produced products—cotton, sugar, rice, and tobacco—were vital to the national economy. At the Constitutional Convention, for example, Oliver Ellsworth of Connecticut, supporting the continuation of the African slave trade, refused to debate the "morality or wisdom of slavery" and simply asserted that "what enriches a part enriches the whole."[8] This was not a direct defense of slavery, but it was an argument that Southerners doubtless liked to hear. Finally, some Northerners joined in racist arguments about blacks that dovetailed with Southern arguments. However, such arguments from Northerners could cut against slavery as well as for it. An assertion that blacks were inferior could support the colonization of African Americans outside the United States, as well as slavery within the United States. Such arguments were also used to oppose the spread of slavery into the West, as some Northerners argued that the vast territories of the United States should become a "white man's" country.

Whatever their tone, Northern defenses of slavery were relatively insignificant for the development of proslavery thought. Thus, in this book, I have focused on the arguments of Southerners, mostly in the late antebellum period.

These defenses were based on religion, politics, economics, history, philosophy, expediency, and science. Most of all, they were rooted in racial theory. This makes sense because slavery in the United States was always racial slavery.

Most Northerners did not accept the explicitly proslavery arguments of their Southern neighbors. Northerners, in general, emphatically rejected the idea that the Bible was proslavery or that the economic value of slavery immunized it from political debate. Some of the proslavery arguments were deeply offensive to the North and influenced few people in the region. For example, by the eve of the Civil War, some Southerners argued that democracy in America was only possible because of slavery. Southerners often pointed to ancient Greece as the "perfect" democracy. It was also, as Southerners noted, a society where the majority of the inhabitants were slaves. Southerners also extolled the virtue of the Roman republic, with its huge slave population. The conclusion for them was that slavery and democratic government went hand in hand. Virtually all Northerners rejected such claims. The North, after all, provided concrete proof that freedom and democracy were not mutually exclusive.

Two arguments, however, resonated well with Northerners and helped to prevent a concerted movement toward emancipation until after the Civil War began. Northerners did not accept all of the conclusions or implications of these arguments, but many in the North accepted their major premises. The first of these defenses was rooted in political and constitutional theory; the second was predicated on racism.

The political/constitutional argument was simple and straightforward. Southerners argued that under the system of federalism and limited government created by the Constitution, the slave states had a right to regulate their own local—or, as they called them, "domestic"—institutions. Furthermore, the argument went, Congress had no power to interfere with slavery where it existed. Most Northern politicians, even those who fervently opposed slavery, accepted this theory of the Constitution. So too did many abolitionists, including William Lloyd Garrison and Wendell Phillips.

The proslavery constitutional theorists were not content with this area of agreement, however, and pushed the argument farther than most Northerners were willing to go. Not satisfied with preventing Congress from interfering with slavery, proslavery jurists, lawyers, and politicians argued that Congress could not ban slavery in the territories and that Congress had an affirmative duty both to protect slavery in the territories and to aid masters in recovering fugitive slaves in the North. They also argued that the free states had an affirmative duty to protect the right of masters to bring slaves with them when visiting or traveling through the free states. The South found support for some of these claims in Chief Justice Roger B. Taney's opinion in *Dred Scott v. Sandford* (1857) and in his concurring opinion in *Prigg v. Pennsylvania* (1842), as well as in opinions by other justices.[9] But these arguments went too far for most Northerners.

From the Revolution to the Civil War, Southerners grounded their defense of slavery on notions of race. Southerners argued that people of African ancestry were inherently biologically inferior and that the racial inferiority of blacks relegated them to permanently diminished status. Most Northern whites—even some opponents of slavery—accepted the Southern argument of racial inferiority, even if they did not accept the Southern conclusion: that this inferiority justified slavery. Indeed, some opponents of slavery argued that because of the racial inferiority of blacks, it was necessary to prevent the spread of slavery into the Western territories.

Because of their devotion to national harmony and preservation of the Union and their acceptance of most of the South's arguments about race, the majority of antebellum Northerners were willing to tolerate and accept the existence of slavery in the South. After all, the political crisis of the 1850s was mostly over the status of slavery and issues of race outside the South: fugitive slaves in the North, the rights of free blacks in the North after the *Dred Scott* decision in 1857, and the expansion of slavery into the territories. Ironically, long after slavery itself had been destroyed, proslavery theories of federalism and national power remained viable. So too did proslavery biblical, theological, and scientific arguments that have since been used to support race discrimination. Thus, even in the twenty-first century, Americans continue to be haunted by the impact of slavery.

This book is designed to help Americans today come to terms with one of the least attractive, yet most important, aspects of our intellectual history: the defenses of slavery articulated by the leading minds of the South between the Revolution and the end of the Civil War. More than a century and a quarter after the demise of slavery, the institution continues to haunt our nation and to challenge our culture. As this book goes to press, organizations and individuals are initiating legal action to consider the "damages" owed to the descendants of slaves. Debates over the place of slavery in our society, and its role in the nation's development, abound. Debates over affirmative action often begin or end with discussions of the role of slavery in creating America's racial divide. In the aftermath of the Supreme Court decision in *Bush v. Gore* (2000), some scholars noted that the electoral college itself was in part created to give the South extra influence in presidential elections based on its slave population.[10] Although a historical subject, slavery—and the defense of slavery—remains a vital issue for modern Americans.

This introduction explores the defenses of slavery common in the United States from the Revolution to the Civil War. Before turning to American slavery, however, it is useful to briefly examine the history of slavery on a worldwide scale. This examination helps us understand why American slaveowners felt a need to develop elaborate defenses of slavery.

THE LEGITIMACY OF SLAVERY IN EARLIER TIMES

The very fact that the Southern master class had to defend its ownership of human beings underscores the "peculiar" nature of American slavery. Masters in earlier times and in other places felt no need to defend the ownership of slaves. In most cultures and at most times, ruling classes accepted that others in society would be treated as inferiors and might be enslaved or oppressed without sparking any moral dilemmas. Plato's "Republic" would have been a slave-owning society, as would Aristotle's perfect state. Romans saw nothing peculiar about slavery and therefore saw no need to defend it. For Rome, as for most of the ancient world, "ideological openness was facilitated by the nakedness of the oppression and exploitation: no 'false consciousness' was necessary or possible."[11] Sir Thomas More's *Utopia,* written in England in 1516, described a slaveholding utopia.

Early Basis of Enslavement

In the classical world, early modern Europe, the Islamic world, much of pre-Columbian America, and most of Africa, the legitimacy of slavery often rested on notions of warfare. Under accepted rules of war, enemies captured in battle could be summarily killed. Those whose lives were spared were, in effect, "socially" or legally "dead" and thus might be enslaved.[12] This also held true for civilians captured in cities, especially if those cities had previously refused to surrender to the conquering army. Thus throughout these slaveholding societies, people from all walks of life might find themselves in some form of bondage if they ended up on the losing side of a military conflict. They might also regain their liberty through ransom or a reversal of military fortune.

Enslavement was also considered to be a legitimate punishment for various crimes. Such enslavement might be temporary or permanent, but it was enslavement nonetheless. Enslavement was also permissible for those who fell into debt. The debtor might sell himself into slavery to relieve his family of the burden of the debt, but he might also sell another family member.

These ideas about slavery affected who could become a slave and what treatment might be given to slaves. Because race or ethnicity was not a determining factor in enslavement due to war, crime, or debt, anyone in these societies might be a potential slave. Similarly, in most of these places, many slaves might potentially become free. In important ways, these notions of enslavement differentiated slavery in the Americas, and especially in the United States, from slavery in the rest of the world.

Who Could Be a Slave?

Before the 1500s and the European settlement of the Americas, slavery was only marginally based on race or ethnicity. Often, slaves were from another ethnic group: Greeks enslaved captured Persians; Romans enslaved captured Carthagenians. But by the same token, Persians enslaved Greeks and Carthagenians enslaved Romans. Although most classical slaves were "barbarians" from other cultures, members of the same ethnic and racial groups also enslaved each other. As the great classical scholar Moses Finley observed, "There were Greek slaves in Greece, Italian slaves in Rome."[13] Similarly, there were Chinese slaves in China, Egyptian slaves in Egypt, Hebrew slaves in ancient Israel, Babylonian slaves in Babylonia, and Russian slaves in Russia. Africans not only enslaved Africans of different ethnic groups, but they also enslaved members of their own communities. Europeans enslaved each other throughout the ancient world and well into the modern period.[14] The nature of slavery was further complicated by the possibility of manumission, through which slaves became free. Because slavery was not tied to race, manumission was easier, and in the ancient world and much of Africa, once free, former slaves and their children were often indistinguishable from other free people. In other words, anyone in the ancient world, Africa, the Islamic world, and early modern Europe might conceivably be a free person, a slave, a free person again, and perhaps even a slaveowner or slave trader, all within one lifetime.

Most strikingly, nowhere in the world before the sixteenth century was enslavement ever confined to a single race or ethnic group. In most premodern societies, enslavement might be the fate of anyone at any time.[15] Historian Carl Deglar notes that "there was a time in antiquity when anyone, regardless of nation, religion, or race, might be a slave."[16] Alan Watson has shown that most legal records of Roman slavery bear on the enslavement of elite slaves who were often from the same class and race as their masters,[17] thus reminding us that it was only in the New World, and particularly in what became the United States, that race became centrally connected to slavery.[18] Indeed, the most striking aspect of Roman slavery, in comparison with slavery in the United States, was the extent to which enslavement had nothing to do with race. Romans were more likely to enslave outsiders—Jews, Syrians, members of various Germanic tribes, Asians—but nevertheless, Romans also enslaved other Romans, and they knew that if captured by enemies, they might in turn be enslaved. Ultimately, what made the ancient world different from the New World, with regard to slavery, was the question of *who* could be enslaved. In the United States, only Africans and their descendants could be enslaved; in the ancient world, enslavement could happen to anyone.[19]

The biblical story of Joseph demonstrates the possibility in the ancient world that anyone could become a slave and that, simultaneously, it was not implausible to believe that someone could rise from enslavement to the highest level of political power. Joseph began his life as the spoiled favorite son of a wealthy Hebrew patriarch. He was sold into slavery by his jealous brothers, dropping dramatically in his social status. Later, he gained favor in the eyes of Pharaoh and was elevated to the highest office in Egypt. He functioned as the Pharaoh's right-hand man, even though he was both a former slave and a foreigner. Whether the story of Joseph is accurate or not (or even happened at all) is irrelevant. The point here is that no one doubted it could have happened, even though Joseph was a Hebrew and a slave living in Egypt.[20]

It is, of course, quite impossible to imagine an African American slave gaining his freedom and, like Joseph, becoming an adviser to a political leader anytime before the Civil War.[21] Unlike "freedmen in the New World," who "carried an external sign of their slave origin in their skin colour, even after many generations," slaves in the ancient world who became free "simply melted into the total population within one or at the most two generations."[22] In Rome, "tens of thousands of freedmen's sons" rose "into a world remote from that of the masses."[23] Even in other parts of the Americas, slavery was not entirely racial. Huge numbers of free people of color were found in much of the Americas. In Haiti, Brazil, and many of the Spanish colonies, the children of white masters and African slave women invariably became free. Only in the United States was this unlikely. Like Rome, throughout the American colonies and nations south of the United States, there were masses of former slaves—whether the mulatto children of masters, the African-born mistresses of Latin American masters, or slaves who earned or won their freedom.

This was impossible—unfathomable—in the United States, where slavery was defined by race. White people in the South were always free. Only blacks could be slaves; whites, no matter how great their misfortune, could never end up enslaved. While courts struggled at the margins to determine who might be black and therefore subject to enslavement,[24] Southern whites never doubted for a moment that, as South Carolina's highest court put it, "by law, every negro is presumed to be a slave."[25]

The Treatment of Slaves

In Europe, the ancient world, the Muslim world, Africa, much of Asia, and parts of pre-Columbian America, the treatment of slaves also differed from the experience in the United States. Because there was no explicit racial tie to slavery, slaves were not always easily identified or singled out. In many places, slaves, especially women, might be integrated into the families of their owners, especially as concubines or even wives, with their children being raised as the children of the master. This could never happen in the United States. On the other hand, however, because many of these slaves were also socially dead—condemned prisoners of war or criminals—they could be killed or tortured with impunity. In Rome, for example, it was not considered a crime to kill a slave. Under biblical law, if a slave died while being punished, there would be no criminal penalty because it was presumed that no master would ever intentionally destroy his own property. Societies throughout pre-Columbian Mexico, Central America, and South America routinely sacrificed slaves in religious ceremonies, while in both ancient China and the ancient Mediterranean world living or freshly executed slaves were often entombed with the bodies of kings and other important people.

In most of the American states, however, it was illegal to murder a slave. American law recognized that slaves had a right to life, and there are scattered instances in which whites, including a few masters, were punished and even executed for murdering slaves. Similarly, by the 1820s, all of the American states had banned certain forms of cruel punishment, such as maiming or castration. However, while the life and even the limbs of slaves might be better protected in the United States, in no American state could they legally marry, enforce a contract (even for their own freedom), or have any legal authority over their own children. Unlike Roman-law societies, the American South discouraged freedom, and by the 1850s, most of the slave states prohibited manumission. Thus, the status and condition of slaves in other places was both much better than in the United States but also much worse, at least in terms of physical safety, because the basis of the slave system was different.

The Evolution of a Religious Rationale for Slavery

Old Testament law had separate rules for the enslavement of Hebrews and non-Hebrews. Hebrew slaves could gain their freedom at various times, including during a "jubilee" year. On the other hand, non-Hebrew slaves were to be kept in bondage for their lifetime. It is not clear, however, whether these distinctions were religious or merely ethnic.

The rise of Christianity and Islam, however, created a strong and explicit religious rationale for slavery: that the slave was a nonbeliever, a pagan, or an infidel and thus not protected by the law of God. Both faiths also discouraged the enslavement of believers, but such ethical considerations, and any rules implementing them, were inconsistently observed or enforced.

Before 1500, the Christian nations of the Mediterranean relied heavily on the importation of enslaved nonbelievers from other parts of Europe and the Middle East. So many Slavic peoples from eastern Europe were enslaved that the term *slave* evolved from the word *Slav.*

The spread of Christianity into eastern Europe undermined this trade because the Catholic Church discouraged the enslavement of believers. In 1363, for example, the government of Florence banned the importation of Christian slaves. During this period, however, Europeans purchased large numbers of non-Christian slaves: Muslims, Circassians, non-Christian Russians, Central Asians, and even some sub-Saharan Africans. For a time, Roman Catholics in Spain enslaved Orthodox Christians from Greece and other parts of the eastern Mediterranean. The Islamic world, meanwhile, enslaved European Christians, as well as Circassians, non-Christian Russians, Central Asians, other Muslims, and, increasingly, sub-Saharan Africans.

For Christians, the religious rationale for slavery was a two-edged sword. On one hand, it placed God on the side of exploration, conquest, and enslavement. Europeans came to the Americas, Africa, Asia, and the Pacific Islands with conversion in mind, and Christian monarchs justified the cost of colonization with an appeal to spreading the faith. First the Spanish and the Portuguese, and then other Europeans, also used religion to justify the enslavement of Indians and Africans. But if the purpose of conquest was conversion, what justified enslavement once these former pagans had been baptized?

In the New World, Anglo-American masters initially believed that conversion would lead to manumission, the freeing of slaves. Thus many masters apparently refused to allow the Church of England to teach and convert their slaves. In 1667, the Virginia legislature felt compelled to pass a statute declaring that the baptism of slaves would not emancipate them. The goal of this act was to "more carefully endeavour the propagation of christianity by permitting" slaves "to be admitted to that sacrament."[26]

This law led to the first defense of slavery in the Anglo-American world. Masters and slave traders alike quickly began to justify the capture and enslavement of Africans on the grounds that they could then be converted to the true faith. Rather than becoming a burden on the masters, Christianity became one of their most important tools for defending slavery. This defense of slavery was not limited to a defense of the importation of slaves from Africa. Although the children of these Africans were born in America, and born as Christians, nineteenth-century masters continued to justify slavery itself on the grounds that it brought Christianity to the "heathens." In part, this justification rested on racist claims that if freed and thus denied the guidance of white masters, African Americans might very well revert to their pre-Christian ways. In the 1850s, proponents of reopening the African slave trade argued that doing so would further allow for the spread of the Gospel.

THE EMERGENCE OF SLAVERY
IN EARLY AMERICA

As we have noted, slavery was found everywhere in the ancient world, and all societies accepted it as a normal social institution. Moreover, slavery thrived in most of Europe until the early modern period. It was still a thriving institution in most of the Mediterranean cultures on the eve of American settlement. The Spanish and Portuguese were fully familiar with slavery, and the first trans-Atlantic slave trade consisted of Columbus taking Carib Indians back to Spain.

But by the time the English had begun to settle America, bondage did not exist in Great Britain or in much of northern Europe. On the continent and in colonies settled by France, Holland, and Denmark, the existing legal structures, based on Roman law, at least allowed for slavery. Of course, Spain and Portugal, also Roman-law societies, brought slavery with them to the New World. Thus, when these nations settled colonies in the New World, they either were familiar with slavery or had a legal heritage that allowed them to quickly adapt their culture to slavery. However, in England, and, by extension, her colonies, there were no laws or precedents that supported slavery.[27]

Culturally, the English claimed to be a "free people," and slavery was clearly antithetical to their institutions. When Englishmen first came to the New World, they in fact had visions of liberating the oppressed peoples of the Americas from the yoke of Spanish oppression.[28] Because they came with these visions of a "free culture," the British settlers did not immediately adopt slavery, and accordingly, slavery grew gradually on the mainland colonies,[29] with little consideration of how this new system of labor might fit in with existing English traditions and institutions.

The first blacks arrived in Virginia before 1620. The traditional date is 1619, although possibly some blacks were in the colony before then.[30] These first Africans were treated as indentured servants, and some eventually became free. By the 1630s, some white Virginians were treating Africans as slaves, but as late as the 1670s, some Africans were gaining their freedom on the ground that they had been imported as indentured servants. Starting in 1660–61, the Virginia legislature began to pass legislation that both recognized slavery and protected the master's interest in his slaves. By 1670, Virginia had begun moving toward a full-blown slave society. The other Southern colonies followed suit. In the Northern colonies, bondage was less pervasive, in part because the religious nature of settlement—Quaker in Pennsylvania and Puritan in New England—was not conducive to having a large population of outsiders. Nevertheless, slaves could be found in every colony; in parts of New York and New Jersey, slavery was especially important to the local economy. Before 1660, the Dutch city of New Amsterdam, which in 1664 became the English settlement called New York City, had a greater percentage of slaves than did Virginia. However, while profitable everywhere in the New World, the demand for cheap labor was greater in the tobacco fields of the Chesapeake and later in the rice fields of South Carolina, than in the rest of the colonies. Thus while a fifth or more of the population of colonial New Jersey and New York consisted of slaves, this population could not match Virginia's, which was about half slave in the colonial period, or later South Carolina's, where by 1739 two-thirds of the population was enslaved. Equally important, large numbers of dissenting Protestants in the Northern colonies, especially Quakers, gave those places a growing population opposed to slavery.

Hostility to slavery was apparent even as slavery began to take root in British America. In 1688, the Quaker meeting in Germantown, Pennsylvania, issued the first known American protest against slavery. These Quakers reminded fellow Christians,

> There is a saying, that we should do to all men like as we will be done ourselves; making no difference of what generation, descent, or colour they are. And those who steal or rob men, and those who buy or purchase them are they not all alike?[31]

The Germantown protest had little resonance beyond the Quaker community, but it did set members of that faith on a path that ultimately led to complete Quaker opposition to slavery. Similarly, the book *The Selling of Joseph,* published by the Puritan lawyer and judge Samuel Sewell in 1701, had little direct effect on American society. Few Americans read the book, and few cared about his plea for the rights of black slaves. But eventually, the descendants of the Puritans, including some who were directly related to Sewell, would become leaders of the abolitionist movement.

These early responses to slavery were not seen as a threat to the institution. This opposition to slavery was mostly personal and local. If

Quakers ceased to own slaves, it would have no effect on the system itself. There was no chance that any of the colonial governments would pass legislation to harm slavery, and even if one did, the British Crown would veto such laws. In the seventeenth and eighteenth centuries, slavery was simply too important to the imperial economy to allow any interference from colonial legislatures. The riches flowing into England from sugar, tobacco, and the African slave trade itself ensured that London would never accept any colonial law that truly, or even potentially, harmed slavery.

Virginia's attempt to stop the importation of African slaves in the 1760s and 1770s illustrates this point. Most white Virginians were not opposed to slavery per se but found the importation of new slaves to be both dangerous to the society and economically damaging. Thus Virginia tried to impose such high taxes on newly imported slaves that it would have been uneconomical to bring them into the colony. The king persistently vetoed these laws, and he similarly ignored a direct petition in 1772 to end the African trade.[32] If the Crown would not let Virginia simply suspend importation, American masters knew full well that the British government would not allow any interference with slavery itself by the colonial legislatures. Thus colonial antislavery efforts could have no political impact; they could only affect individuals and narrowly defined groups, such as the Quakers and Methodists.

Support for this understanding of the relationship between slavery and the British Empire also came from the highest court in England. In *Somerset v. Stewart,* decided in 1772, Lord Chief Justice Mansfield ruled that a slave brought into Great Britain could not be held in bondage against his will because there was no statutory law creating slavery or supporting its existence in England. Lord Mansfield was careful, however, to limit the reach of his decision to the importation of slaves into the British Isles, asserting that his court would uphold business agreements involving slavery in the colonies. Mansfield declared that "contract for sale of a slave is good here; the sale is a matter to which the law properly and readily attaches," and thus the English courts would "maintain the price according to the agreement."[33] The point was clear. England would support the buying and selling of slaves where bondage was legal, such as in the American colonies. The only limitation on slavery occurred if the master brought the slave back to Britain and the slave resisted being returned to bondage in the Americas.

Complementing the paucity of challenges to slavery in the colonial period was the imperial social structure, which implicitly justified bondage. The American colonies were part of a larger empire built on distinctive classes and social hierarchy. Americans fully understood that some men were born to lead and rule; others were born to follow and obey. At the top of British society was a monarch; at the bottom there had been serfs and peasants in earlier times, and by the time of American settlement, a growing population of urban poor, as well as the despised Irish, who were seen by most Englishmen as contemptible at best. New World settlement simply added new layers to this class structure: white and black indentured servants, some Indian slaves, and then black slaves. Indeed, a challenge to colonial slavery was implicitly a challenge to the entire social order of the British Empire. Before the American Revolution, such a challenge was unthinkable. Thus on the eve of the Revolution, opposition to slavery in America was narrowly limited to members of some religious groups who, for the most part, were concerned with cleansing themselves and their co-religionists of the taint of slaveholding. Otherwise, whites understood slavery to be an integral part of the society and life of the colonies and a central factor in the economy of the entire British Empire. It also fit well into the social hierarchy of the society.

In sum, before the Revolution, most of the Anglo-American world, and almost all of the rest of the Western world, generally accepted black slavery (as long as it was limited to the colonies), and the few attacks on slavery were religious and not terribly effective. There was no need to defend slavery because there were no serious threats to slavery.

THE AMERICAN REVOLUTION THREATENS SLAVERY

All this changed with the American Revolution. By freeing the colonies from British rule, the Revolution set the stage for formidable attacks on slavery and in turn necessitated a strong defense of slavery. The threats to slavery were ideological, political, and social.

The Ideological Threat

As Americans fought for their own liberty, many wondered about the morality of holding others in bondage. The groundwork laid by Quakers, Methodists, and other religious opponents of slavery now had a political context. The clarion call of the Declaration of Independence—

that all people were "created equal" and entitled to "liberty"—surely undermined the legitimacy of slavery. If people were truly "equal," then slavery might be truly illegitimate.

During the Revolution, whole states accepted this ideology and implemented it to undermine slavery. For example, Massachusetts declared in its 1780 constitution that all people were born "free and equal," and the courts quickly interpreted this to abolish all slavery in the state.

Pennsylvania's Gradual Abolition Act of 1780 began with a stirring preamble that tied ending slavery to the struggle against the "tyranny of Great-Britain," noting that slavery "deprived" blacks "of the common blessings that they were by nature entitled to."[34] Such an argument clearly and directly threatened slavery. It was only a matter of time before this ideological commitment to liberty began to affect national politics.

In addition to these actions by state governments, there were the decisions of hundreds, perhaps thousands, of individuals who acted on the revolutionary ideology by manumitting their slaves. Many masters in the North allowed their male slaves to enlist in the revolutionary militias and armies, gaining their freedom while fighting for the liberty of the nation.

The Political Threat

The political threat to slavery was directly tied to the ideology of the Revolution. The political threat to slavery after the Revolution came from two sources: the new state governments and the new national government that emerged first under the Articles of Confederation and later under the Constitution. Opponents of slavery could now direct their protests to popularly elected legislators, who, independent of the Crown, might respond to the pleas of those who found human bondage to be immoral and in violation of the natural rights theories of the Revolution.

Before the Revolution was over, the new state governments, now independent and free to act without interference from London, embarked on what has been called the "First Emancipation."[35] Massachusetts implicitly ended slavery in its 1780 constitution, and in the *Quock Walker Cases* (1781–1783), the state's highest court affirmed this result. New Hampshire adopted virtually identical language in its constitution of 1783, and by 1790, there were no slaves in that state. Vermont, which would become the fourteenth state, banned slavery in its constitution of 1777, and this clause remained when Vermont joined the Union in 1791. In 1780, Pennsylvania took steps to end slavery through the passage of a gradual emancipation act. Under this law, no new slaves could be brought into the state, and the children of all existing slaves would be free at birth. Connecticut and Rhode Island adopted similar legislation in 1784, the year after the Revolutionary War ended, as did New York in 1799 and New Jersey in 1804. While no slaves were emancipated directly under these laws, the statutes put slavery on the road to extinction, and very quickly it ceased to be an important social or economic institution in these states, even though in some places a few individuals were held as slaves as late as the 1840s.

The North's move to abolition did not directly threaten slavery in the South, but these laws did put the South on notice that half the country, more or less, was moving to end slavery. This movement clearly put some pressure on the rest of the nation to follow suit or to explain why it would not.

The second threat to slavery from political independence came with the creation of a national government. As the free states of the North emerged, it became clear that more than half of the seats in the national Congress would represent districts that contained no slaves and, more importantly, no slaveowners. Thus Southerners faced the prospect of being outvoted in a national legislature by representatives who had no direct interest in slavery and who might be ideologically and morally opposed to the South's most important social and economic institution. Without the stabilizing power of Great Britain, with its proslavery policies, the American slave states after the Revolution faced potential political pressures from a national government.

The Social Threat

The social threat to slavery during the Revolutionary Era came from two quite separate sources: religion and the military conflict.

The religious revivals that preceded the Revolution—collectively known as the Great Awakening—stimulated serious antislavery sentiment. By the time of the Revolution, antislavery had firmly taken root among Quakers. Some, like John Woolman and Anthony Benezet, had begun to agitate for an end to the African slave trade and also an end to slavery itself. The Quakers were few in number and influential mostly in Pennsylvania and New Jersey, but their arguments, based on Christian values, resonated among members of various pietistic faiths and, to a lesser but still significant degree, among Puritans and their descendants and among members of various evangelical faiths. The founder of the Methodist Church, John Wesley, was unalterably opposed to slavery, and initially his church would not accept slaveowners as members. The Methodist Church would remain opposed to slavery well into the nineteenth century, even though millions of Southern whites, including a considerable number of slaveowners, joined the church. Eventually, slavery would lead to the church splitting into Southern and Northern branches.

These religiously motivated opponents of slavery organized the first institutional assaults on slavery, through the creation of what were called at the time "abolition societies." These societies, found throughout the North as well as the Upper South, agitated for gradual abolition acts, bans on the African slave trade, and greater rights for free blacks. Once abolition acts and bans on the importation of slaves were in place, these organizations pushed for their strict enforcement.

The social threat also came from the realities of the Revolutionary War. Initially, the national government opposed the enlistment of black troops. General Washington, one of the nation's most important slaveowners, was an early opponent of black troops. But he soon changed his mind as manpower needs and the obvious skill and bravery of some black soldiers led him to the conclusion that black enlistment was in the best interest of the young nation. Seeing free black soldiers in action undermined Washington's racial prejudice and ultimately his support for slavery itself. In New England, the Middle States, and even Virginia, hundreds of slaves gained their freedom by serving in the army.[36] Free blacks posed a threat to slavery because they were living proof that blacks could be useful citizens once they were no longer held in bondage.

The Threat to Racial Solidarity

These three developments and changing attitudes led to the greatest threat of all to slavery: the possibility that a large number of Americans would accept the fundamental equality of blacks. If this happened, the basis of slavery itself would be undermined.

The political changes threatened white supremacy. A number of Revolutionary Era constitutions allowed all "free" men to vote. As slavery ended in much of the North, the free black population grew, and African American men began to vote in most of New England and throughout the Middle States. North Carolina also allowed all free men to vote, and the small free black population there exercised this right.

The ideology of the Revolution, with its emphasis on natural rights and "equality," surely challenged the racial basis of slavery. If all people were "created equal," then it was truly immoral and wrong to enslave some of them. If all people were entitled to "Life, Liberty, and the Pursuit of Happiness," then blacks must also be entitled to these rights.

The enlistment and arming of blacks undermined the claim of Southerners that they had a right to deprive these people of their liberty. The heroism of blacks proved, at least to some whites, that African Americans had earned a place at the political table.

Similarly, the Great Awakening implicitly threatened slavery by raising the religious and moral consciousness of the nation. If all souls are worth saving, then surely there is something wrong with enslaving the bodies that contain those souls.

THE EMERGENCE OF PROSLAVERY THOUGHT

In the years immediately following the Revolution, slaveowners began to offer defenses of slavery. For the first time, a defense of slavery seemed necessary. Before the Revolution, there was no need to defend slavery per se. As one more level of social status in the British Empire, slavery fit perfectly well into a society built on hierarchy. But with hierarchy under attack, American masters had to develop some explanation for why they continued to hold slaves. During the Revolution, the British intellectual Samuel Johnson asked, "How is it that we hear the loudest *yelps* for liberty among the drivers of negroes?"[37] The move toward abolition in the North suggested that some Americans agreed with the implications of Johnson's question. The onus was now on the slaveowners of the new nation to answer that question.

Fittingly, perhaps, as well as ironically, the most important early defense of the institution came from a man most remembered for his articulation of the rights of man and the fundamental importance of liberty: Thomas Jefferson. Equally ironic was the defense of slavery that developed at the Philadelphia Convention in 1787, which drafted a national constitution for a "free people."

Jefferson's Defense of Slavery

In the Declaration of Independence, Thomas Jefferson had set out, unintentionally perhaps, the argument for abolition: "We hold these Truths to be self-evident, that all Men are created equal, that they are

R UN away from the fubfcriber in *Albemarle*, a Mulatto flave called *Sandy*, about 35 years of age, his ftature is rather low, inclining to corpulence, and his complexion light; he is a fhoemaker by trade, in which he ufes his left hand principally, can do coarfe carpenters work, and is fomething of a horfe jockey; he is greatly addicted to drink, and when drunk is info-lent and diforderly, in his converfation he fwears much, and in his behaviour is artful and knavifh. He took with him a white horfe, much fcarred with traces, of which it is ex-pected he will endeavour to difpofe; he alfo carried his fhoe-makers tools, and will probably endeavour to get employment that way. Whoever conveys the faid flave to me, in *Albemarle*, fhall have 40 s. reward, if taken up within the county, 4 l. if elfewhere within the colony, and 10 l. if in any other colony. from
                          THOMAS   JEFFERSON.

Thomas Jefferson placed this notice about Sandy, a slave who ran away from one of his plantations, in the *Virginia Gazette* (Williamsburg), September 14, 1769. Virginia Historical Society, Richmond.

endowed by their Creator with certain unalienable Rights, that among these are Life, Liberty, and the Pursuit of Happiness."

A few years after drafting the Declaration, Jefferson developed the outlines of a number of important proslavery arguments that countered his assertions of equality. While Jefferson was often ambivalent about slavery and condemned it when writing letters to known opponents of the institution, in his *Notes on the State of Virginia* he used arguments based on history, science, political theory, practical necessity, and, most of all, race to justify the continued enslavement of Africans. In the nineteenth century, numerous defenders of slavery would elaborate on the themes that Jefferson had set out.[38]

Jefferson argued in the *Notes* that blacks were inherently inferior to whites in their mental abilities and their moral virtues. He would not speculate on whether blacks were "originally a distinct race, or made distinct by time and circumstances," but whatever the cause, he asserted that they were "inferior to the whites in ... body and mind." He claimed that he had never found a black who "had uttered a thought above the level of plain narration; never seen an elementary trait of painting or sculpture." He found "no poetry" among blacks.

Jefferson conceded that blacks were brave, but this "may perhaps proceed from a want of forethought, which prevents their seeing a danger till it be present." He offered pseudo-scientific theories of race, speculating that blackness might come "from the color of the blood" or that black women might breed with the "Oranootan." He asserted, without offering any proof, that black men preferred white women as their sexual partners. But their sexuality, like everything else about blacks, was less human and more animalistic. "They are more ardent after their female," he wrote, "but love seems with them to be more an eager desire, than a tender delicate mixture of sentiment and sensation. Their griefs are transient." Indeed, he found that

> in general, their existence appears to participate more of sensation than reflection. To this must be ascribed their disposition to sleep when abstracted from their diversions, and unemployed in labour. An animal whose body is at rest, and who does not reflect, must be disposed to sleep of course. Comparing them by their faculties of memory, reason, and imagination, it appears to me that in memory they are equal to the whites; in reason much inferior, as I think one could scarcely be found capable of tracing and comprehending the investigations of Euclid; and that in imagination they are dull, tasteless and anomalous.

Initiating a historical argument that would become a mainstay of proslavery thought, Jefferson noted that ancient Rome had also been a slaveholding society. However, Jefferson noted that many Roman slaves achieved great accomplishments because "they were of the race of whites"; American slaves could never achieve such distinction because they were not white.

Being unequal, blacks could never, in Jefferson's mind, survive in competition with whites. At the time, free black men could vote in the states surrounding Virginia: Pennsylvania, Maryland, and North Carolina. Nevertheless, Jefferson fervently believed that blacks could never be the political equals of whites and must never be allowed to vote or to participate in public life. As Jefferson saw it, if emancipated, former slaves would become a permanent class of peasants or serfs. This would undermine American democracy. Thus Jefferson asserted that if slavery were to end, the slaves themselves would have to be exiled, perhaps sent to the Caribbean, Africa, or some remote part of the American continent.

Jefferson justified such a wholesale removal of African Americans on two grounds. First, he asserted that the "deep rooted prejudices entertained by the whites; ten thousand recollections, by the blacks, of the injuries they have sustained; new provocations; the real distinctions which nature has made" would lead to "the extermination of the one or the other race." To avoid this race war, Jefferson thought it was necessary to ship all ex-slaves, and indeed all free blacks, out of the country. He also feared that if free blacks stayed in the United States, they might intermarry with whites. This, Jefferson believed, would lead to "staining the blood" of the master class. Thus even if there were no race war, Jefferson asserted that blacks, if freed, had "to be removed beyond the reach of mixture."

But if this happened, who would then do the work necessary to maintain the American economy? Jefferson fully understood that slaves provided the labor that made the Southern economy possible. He suggested that the nation might import European workers and remove slaves, but he realized the utter impracticality of this. Europeans were unwilling to come to America as exploited laborers, and the nation had neither the money nor the ships to send its black population back to Africa or even to some closer foreign destination. Moreover, Jefferson understood that most Southern masters were unwilling to part with their slaves and the lifestyle that came with being a master.

Jefferson's fears of either a race war or the opposite, interracial love and marriage, combined with the need for brute labor, led to this early and incredibly important defense of slavery. Jefferson's *Notes* contain four proslavery themes: First, since antiquity slavery had been an accepted social and economic institution in all of the great nations of the world, including Rome and Greece. Second, ending slavery would lead to chaos and destruction of civilized society. Third, the Southern economy depended on slave labor, and there was really no viable alternative to this labor. Finally, blacks were genetically inferior to whites and at the same time innately predisposed to sexual immorality. They were, in essence, a dangerous class that had to be controlled at all times. Slavery was obviously the most effective, most efficient, and most profitable way to control the Africans and their descendants living in the United States.

Proslavery Arguments at the Constitutional Convention

Like Jefferson, the Southern delegates to the Constitutional Convention articulated a number of defenses of slavery that would later be developed by proslavery theorists in the antebellum period. Just a few years after Jefferson wrote his *Notes on the State of Virginia,* delegates from South Carolina and other slave states at the Constitutional Convention offered a series of defenses of slavery, setting out why the Constitution had to protect slavery and the slave trade. In a closed convention where the delegates were sworn to secrecy, there was relatively little need for political posturing. The delegates also probably had little expectation that they could change any minds on the morality of slavery. Thus they offered, for the most part, practical, economic, political, and historical arguments in favor of slavery. In many ways, these were the South's strongest arguments—along with the racial ones that Jefferson pioneered—in the long debate over slavery. In essence, the proslavery delegates did not ask their Northern colleagues to support slavery, to like it, or even to acknowledge that it was morally legitimate. Instead, they set out why, from a practical standpoint, it was in the self-interest of Northerners to accept and even to protect slavery.

One of the most vocal defenders of slavery at the Convention was Charles Pinckney of South Carolina. He asserted that there was "a solid distinction as to interest between the southern and northern states." He noted that the Carolinas and Georgia "in their Rice and Indigo had a peculiar interest which might be sacrificed" if they did not have sufficient power in any new Congress.[39] In a later debate, Pinckney's more famous cousin, General Charles Cotesworth Pinckney, declared that the South did not require "a majority of representatives" in Congress, "but [he] wished them to have something like an equality." Otherwise, the Southern states would "be nothing more than overseers for the Northern States." Similarly, Hugh Williamson of North Carolina argued that if the North had a majority in Congress, "the Southern Interest must be extremely endangered."[40] Later, Pierce Butler of South Carolina claimed that "the labour of a slave in South Carolina was as productive and valuable as that of a freeman in Massachusetts" and that because the national government "was instituted principally for the protection of property," slaves should be counted for representation.[41] Even Virginia's Edmund Randolph, who "lamented that such a species of property existed," nevertheless "urged strenuously that express security ought to be provided for including slaves in the ratio of Representation."[42]

The Southern delegates also made clear that the alternative to denying representation for slavery was an end to the Union. William R. Davie warned that his state, North Carolina, would "never confederate" unless slaves were counted for representation and that if slaves were not counted for apportionment, "the business [of the Convention] was at an end."[43]

The threat of disunion, which would mark proslavery political thought until 1861, was also apparent during the debate over the slave trade. South Carolina's John Rutledge told the Convention that the "true question at present is whether the Southern States shall or shall not be parties to the Union." The implied threat of secession was clear. He then told the Northern delegates that if they would "consult their interest," they would "not oppose the increase of slaves which will increase the commodities of which they will become the carriers."[44] General Pinckney also argued that if the Constitution failed to protect the slave trade, his "personal influence . . . would be of no avail towards obtaining the assent" of his home state in favor of the Constitution. Shifting from the implied threat of political instability, Pinckney then reiterated the economic argument. More slaves would produce more goods, and that result would help not only the South, but also Northern states involved in "the carrying trade." Pinckney declared that a prohibition of the slave trade would be "an exclusion of S. Carolina from the Union," because "S. Carolina and Georgia cannot do without slaves." General Pinckney's younger cousin, Charles Pinckney, argued on the basis of history that there was nothing wrong with slavery and, citing ancient Rome and Greece, declared that slavery was "justified by the example of all the world."[45]

The arguments here were clear: The economic interests of the South, based on slavery, had to have special protection in the Constitution. This was an early version of the assertions that "Cotton Is King" and that no power in the world could make war on cotton. Here, in a pre-cotton economy, Southerners were simply arguing that the contributions of slavery to the national economy were so great that the rest of the nation could not live without slavery and therefore had to give slavery special constitutional protections. A number of clauses of the Constitution, including the three-fifths clause, the provision for the electoral college, the protection of the African slave trade, and the fugitive slave clause, would eventually do this.

There was, of course, a logical inconsistency in these arguments. If cotton or tobacco or any other slavery-based product had truly been "king," then no politicians would have dared attack it. However, the point of these economic arguments was always to warn the opponents of slavery that attacks on the institution would be very costly.

With such arguments, the Southern delegates, like Jefferson, ably defended their most important economic and social institution. They set out what would become major themes of proslavery thought: that slavery had been a prominent institution in the great societies of the classical period; that all the world allowed and supported slavery; that slavery was vital to the national economy; and most importantly, that the very survival of the national Union depended on great deference being shown to slavery.

The Founding and the Need for a Proslavery Argument

In summing up the entire Constitution, General Pinckney, who had been one of the ablest defenders of slavery at the Convention, proudly told the South Carolina House of Representatives:

> We have a security that the general government can never emancipate them, for no such authority is granted and it is admitted, on all hands, that the general government has no powers but what are expressly granted by the Constitution, and that all rights not expressed were reserved by the several states.[46]

This powerful South Carolina planter boasted, "In short, considering all circumstances, we have made the best terms for the security of this species of property it was in our power to make. We would have made better if we could; but on the whole, I do not think them bad."[47]

Pinckney was of course correct. The Constitution he helped create protected slavery in numerous ways. But it also created the seeds of a new and powerful threat to slavery, especially when combined with the libertarian ideology of the Revolution. In a stronger, "more perfect Union," the interests of the slave states would have to be balanced against those of the free states and against the interests of the nation as a whole. Moreover, as part of a federal Union, South Carolina and other slave states would have to contend with the ideas and beliefs of Americans from the emerging free states who increasingly challenged the religious, moral, political, and social legitimacy of slavery.

THE OUTLINES OF ANTEBELLUM PROSLAVERY THOUGHT

Between 1820 and the start of the Civil War in 1861, Southerners developed a variety of defenses of slavery that were rooted in traditional academic, professional, and political categories commonly understood by most educated Americans. This defense also responded, in kind, to attacks on slavery. Southerners turned to theology, history, political theory, law, science, and economics to defend the central institution of their society. They expressed their views in almost every conceivable form, including sermons and speeches delivered orally and then published; popular essays and learned articles on the Bible, history, and philosophy; economic analyses of labor, management, and production; books and articles in scientific and medical journals on all manner of subjects, from anthropology to zoology; contemporary descriptions of Haiti and other places where slavery had been abolished; legal treatises and judicial opinions; and novels, short stories, poems, and book reviews.

The common themes of this literature included arguments on black inferiority; that slavery is both universal and natural in all societies; and that Southern slavery is the most humane system of slavery ever devised because it protects and nurtures the slaves, who are inferior beings in need of care and supervision.

All of these arguments could not fit into a single, coherent defense of slavery. Some were mutually exclusive. For example, the largest single body of proslavery literature is based on religious defenses of slavery. Such defenses appealed to the overwhelmingly Protestant, often evangelical, Southern population. They were also aimed at the South's Protestant counterparts in the North and in Great Britain. But these religious defenses of slavery were often incompatible with the proslavery arguments based on science, medicine, and anthropology, which attracted some of the sharpest minds of the South.

One important debate illustrates this conflict between religion and science. Southern ministers and their allies argued that all humans were the descendants of Adam and Eve and existed as a result of a single creation, as described in the Bible. These ministers claimed that blacks were the descendants of Noah's son Ham and Noah's grandson Canaan. After the flood, according to the biblical story, Noah cursed Canaan, and proslavery ministers claimed that the biblical "curse of Canaan" was that Canaan and all his descendants became black and were doomed forever to be "servants" of their brothers.[48]

Many mid-nineteenth-century scientists argued that this biblical literalism was nonsense. They rejected the whole notion of monogenesis and asserted that blacks had in fact been separately created. Some of these scientists argued that blacks were in fact a separate species of beings, somewhere on the evolutionary scale between the great apes and humans. These scientists asserted that blacks had a different anatomy than whites and were even susceptible to different diseases. Many in the overwhelmingly Protestant and evangelical South rejected the scientific arguments and stuck to their biblical defense. However, this forced them into a debate over the Bible with Northern ministers, who had their own biblical arguments on the immorality of slavery. In the North, at least, and in much of the rest of the world, the antislavery biblical argument neutralized or defeated the proslavery biblical argument in the struggle for public opinion outside of the South. The antislavery forces focused on the Golden Rule—"Do unto others as you would have them do unto you"—to make the persuasive point that slavery was antithetical to the spirit of Christianity. The result was that by fighting the intellectual debate over slavery with biblical arguments, the South was in fact fighting the antislavery forces on their strongest ground.

Ironically, opponents of slavery had few scientific arguments of their own, and thus in convincing outsiders, the scientific arguments may have been the strongest in the South's intellectual arsenal.[49] But many of the most prominent Southerners refused to use these arguments because they were in conflict with Scripture.

Some proslavery theorists tried to please both the scientists and the clergy, asserting a single creation but searching the Bible for an explanation of the origin of the races. Some claimed that when God cursed Cain for killing Abel, he made Cain black. This theory, however, was relatively weak because it did not explain the existence of other races. Some Southerners argued that the different races emerged when God transformed the builders of the Tower of Babel. The most common explanation for the existence of blacks was the story of Noah and the curse of Canaan. Dr. Samuel Cartwright of New Orleans was perhaps the most creative of all. He argued that blacks and all other nonwhites were among the "other creatures" that God placed in the Garden of Eden before the creation of Adam. Cartwright claimed that the biblical story of Eve and the Tree of Knowledge had not involved a serpent but rather "the *negro gardener*" who handed Eve the apple.[50] Beyond the disputes between the scientists and the clergy, important proslavery thinkers differed substantially among themselves about other issues. Many proslavery theorists, like Thomas Jefferson and George Fitzhugh, had a strong animus against capitalism, industrial society, urbanization, and market economies. These Southern leaders extolled the virtues of an agrarian, noncapitalist society. On the other hand, the fiercely proslavery James D. B. De Bow, editor of *De Bow's Commercial Review of the South and Western States,* was a forceful advocate of Southern industrialization. Similarly, those who advocated that "Cotton Is King," such as Senator James Henry Hammond, implicitly endorsed the importance and power of world markets.

The defense of slavery that allowed it to coexist with American democracy relied on numerous theories and factual assertions based on a wide variety of perspectives, philosophies, and principles. This defense also responded, in kind, to attacks on slavery. Southerners used religion, history, constitutional and legal arguments, census data, science, and economics to defend slavery. They wrote sermons, gave speeches, published essays, and prepared scientific articles that not merely defended slavery against its opponents, but also aggressively argued that the institution was a blessing, a benefit, a "positive good" for the masters, the slaves, the nonslaveholding whites, and indeed the entire society.

In addition, the South also turned to a cultural defense of slavery. Using short stories, novels, book reviews, and poems, Southerners offered a romantic fictionalized portrayal of slavery to counter growing Northern hostility. The literature was sometimes explicitly political. William J. Grayson's "The Hireling and the Slave," for example, was a fifty-page poem comparing the lot of the slave to that of the hired worker in a free market. The message was clear: A slave was protected from the cruelties of the market, while the free worker was not. Other literary works were romantic portrayals of happy slaves and kind masters. In the 1850s, Southern intellectuals and novelists combined harsh reviews with not particularly successful novels in a failed attempt to counter the most successful cultural assault on slavery, Harriet Beecher Stowe's best-selling novel, *Uncle Tom's Cabin.* In his *Uncle Tom's Cabin and American Culture,* Thomas F. Gossett lists twenty-seven proslavery works in response to Stowe's novel between 1852 and the Civil War.[51] Southerners produced a number of stories and novels modeled on Stowe's masterpiece but written to provide a sympathetic view of slavery. Ultimately, whatever the form—a scientific paper, a sermon, a poem, or a speech—the most important defenses of slavery rested on history, religion, economics, political and constitutional arguments, social necessity, and science and medicine. Tied to all of these defenses, and woven throughout them, were arguments and discussions about race. Law, literature, theology, and all other disciplines and arts were applied to these defenses.

The Historical and Classical Defense

From the Revolution until the Civil War, many Americans looked to Greece and Rome—the first democracy and the first republic—as models for their own emerging democratic republic. Greek revival architecture and references to Roman society and culture were common in this period. Statues and paintings of George Washington and other national leaders often portrayed them in Roman togas. Thus it is not surprising that Southern defenders of slavery developed a historical defense based on the argument that slavery was a central institution in ancient Greece and Rome. Southerners in fact argued that all great societies—as well as democracy, higher learning, and even civilization itself—relied on slavery. The proponents of this view noted that the great classical philosophers, especially Plato and Aristotle, assumed that slavery was an integral part of any great society. Southerners pointed to the accomplishments of the Greek democracy and the grandeur of the Roman republic to make the point that truly great cultures and societies not only accepted slavery, but depended on it. These Southerners noted that slavery allowed the leaders of a society to avoid manual labor and gave them time to devote to affairs of state. Thus classical support for slavery dovetailed with the notion, asserted by many Southerners, that slavery was a prerequisite to a ruling elite within a democratic society. As the historian David Brion Davis noted, "Living in a society that increasingly dissociated culture and public service from the slightest taint of manual labor," Aristotle "saw slavery as a necessary means of supplying the wants of life."[52] Southern whites heartily agreed with such observations.

The logic of this argument was illustrated, in the minds of Southerners, by the contribution to national life made by the great planter-politicians like George Washington, George Mason, Thomas Jefferson, and General Charles Cotesworth Pinckney. In the antebellum era, this sort of contribution continued with leaders like Andrew Jackson, James Polk, John C. Calhoun, and Henry Clay. Such men could devote their lives to public service because they had slaves to provide for their economic needs, just as the great slaveholding citizens of Greece and Rome could devote their lives to public service.

Southerners often turned to the ancient world to justify their modern institution. In looking at the ancient world, they found support from some of the most important thinkers in Western culture. Plato, for example, opposed the enslavement of fellow Greeks, and in *The*

Republic he rejected the enslavement of citizens as punishment for crimes. Significantly, however, Plato and other Greek philosophers took for granted the enslavement of non-Greeks—barbarians—and in fact "had come to believe that the inferiority of barbarians could be seen in their willingness to submit to despotic and absolutist rulers."[53] Barbarians were, in effect, a "slavish people" who were unfit for self-government but were naturally suited for bondage. This meant that in their own countries they would be perpetually ruled by tyrants, but also that if manumitted in Greece they could not possibly govern themselves either. Similarly, Aristotle "built his entire argument" for slavery "around Plato's theory of natural inferiority."[54] Indeed, he believed that Greeks should find a different "race" of people—that is non-Greeks—to serve as their slaves.[55]

Southern defenders of democracy and slavery, like Thomas Jefferson, instinctively understood this concept. The Greek ideas of natural slavishness dovetailed perfectly with Southern notions of slavery. One need only substitute "black" or "African" for barbarian, and Southerners easily and quickly recognized that the great thinkers of ancient Greece were truly their allies. An important illustration of this comes from *An Inquiry into the Law of Negro Slavery,* written by Thomas R. R. Cobb, a cofounder of the first law school in Georgia. In this treatise, Cobb quoted Plato, Euripides, Juvenal, and other classical writers to teach his readers that slavery, especially Negro slavery, was accepted by the greatest minds of Western culture. Tying race to history, Cobb insisted that at an "early day" the "negro was commonly used as a slave at Rome." Implicitly comparing the South to the Roman Republic, he noted that "for her footmen and couriers" the Roman "wife preferred always the negroes" and that "Negroes, being generally slaves of luxury, commanded a very high price." Similarly, Cobb asserted that in Ancient Israel "many" of the slaves "were Africans of negro extraction" and that "among the Egyptians . . . there were numbers of negro slaves." Making similar claims for Assyria and Alexander the Great's empire, he concluded, "The negro was a favorite among slaves" in the ancient world.[56] While there is no historical support for these ideas, Cobb's assertions went unchallenged by most readers, who had little knowledge of or access to any serious works about ancient history. Most importantly, Cobb's historical claims, however factually inaccurate, illustrate the way Southerners used (or misused) history to support the idea of slavery in general, and of racially based slavery in particular.

The Religious Defense

The holiness of ancient Israel was the starting place for the religious defense of slavery. Most of the biblical patriarchs, beginning with Abraham, were slaveowners. In testing Job, God allowed all of his slaves to be taken from him, and in rewarding Job for his piety, God made sure that Job had more slaves than before. Leviticus set out elaborate laws for governing slaves, but nowhere did the texts even implicitly condemn slavery. On the contrary, the law of the Old Testament *assumed* the existence of slavery and only attempted to regulate it. A minor example of this illustrates the point in a way that Southern slaveowners surely understood. Leviticus declared that "whosoever lieth carnally with a woman, that *is* a bondmaid, betrothed to an husband, and not at all redeemed, nor freedom given her; she shall be scourged, they shall not be put to death, because she was not free."[57] The punishment for adultery—that is, sexual relations with another man's wife—was execution of both parties. But sexual relations with another man's slave woman, even if she were married, would not lead to any punishment for the man because the slave's marriage was not recognized by the law in the same way that a free person's marriage was. The slave woman would not be executed but only scourged. This passage also assumed, without comment or explanation, that male masters were free to have sex with their female slaves. If God ordained slavery in the Old Testament—and even explained how to deal with sex between slave women and free men— then how, Southerners asked, could there be any moral taint from owning slaves?

Proslavery theorists were equally at home turning to the New Testament for support. Paul's "Letter to Philemon" explicitly endorsed the return of fugitive slaves. The Corinthian letters proclaimed that slaves should be satisfied with their lot: "For he that is called in the Lord, *being* a servant, is the Lord's freeman; likewise he that was called, *being* free, is Christ's servant."[58] Southern ministers defended slavery with countless sermons on these and other texts. They were certain that the Bible, both the Old and New Testaments, supported their system of bondage.

While noting that the Bible supported slavery, they also urged masters to apply Christian principles to their treatment of slaves. Ministers argued for moderate punishment, sufficient food, decent housing, and even giving slaves leisure time, including an observance of the Sabbath.

From the beginning of slavery in the Anglo-American world, one defense of bondage had been that it allowed for the conversion of pagans. This continued after the slave trade had ended. "The Duties of Christian Masters," published by the Baptist State Convention of Alabama, exhorted masters to care for the souls, as well as the bodies, of slaves. The author advised,

> Short portions of Divine truth should be read and explained, and their particular application to them urged with kindness and faithfulness. Let the master exercise his judgment, that his servants may be benefitted by his wise arrangements for their spiritual well-being.[59]

The religious arguments for slavery dovetailed with racist assumptions of whites. Southern ministers accepted the idea that only through enslavement could Christian morality be imposed on blacks. While supporting slavery, ministers also encouraged masters to respect slave marriages when at all possible and, of course, to avoid sexual exploitation of slaves. Their argument was a strong one: If Southern slavery was humane and generous and rooted in Christianity, then it could be easily justified to the entire world as an institution beneficial, not only to the master class, but also to the slaves themselves. Southern masters, in other words, could do well by doing good.

Finally, Southern religious leaders offered a biblical defense of black enslavement. As already noted, slaveowners turned to the story of Noah to explain the origins of blacks and to legitimize slavery. After the flood, Noah was "drunk and uncovered himself inside his tent." His son Ham "saw his father's nakedness, and told his two brothers outside." When Noah awoke, he cursed Ham's son, Canaan, declaring "Accursed be Canaan. He shall be his brothers' meanest slave." He then blessed his other sons, declaring "may Canaan be his slave."[60] Slaveowners argued that part of the "curse of Ham" was that he became black. Hence the Bible taught that slavery was legitimate and that race justified slavery. Southern ministers retold and explained this biblical story throughout the antebellum period.

The Economic Argument

Before the Civil War, numerous defenders of slavery stressed its importance to the American economy. In urging the admission of Kansas as a slave state, Senator James Henry Hammond of South Carolina argued that "the strength of a nation depends in a great measure upon its wealth," which was created by its exports. He estimated that about two-thirds of America's exports were either produced by slave labor, like raw cotton, or were manufactured goods tied to slavery, like cotton cloth. In addition, he noted that much of the North's industrial production was based on the cotton, tobacco, and hemp that the South produced. Furthermore, he asserted that much of England's economy was tied to the Southern production of cotton. Equating attacks on slavery with attacks on the productions of slave labor, Hammond was emphatic: "No, sir, you dare not make war on cotton. No power on earth dares make war upon it. Cotton is king."[61] Southerners also argued that slavery created a more stable economy than free labor. Free people could be put out of work in an economic downturn, as the poem "The Hireling and the Slave" makes clear. Similarly, they might strike for higher wages in flush times. But slaves were always employed and never went on strike. Thus some Southerners argued that slavery was actually a humane alternative to the harshness of the marketplace. The economics of slavery, they asserted, allowed for a paternalistic protection of slaves that capitalism did not provide for workers. If the factory owner went bankrupt, the workers would suffer; but if the master went bankrupt, the slaves would be sold to a new master, who would "care" for them.

Finally, slavery was of course extremely profitable. Profit, in the end, is a measure of the economic value of any system. Masters did not assert, too boldly, that their system was highly profitable. That would have been out of character with their culture and their self-proclaimed status as gentlemen. But it *was* profitable, highly profitable, and most Americans knew it. The best defense of slavery in the end may very well have been the lifestyle of the planter class. In a nation where "money talks," the profits of slavery were very loud.

The Legal Defense

The legal defense of slavery, like the American system of government, had a state component and a federal component. It also had a theoretical component. Legal theorists like Thomas R. R. Cobb offered arguments based on property, history, and the needs of a stable society, both to defend the existing slave system and to show what laws were necessary to preserve the system. Proslavery legal theorists like Cobb argued that blacks were inferior to whites, and thus there had to be special laws and special punishments for both free blacks and slaves. If blacks were inherently a criminal element, as proslavery

Recently liberated slaves photographed at work in a South Carolina sweet potato field in 1862. Some of the men are wearing discarded Union military uniforms.
Collection of the New-York Historical Society.

theorists asserted, then the law had to be harsh and strict in keeping such people in their place.

State judges provided decisions, analysis, and precedents designed to protect slavery. Some of the case law was directed at protecting slave property *within* the South. For example, in *State v. Hale*,[62] the North Carolina Supreme Court upheld the prosecution of a white man for beating a slave owned by someone else. The court noted that such offenses were

> usually committed by men of dissolute habits, hanging loose upon society, who, being repelled from association with well disposed citizens, take refuge in the company of slaves, whom they deprave by their example, embolden by their familiarity, and then beat,

under the expectation that a slave dare not resent a blow from a white man.

Decisions like *State v. Hale* protected the property interest of the master in a slave but permitted the punishment of whites who harmed slaves. At the same time, in cases like *State v. Mann,*[63] the courts affirmed the right of masters to treat a slave however they wished, short of murder. The purpose of slavery, according to the legal systems of the Southern states, was to benefit the master. As North Carolina's Chief Justice Thomas Ruffin asserted: "The end is the profit of the master, his security and the public safety; the subject, one doomed in his own person and his posterity, to live without knowledge and without the capacity to make anything his own, and to toil that another may reap the fruits." Because of this, "the power of the master must be absolute to render the submission of the slave perfect." The majesty of the law, and the power of the courts, secured to the master the power to coerce the slave. The legal system defended slavery, affirming that the courts could not "allow the right of the master to be brought into discussion in the courts of justice. The slave, to remain a slave, must be made sensible that there is no appeal from his master; that his power is in no instance usurped; but is conferred by the laws of man at least, if not by the law of God."[64]

State courts and legislatures also provided for the punishment of whites or free blacks who challenged slavery. As early as the 1820s, the Southern states limited freedom of speech, press, assembly, and even movement for people who opposed slavery. The South increasingly became a closed society when it came to bondage. Debate over the justice or morality of slavery was simply not allowed, and the legal system provided a forum to punish those who violated the rules. At the federal level, the master class turned to the U.S. Constitution for the protection of slavery. Under the Constitution, masters could regain their fugitive slaves and rely on the national government to protect their property interest in their slaves. Neither slaves nor free blacks could hope for any legal protection from the U.S. Constitution. In *Dred Scott v. Sandford,*[65] Chief Justice Roger B. Taney constitutionalized this theory while nationalizing Southern concepts of race. He found that under the Constitution blacks "had no rights which the white man was bound to respect."[66] Applying a rigorous, although not necessarily accurate, argument to determine the rights of blacks under the Constitution based on the intentions of the framers, Taney found "that neither the class of persons who had been imported as slaves, nor their descendants, whether they had become free or not, were then acknowledged as a part of the people, nor intended to be included in the general words used in that memorable instrument."[67]

Proslavery Science and Medicine

Scientists, physicians, and anthropologists offered their own defenses of slavery. Some of these defenses were implicit. Northern scholars, like Samuel G. Morton of Philadelphia, argued that blacks were a separate species from whites and biologically and intellectually inferior to whites. Morton did not talk about slavery but limited his discussions to "science" as he understood it. Although he made no direct comments about slavery, he was of course fully aware that others would use his scientific "discoveries" to support the institution.

More directly concerned with slavery were two Southern physicians: Samuel Cartwright of New Orleans and Josiah C. Nott of Mobile, Alabama. Both were significant figures in the medical communities of the antebellum South. They contributed numerous articles to Southern medical journals on subjects that had nothing to do with slavery. Nott, an expert on yellow fever, posited the theory, which proved to be correct, that the disease was transmitted to humans through an intermediate host. Dr. Walter Reed would later use Nott's theories to solve the mystery of the spread of both yellow fever and malaria.

Nott and Cartwright also wrote extensively on the connections between science, race, and slavery. Cartwright was well known as a "Negro" doctor who specialized in treating slaves. Masters throughout Louisiana as well as other parts of the deep South brought their slaves to him for care. Cartwright thus observed slaves, and blacks, and reached what he believed to be scientific discoveries about blacks.

He argued that blacks and whites had significant anatomical differences that made blacks suited for slavery. He wrote that a black had more nerve endings than other people but that "the brain being ten per cent less in volume and weight, he is, from necessity, more under the influence of his instincts and *animality,* than other races of men and less under the influence of his reflective faculties."[68] This, Cartwright believed, made blacks more suited to slavery than members of other races. Cartwright also believed that blacks suffered from diseases that whites could not catch. He identified "Dysaethesia Aethiopis" as an illness which caused slaves to misbehave, as if by compulsion. Another disease, "Drapetomania" affected the minds of slaves, "causing negroes to runaway."

Cartwright's scientific observations led him to defend slavery because in his mind, slavery protected the inferior race, which he believed could not survive in freedom. Josiah Nott was equally certain of the justice of slavery, but he rejected Cartwright's acceptance of blacks as merely an inferior group within the human family. Nott concluded that blacks were actually a separate species from whites that God had created solely to be the slaves of whites.[69] For Nott, black inferiority was "a fixed law of nature,"[70] and thus slavery was not only logical, but moral. Nott and Cartwright are only the best known of numerous scientists who made consistent arguments in favor of slavery based on the view that blacks were particularly suited to bondage and that they could not survive as free people.

The Political Defense

The political defense of slavery proceeded from the assumption that any attack on slavery would lead to a civil war and that the American political and constitutional system was based implicitly on an understanding that slavery was sacrosanct. In addition, proslavery theorists argued that slavery ultimately made democracy work. Such theorists as Senator James Henry Hammond and George Fitzhugh claimed that the greatest threat to democracy came from class warfare that destabilized the economy and threatened a peaceful and harmonious implementation of laws. But Southern theorists asserted that slavery eliminated this problem by elevating all free people to the status of "citizen" and by removing the lowest classes of society—what Hammond called "the mudsill"—from the political process.[71] Those who would most threaten economic stability and political harmony—the lower classes—were not allowed to undermine democratic society because they were not allowed to participate in it. Thus the rights of life, liberty, and happiness proclaimed in the Declaration of Independence could be universally applied to white Americans precisely because they were not applied to blacks.

Proslavery theorists also questioned the legitimacy of politicians who attacked slavery. David Christy, writing on the eve of the Civil War, asserted that "the dropping of the negro question, in American politics would at once destroy the prospects of thousands of aspirants to office. In ninety-nine cases out of a hundred, the clamor against slavery is made only for effect."[72]

A subset of the political defense of slavery involved Southern responses to the Declaration of Independence itself. Some Southerners categorically rejected the entire ideology of the Declaration. In 1826, the Virginia politician John Randolph of Roanoke asserted that the Declaration was "a most pernicious falsehood."[73] Edmund Ruffin, one of the South's earliest secessionists, thought the Declaration was a dangerous document. John C. Calhoun labeled the idea of equality a "false doctrine," only "hypothetically true," that had been "inserted" in the Declaration of Independence "without any necessity."[74] James Henry Hammond of South Carolina sneered at the "fine sounding and sentimental" language of the Declaration.[75]

In 1854, George Fitzhugh provided an elaborate proslavery attack on the Declaration. Fitzhugh believed that the United States was founded on "abstractions" that were "professed falsely."[76] He candidly asserted that "men are not born physically, morally or intellectually equal" and, contrary to the ideology of the Declaration, "their natural inequalities beget inequalities of rights." All blacks, he believed, were born "weak in mind or body,"[77] and because of this, "nature has made them slaves; all that law and government can do, is to regulate, modify and mitigate their slavery." He argued that on historical grounds "life and liberty" are not "inalienable"; they have been sold in all countries, and in all ages, and must be sold so long as human nature lasts." Slavery, in Fitzhugh's mind, was not peculiar but fundamental to society. He believed the North, not the South, had a peculiar institution: freedom. He argued that the purpose of government was "to restrict, control and punish man in the pursuit of happiness." Thus the preamble to the Declaration was "verbose, newborn, false, and unmeaning." The Declaration was "exuberantly false" and "fallacious."[78] Fitzhugh and other proslavery theorists argued that all men were not created equal, but that inequality was natural and universal. Rejecting the Declaration and its theories of equality, many Southerners instead developed their own proslavery arguments, ultimately asserting that slavery was a positive good for the slave and the master.[79]

Other Southerners continued to endorse the Declaration but denied that it could affect slavery. Some Southerners took a high road by arguing that the Declaration—like its Virginia counterpart—only applied to citizens or political communities. Slaves were naturally excluded from these.[80] One Virginia congressman argued that "no ingenuity" could "torture the Declaration of Independence into having the remotest allusion to the institution of domestic slavery."[81] Alexander Stephens, the future vice president of the Confederate States of America, believed that the framers had established "the first great principles of self-government by the governing race."[82]

The key for Stephens and other Southern supporters of the Declaration was of course race. Race made it possible for slaveowners to accept the credo of America because they could reject its application to their own slaves. Thus one Louisiana slaveowner affirmed that all men were created "free and equal as the Declaration of Independence holds they are."[83] He then added, "But all men, niggers, and monkeys *aint.*"[84]

While Calhoun, Fitzhugh, and other white Southerners rejected the Declaration because it undermined slavery, other masters "frequently made the Fourth of July a holiday for their slaves."[85] Slaves at a barbecue to celebrate the signing of the Declaration of Independence may seem ironic, but for such masters it was not. Masters considered slavery a benefit to the slaves, who were, in their eyes, racially inferior. Thus masters celebrated independence with their slaves because it was independence from Britain that allowed the American slaveowners to develop the political and legal system that perpetuated and strengthened slavery—a slavery that they claimed was a positive good for slaves as well as masters.

RACIAL THEORY AND IDEOLOGY: THE KEY TO PROSLAVERY THOUGHT

In the end, the key to the proslavery argument was race. It was the basis for all other defenses of slavery. Indeed, the racial argument was the "mudsill" of proslavery theory, just as Senator Hammond proclaimed that slavery was the mudsill of Southern society. Ultimately, all of the Southern defenses of slavery came back to race. This was necessary for two reasons. First, in the end only race could counter the obvious point that slavery contradicted the egalitarian and free-labor basis of American society. Second, if race was not the ultimate basis of slavery, then all of the arguments in favor of slavery might also be applied to poor whites or to immigrant whites. Other societies that accepted class distinctions as inevitable allowed for the enslavement of their own people, even though "outsiders" were most often enslaved. But in the United States, formal, recognized class distinctions among whites were unacceptable. Outsiders or immigrants, moreover, were constantly being brought into the society as full citizens. Thus only race could justify slavery.

The racial defense of slavery was based on two interrelated arguments: First, blacks were inferior to whites and were indeed better off as slaves. Second, if freed, people of African ancestry could not survive in the United States or live in peace with whites. The racial argument was tied to all other arguments defending slavery because for Americans, "race has always been the central reality of slavery."[86]

Because slavery in the United States "was black slavery," the study of slavery remains current and vital, and "even a purely historical study of an institution now dead for more than a century cannot escape being caught up in the urgency of contemporary black-white tensions."[87] Ultimately, Southerners turned to history, religion, and science to defend the concept of race as a justification for slavery. Using science or the Bible or both, Southerners strove mightily to demonstrate why blacks were "inferior" to whites.

Although slavery ended in 1865, many of the arguments about racial inferiority used to defend slavery remained part of America's intellectual culture and social mores. These proslavery arguments were recast and used to defend segregation, inequality, and the exploitation of blacks well into the twentieth century. To this day, remnants of proslavery thought can be found in our public discourse as well as private conversation. To understand how slavery shaped American history and continues to affect American society, we must examine the nature of proslavery thought.

NOTES

[1] U.S. Constitution, preamble.

[2] See, for example, Paul Finkelman, *Slavery and the Founders: Race and Liberty in the Age of Jefferson*, 2d ed. (Armonk, N.Y.: M. E. Sharpe, 2001).

[3] Ibid.; and William M. Wiecek, "Slavery and Abolition before the United States Supreme Court, 1820–1860," *Journal of American History* 65 (1979): 34–59. More generally, see William M. Wiecek, *The Sources of Antislavery Constitutionalism in America, 1760–1848* (Ithaca, N.Y.: Cornell University Press, 1977).

[4] A number of Northern states adopted "gradual emancipation" schemes, which freed the children of existing slaves. Thus, as late as the 1840s, a few hundred, mostly very old, slaves could be found in Pennsylvania, New Jersey, and Connecticut. Similarly, some people were held as slaves in Illinois until 1847. However, despite these anomalies, slavery after 1804 was a *Southern* institution.

[5] See, for example, Chief Justice Marshall's opinion in *The Antelope,* 23 U.S. (10 Wheat.) 66 (1825) upholding the legality of the African slave trade under international law. For a discussion of this case, see Robert Cover, *Justice Accused: Antislavery and the Judicial Process* (New Haven, Conn.: Yale University Press, 1977), 102–4. See also Wiecek, "Slavery and Abolition."

[6] *Dred Scott v. Sandford,* 60 U.S. (19 How.) 393 (1857). See also Paul Finkelman, *Dred Scott v. Sandford: A Brief History with Documents* (Boston and New York: Bedford/

St. Martin's, 1995). For a discussion of the many ways in which the Constitution protected slavery, see Finkelman, *Slavery and the Founders,* 3–36.

[7]Max Farrand, ed., *The Records of the Federal Convention of 1787,* rev. ed. (New Haven, Conn.: Yale University Press, 1966), 2:369–70.

[8]Ibid., 2:363–65.

[9]See Paul Finkelman, *"Prigg v. Pennsylvania:* Understanding Justice Story's Pro-Slavery Nationalism," *Journal of Supreme Court History* 2 (1997): 51–64; and Finkelman, *Dred Scott v. Sandford: A Brief History.*

[10]Paul Finkelman, "The Proslavery Origins of the Electoral College," *Cardozo Law Review* 23 (2002): 1145–57.

[11]Moses I. Finley, *Ancient Slavery and Modern Ideology* (New York: Viking, 1980), 117.

[12]On the concept of social death, see Orlando Patterson, *Slavery and Social Death* (Cambridge, Mass.: Harvard University Press, 1982).

[13]Finley, *Ancient Slavery,* 118.

[14]In the 1940s, Germans enslaved their fellow countrymen (as well as Russians, Poles, and other Europeans). Those sent to German industries as slaves or to German slave labor camps (as opposed to death camps like Auschwitz) were often physically indistinguishable from those who commanded their labor. However, under German theories of race, those enslaved were designated as members of different races or as politically corrupted.

[15]For example, see Patterson, *Slavery and Social Death.*

[16]Carl N. Deglar, "The Irony of American Negro Slavery," in Harry P. Owens, ed., *Perspectives and Irony in American Negro Slavery* (Jackson: University of Mississippi Press, 1976), 19.

[17]Alan Watson, "Seventeenth Century Jurists, Roman Law, and Slavery," in Paul Finkelman, ed., *Slavery and the Law* (Madison, Wis.: Madison House, 1997), 367–78.

[18]Race-based slavery existed in other New World societies, but in most, like Haiti and Brazil, there were large numbers of free people of color, often of mixed race parentage, as well as substantial numbers of free people of African birth or wholly of African ancestry. By contrast, on the eve of the Civil War, 95 percent of all people with any African ancestry were slaves.

[19]Finley, *Ancient Slavery,* 118, 119.

[20]Gen. 37:39–41.

[21]A unique exception to this may have been William Goyens, a free person of mixed ancestry who was an informal adviser to Sam Houston during the early days of the Texas Republic.

[22]Finley, *Ancient Slavery,* 97–98.

[23]This was also a result in Africa, where "slaves could often anticipate the gradual assimilation of their descendants into the social mainstream." James Oakes, *Slavery and Freedom: An Interpretation of the Old South* (New York: Random House, 1990), 32.

[24]For example, see *Gobu v. Gobu,* 1 N.C. 188 (1802); *Hudgins v. Wrights,* 11 Va. (1 Hen. & M.) 134 (1806); and *Adelle v. Beauregard,* 1 Mart. 183 (La. 1810).

[25]*State v. Harden,* 29 S.C.L. (2 Speers) 151n, 155n (1832).

[26]"An Act declaring that baptisme of slaves doth not exempt them from bondage," 2 *Hening's Statutes at Large* 260 (1667).

[27]Alan Watson, *Slave Law in the Americas* (Athens: University of Georgia Press, 1989).

[28]See, generally, Edmund Morgan, *American Slavery, American Freedom* (New York: W. W. Norton, 1975).

[29]Slavery also grew slowly at first on Barbados, where the British first used white servants as their labor force.

[30]William Thorndale, "The Virginia Census of 1619," *Magazine of Virginia Genealogy* 33 (1995): 155–71, suggests that blacks arrived before the summer of 1619; however, Martha W. McCartney, "An Early Virginia Census Reprised," *Quarterly Bulletin of the*

Virginia Archaeological Society 54 (1999): 178–96, argues that Thorndale's evidence is misdated.

    [31]"The Germantown Protest against Slavery" (1688), reprinted in Kermit Hall, William Wiecek, and Paul Finkelman, *American Legal History*, 2d ed. (New York: Oxford University Press, 1996), 35–36.

    [32]W. E. B. Du Bois, *The Suppression of the African Slave Trade, 1638–1870* (Cambridge, Mass.: Harvard University Press, 1896), 12–14.

    [33]*Somerset v. Stewart*, 1 Lofft (G.B.) 1 (1772); 12 Geo. 3 1772 K.B.

    [34]"An Act of the Gradual Abolition of Slavery," Act of Mar. 1, 1780, reprinted in Paul Finkelman, *The Law of Freedom and Bondage* (Dobbs Ferry, N.Y.: Oceana Press, 1986), 42–43.

    [35]See, generally, Arthur Zilversmit, *The First Emancipation: The Abolition of Slavery in the North* (Chicago: University of Chicago Press, 1967); and Gary B. Nash and Jean Soderlund, *Freedom by Degrees: Emancipation in Pennsylvania and Its Aftermath* (New York: Oxford University Press, 1991).

    [36]Thousands of other slaves gained freedom for themselves and their families by joining the British Army.

    [37]Quoted in Robinson, *Slavery in the Structure of American Politics, 1765–1820* (New York: Harcourt Brace, 1971), 80.

    [38]*Notes on the State of Virginia by Thomas Jefferson, with Related Documents*, ed. David Waldstreicher (Boston and New York: Bedford/St. Martin's, 2002). These quotations are taken from pp. 175–81. The entire passage is reprinted as Document 1. On Jefferson as a scientist, see Silvio A. Bedini, *Thomas Jefferson: Statesman of Science* (New York and London: Macmillan, 1990), esp. pp. 89–124.

    [39]Farrand, ed., *Records*, 1:516, 510.

    [40]Ibid., 1:566–67.

    [41]Ibid., 1:580–81.

    [42]Ibid., 1:594.

    [43]Ibid., 1:593.

    [44]Ibid., 1:363–65.

    [45]Ibid., 1:371–75.

    [46]Pinckney quoted in Jonathan Elliot, ed., *The Debates in the Several State Conventions on the Adaptation of the Federal Constitution*, 5 vols. (Philadelphia: J. B. Lippincott, 1896), 4:286. Patrick Henry, using any argument he could find to oppose the Constitution, feared that "among ten thousand implied powers which they may assume, they may, if we be engaged in war, liberate every one of your slaves if they please." Elliot, ed., *Debates*, 3:589. Ironically, the implied war powers of the president *would* be used to end slavery, but only after the South had renounced the Union.

    [47]Elliot, ed., *Debates*, 4:286.

    [48]"And he [Noah] said: Cursed be Canaan; a serve of servants he shall be unto his brethren.

    "And he said, Blessed be the Lord God of Shem; and Canaan shall be his servant.

    "God shall enlarge Japheth, and he shall dwell in the tents of Shem; and Canaan shall be his servant." Gen. 9:25–27.

    [49]See, for example, William R. Stanton, *The Leopard's Spots: Scientific Attitudes toward Race in America, 1815–1860* (Chicago: University of Chicago Press, 1960); Josiah Nott, *Types of Mankind* (1854); and various articles in Paul Finkelman, ed., *Articles on American Slavery*, vol. 11, *Religion and Slavery* (New York: Garland, 1989).

    [50]Samuel Cartwright, "The Unity of the Human Race Disproved by the Hebrew Bible," *De Bow's Review*, 29 (1860): 130.

    [51]Thomas F. Gossett, *Uncle Tom's Cabin and American Culture* (Dallas: Southern Methodist University Press, 1985), Chap. 12.

    [52]David Brion Davis, *Problem of Slavery in Western Culture* (Ithaca, N.Y.: Cornell University Press, 1964), 70.

[53] Ibid., 66–67.

[54] Ibid., 70.

[55] Ibid., 72.

[56] Thomas R. R. Cobb, *An Inquiry into the Law of Negro Slavery in the United States of America, To Which Is Prefixed an Historical Sketch of Slavery* (Philadelphia: T. & J. W. Johnson; Savannah: W. Thorne Williams, 1858), xl, lxxxi, lxvi, lxxxiii, lxvii.

[57] Lev. 19:20. I have used the King James Version of the Bible throughout this introduction because it was the most common in the United States at this time. A more modern translation would have, in fact, given greater support to slaveowners: "If a man sleeps with a woman as though married to her, she being another's concubine slave not yet purchased or given freedom, then the man is to be answerable for infringement of rights, but he shall not be put to death, since she was not a free woman." *The Jerusalem Bible: Reader's Edition* (Garden City, N.Y.: Doubleday, 1966), 128.

[58] 1 Cor. 7:22. The alternative, modern translation is more blunt. "A slave, when he is called in the Lord, becomes the Lord's freeman; and a freeman called in the Lord becomes Christ's slave." *New Jerusalem Bible*, 1 Cor. 7:22.

[59] Rev. A. T. Holmes, "The Duties of Christian Masters," reprinted in Holland N. McTyeire, ed., *Duties of Masters to Servants* (Charleston, S.C.: Southern Baptist Publication Society, 1851), 149.

[60] Gen. 9:18–25.

[61] James Henry Hammond, *Congressional Globe*, 35th Cong., 1st sess., Mar. 6, 1858, 61.

[62] 2 Hawks (N.C.) 582 (1823).

[63] 2 Dev. L. Rep. (N.C.) 263 (1829).

[64] *State v. Mann*, 13 N.C. at 266, 267.

[65] *Dred Scott v. Sandford*, 60 U.S. (19 How.) 393 (1857). See also Finkelman, *Dred Scott v. Sandford: A Brief History.*

[66] Ibid., 407.

[67] Ibid.

[68] Quoted in William Sumner Jenkins, *Pro-Slavery Thought in the Old South* (Chapel Hill: University of North Carolina Press, 1935), 250–51.

[69] Reginald Horsman, *Josiah Nott of Mobile: Southerner, Physician, Racial Theorist* (Baton Rouge: Louisiana State University Press, 1987), 82.

[70] Ibid., 125.

[71] James Henry Hammond, "Speech on the Admission of Kansas," U.S. Senate, *Congressional Globe*, 35th Cong., 2nd sess., Mar. 4, 1858, 961–62.

[72] David Christy, "Preface to the Third Edition," in E. N. Elliot, ed., *Cotton Is King and Proslavery Arguments* (Augusta, Ga.: Pritchard, Abbott & Loomis, 1860), 24.

[73] Quoted in Jenkins, *Pro-Slavery Thought in the Old South*, 60.

[74] John W. Blassingame, ed., *The Frederick Douglass Papers*, Series 1: *Speech, Debates, and Interviews, 1847–54* (New Haven, Conn.: Yale University Press, 1982), 488, n. 15.

[75] Quoted in Harvey Wish, *George Fitzhugh: Propagandist of the Old South* (Baton Rouge: Louisiana State University Press, 1943), 96.

[76] George Fitzhugh, *Sociology for the South, or the Failure of Free Society* (1854), 177; quotations in the rest of this paragraph are from pp. 177–78, 179, 180, 182.

[77] Ibid., 178. Fitzhugh also believed that some whites were born "weak in mind" and that they too might be legitimately enslaved.

[78] Ibid., 182.

[79] See, generally, Jenkins, *Pro-Slavery Thought in the Old South;* and Eugene D. Genovese, *The World the Slaveholders Made* (New York: Pantheon, 1969).

[80] Jenkins, *Pro-Slavery Thought in the Old South*, 156–57. In *Hudgins v. Wrights*, 11 Va. (1 Hen. & M.) 134 (1806), Virginia's highest court applied this analysis to similar language in Virginia's Declaration of Rights.

[81] Quoted in James Oakes, *The Ruling Race: A History of American Slaveholders* (New York: Knopf, 1982), 143.

[82] Ibid.
[83] Ibid.
[84] Ibid.
[85] Ibid., 142.
[86] David Brion Davis, "Slavery and the American Mind," in Harry P. Owens, ed., *Perspectives and Irony in American Slavery* (Oxford: University Press of Mississippi, 1976), 59.
[87] Finley, *Ancient Slavery,* 11.

PART TWO

The Documents

Politics, Economics, and Proslavery Thought

1

THOMAS JEFFERSON

Notes on the State of Virginia

1787

Thomas Jefferson (1743–1826) wrote his Notes on the State of Virginia *for private circulation among French intellectuals. He authorized its publication in 1787. In the middle of his section on Virginia's laws, Jefferson noted a proposed bill for the gradual emancipation of slaves in Virginia. This bill had in fact never been proposed in the Virginia legislature, and despite Jefferson's claims to the contrary, there is no evidence that he ever supported such a bill. Writing about the bill as if it were still pending in the legislature, Jefferson began a larger discussion of slavery in which he set out many of the arguments that Southerners would develop into a full-blown proslavery defense in the first half of the nineteenth century.*

The bill reported by the revisors* does not itself contain this proposition [to emancipate all slaves born after passing the act]; but an amendment containing it was prepared, to be offered to the legislature whenever the bill should be taken up, and further directing that they

---

revisors: The legislative committee appointed to revise the laws of Virginia, chaired by Jefferson.

From *Notes on the State of Virginia by Thomas Jefferson, with Related Documents,* ed. David Waldstreicher (Boston and New York: Bedford/St. Martin's, 2002), 175–81. Unless otherwise noted, footnotes with symbols are by David Waldstreicher.

N   O   T   E   S

ON THE

STATE OF VIRGINIA,

WRITTEN BY

THOMAS JEFFERSON.

ILLUSTRATED WITH

A MAP, including the States of VIRGINIA, MARY-
LAND, DELAWARE and PENNSYLVANIA.

L O N D O N:

PRINTED FOR JOHN STOCKDALE, OPPOSITE
BURLINGTON-HOUSE, PICCADILLY.

M.DCC.LXXXVII.

The title page of the 1787 edition of Jefferson's *Notes on the State of Virginia,* published in London.
Benjamin Franklin Collection, Yale University Library.

[the slave children] should continue with their parents to a certain age, then be brought up, at the public expense, to tillage, arts or sciences, according to their geniuses, till the females should be eighteen, and the males twenty-one years of age, when they should be colonized to such place as the circumstances of the time should render most proper, sending them out with arms, implements of household and of the handicraft arts, seeds, pairs of the useful domestic animals, &c. to declare them a free and independent people, and extend to them our alliance and protection, till they shall have acquired strength; and to send vessels at the same time to other parts of the world for an equal number of white inhabitants; to induce whom to migrate hither, proper encouragements were to be proposed. It will probably be asked, Why not retain and incorporate the blacks into the state, and thus save the expense of supplying, by importation of white settlers, the vacancies they will leave? Deep-rooted prejudices entertained by the whites; ten thousand recollections, by the blacks, of the injuries they have sustained; new provocations; the real distinctions which nature has made; and many other circumstances, will divide us into parties, and produce convulsions which will probably never end but in the extermination of the one or the other race. — To these objections, which are political, may be added others, which are physical and moral. The first difference which strikes us is that of color. Whether the black of the negro resides in the reticular membrane between the skin and scarf–skin, or in the scarf–skin itself; whether it proceeds from the color of the blood, the color of the bile, or from that of some other secretion, the difference is fixed in nature, and is real as if its seat and cause were better known to us. And is this difference of no importance? Is it not the foundation of a greater or less share of beauty in the two races? Are not the fine mixtures of red and white, the expressions of every passion by greater or less suffusions of color in the one, preferable to that eternal monotony which reigns in the countenances, that immovable veil of black which covers all the emotions of the other race? Add to these flowing hair, a more elegant symmetry of form, their own judgment in favor of the whites, declared by their preference of them, as uniformly as is the preference of the Oranootan[1] for the black women over those of his own species. The circumstance of superior beauty, is thought worthy attention in the propagation of our horses, dogs, and other domestic animals; why not in that of man? Besides those of color, figure and hair, there are other physical distinctions proving a difference of race. They have less hair on the face and body. They secrete less by the kidneys, and more by the glands of the skin, which gives them a very strong and disagreeable odor. This greater degree of transpiration renders them more tolerant of heat, and less so of cold, than the whites. Perhaps, too, a difference of structure in the pulmonary apparatus, which a late

[1] *Oranootan:* orangutan.

ingenious experimentalist has discovered to be the principal regulator of animal heat, may have disabled them from extricating, in the act of inspiration, so much of that fluid from the outer air, or obliged them in expiration, to part with more of it. They seem to require less sleep. A black, after hard labor through the day, will be induced by the slightest amusements to sit up till midnight, or later, though knowing he must be out with the first dawn of the morning. They are at least as brave, and more adventuresome. But this may perhaps proceed from a want of forethought, which prevents their seeing a danger till it be present. When present, they do not go through it with more coolness or steadiness than the whites. They are more ardent after their female; but love seems with them to be more an eager desire, than a tender delicate mixture of sentiment and sensation. Their griefs are transient. Those numberless afflictions, which render it doubtful whether Heaven has given life to us in mercy or in wrath, are less felt, and sooner forgotten with them. In general, their existence appears to participate more of sensation than reflection. To this must be ascribed their disposition to sleep when abstracted from their diversions, and unemployed in labor. An animal whose body is at rest, and who does not reflect, must be disposed to sleep of course. Comparing them by their faculties of memory, reason, and imagination, it appears to me that in memory they are equal to the whites; in reason much inferior, as I think one could scarcely be found capable of tracing and comprehending the investigations of Euclid; and that in imagination they are dull, tasteless and anomalous. It would be unfair to follow them to Africa for this investigation. We will consider them here on the same stage with the whites, and where the facts are not apocryphal on which a judgment is to be formed. It will be right to make great allowances for the difference of condition, of education, of conversation, of the sphere in which they move. Many millions of them have been brought to, and born in America. Most of them, indeed, have been confined to tillage, to their own homes, and their own society; yet many have been so situated, that they might have availed themselves of the conversation of their masters; many have been brought up to the handicraft arts, and from that circumstance have always been associated with the whites. Some have been liberally educated, and all have lived in countries where the arts and sciences are cultivated to a considerable degree, and have had before their eyes samples of the best works from abroad. The Indians, with no advantages of this kind, will often carve figures on their pipes not destitute of design and merit. They will crayon out an animal, a plant, or a country, so as to prove the existence of a germ in their minds which only wants cultivation. They astonish you with strokes of the most sublime oratory; such as prove their reason and sentiment strong, their imagination glowing and elevated. But never yet could I find that a black had uttered a thought above the level of plain narration; never seen even an elementary trait of painting or sculpture. In music they are more generally gifted than the whites with accurate ears for tune and time, and they have been found capable of imagining a small catch.* Whether they will be equal to the composition of a more extensive run of melody, or of complicated harmony, is yet to be proved. Misery is often the parent of the most affecting touches in poetry.—Among the blacks is misery enough, God knows, but no poetry. Love is the peculiar oestrum[2] of the poet. Their love is ardent, but it kindles the senses only, not the imagination. Religion, indeed, has produced a Phyllis Whately; but it could not produce a poet.† The compositions published under her name are below the dignity of criticism. The heroes of the Dunciad are to her as Hercules to the author of that poem.‡ Ignatius Sancho has approached nearer to merit in composition; yet his letters do more honor to the heart than the head.§ They breathe the purest effusions of friendship and general philanthropy, and shew how great a degree of the latter may be compounded with strong religious zeal. He is often happy in the turn of his compliments, and his style is easy and familiar, except when he affects a Shandean fabrication of words.‖ But his imagination is wild and extravagant, escapes incessantly from every restraint of reason and taste, and, in the course of its vagaries, leaves a tract of thought as incoherent and eccentric as is the course of a meteor through the sky. His subjects should often have led him to a process of sober reasoning: yet we find him always substituting sentiment for demonstration. Upon the whole, though we admit him to the first place among those of his own color who have presented themselves to the public judgment, yet when we compare him with the writers of the race among whom he lived, and particularly with the epistolary class, in which he has taken his own stand, we are compelled

---

*The instrument proper to them is the banjo, which they brought hither from Africa, and which is the original of the guitar, its chords being precisely the four lower chords of the guitar. [Jefferson's note.]

[2]*oestrum:* as used here, stimulus.

†Phillis Wheatley, a Massachusetts slave born in Africa, author of *Poems on Various Subjects, Religious and Moral* (London, 1773).

‡Alexander Pope, *The Dunciad* (London, 1728).

§Ignatius Sancho, *Letters of Ignatius Sancho,* 2 vols. (London, 1782).

‖Laurence Sterne, *The Life and Opinions of Tristram Shandy, Gentleman* (London, 1757–71).

to enroll him at the bottom of the column. This criticism supposes the letters published under his name to be genuine, and to have received amendment from no other hand; points which would not be of easy investigation. The improvement of the blacks in body and mind, in the first instance of their mixture with the whites, has been observed by every one, and proves that their inferiority is not the effect merely of their condition of life. We know that among the Romans, about the Augustan age especially, the condition of their slaves was much more deplorable than that of the blacks on the continent of America. The two sexes were confined in separate apartments, because to raise a child cost the master more than to buy one. Cato, for a very restricted indulgence to his slaves in this particular, took from them a certain price. But in this country the slaves multiply as fast as the free inhabitants. Their situation and manners place the commerce between the two sexes almost without restraint.—The same Cato, on a principle of economy, always sold his sick and superannuated slaves. He gives it as a standing precept to a master visiting his farm, to sell his old oxen, old wagons, old tools, old and diseased servants, and every thing else become useless. . . . The American slaves cannot enumerate this among the injuries and insults they receive. It was the common practice to expose in the island of Aesculapius, in the Tyber, diseased slaves, whose cure was like to become tedious. The Emperor Claudius by an edict gave freedom to such of them as should recover, and first declared, that if any person chose to kill rather than to expose them, it should be deemed homicide. The exposing them is a crime, of which no instance has existed with us; and were it to be followed by death, it would be punished capitally. We are told of a certain Vedius Pollio, who, in the presence of Augustus, would have given a slave as food to his fish, for having broken a glass. With the Romans, the regular method of taking the evidence of their slaves was under torture. Here it has been thought better never to resort to their evidence. When a master was murdered, all his slaves in the same house, or within hearing, were condemned to death. Here punishment falls on the guilty only, and as precise proof is required against him as against a freeman. Yet notwithstanding these and other discouraging circumstances among the Romans, their slaves were often their rarest artists. They excelled, too, in science, insomuch as to be usually employed as tutors to their master's children. Epictetus, Diogenes, Phaedon, Terence, and Phedrus, were slaves. But they were of the race of whites. It is not their condition then, but nature, which has produced the distinction.— Whether further observation will or will not verify the conjecture, that nature has been less bountiful to them in the endowments of the head, I believe that in those of the heart she will be found to have done them justice. That disposition to theft with which they have been branded, must be ascribed to their situation, and not to any depravity of the moral sense. The man, in whose favor no laws of property exist, probably feels himself less bound to respect those made in favor of others. When arguing for ourselves, we lay it down as a fundamental, that laws, to be just, must give a reciprocation of right: that, without this, they are mere arbitrary rules of conduct, founded in force, and not in conscience; and it is a problem which I give to the master to solve, whether the religious precepts against the violation of property were not framed for him as well as his slave? And whether the slave may not as justifiably take a little from one who has taken all from him, as he may slay one who would slay him? That a change in the relations in which a man is placed should change his ideas of moral right and wrong, is neither new nor peculiar to the color of the blacks. Homer tells us it was so 2600 years ago:

Jove fix'd it certain, that whatever day
Makes man a slave, takes half his worth away.

But the slaves of which Homer speaks were whites. Notwithstanding these considerations, which must weaken their respect for the laws of property, we find among them numerous instances of the most rigid integrity, and as many as among their better instructed masters, of benevolence, gratitude, and unshaken fidelity.—The opinion that they are inferior in the faculties of reason and imagination, must be hazarded with great diffidence. To justify a general conclusion, requires many observations, even where the subject may be submitted to the Anatomical knife, to Optical glasses, to analysis by fire, or by solvents. How much more then where it is a faculty, not a substance, we are examining; where it eludes the research of all the senses; where the conditions of its existence are various, and variously combined; where the effects of those which are present or absent bid defiance to calculation; let me add too, as a circumstance of great tenderness, where our conclusion would degrade a whole race of men from the rank in the scale of beings which their Creator may perhaps have given them. To our reproach it must be said, that though for a century and a half we have had under our eyes the races of black and of red men, they have never yet been viewed by us as subjects of natural history. I advance it therefore as a suspicion only, that the blacks, whether originally a distinct race, or made distinct by time and circumstances, are inferior to the whites in the endowments both of body and mind. It is not against experience to suppose that different species of the same genus, or varieties of the same species, may possess different qualifications. Will not a lover of natural history then, one who views the gradations in all the races of animals with the eye of philosophy, excuse an effort to keep those in the department of man as distinct as nature has formed them? This unfortunate difference of color, and perhaps of faculty, is a powerful obstacle to the emancipation of these people. Many of their advocates, while they wish to vindicate the liberty of human nature, are anxious also to preserve its dignity and beauty. Some of these, embarrassed by the question, "What further is to be done with them?" join themselves in opposition with those who are actuated by sordid avarice only. Among the Romans emancipation required but one effort. The slave, when made free, might mix with, without staining the blood of his master. But with us a second is necessary, unknown to history. When freed, he is to be removed beyond the reach of mixture.

2

JOHN C. CALHOUN

Speech in the U.S. Senate

1837

John C. Calhoun (1782–1850) of South Carolina was the most important proslavery politician in the country before his death, which took place in the midst of the debates over the Compromise of 1850. Calhoun had a distinguished career in public service as a congressman, senator, cabinet member, and vice president under both John Quincy Adams and Andrew Jackson.

In this speech, Calhoun responds to antislavery petitions sent to the Senate by abolitionist groups. He refuses to concede that slavery is in the

John C. Calhoun, "Speech on the Reception of Abolition Petitions, Delivered in the Senate, February 6th, 1837," in Richard R. Crallé, ed., *Speeches of John C. Calhoun, Delivered in the House of Representatives and in the Senate of the United States* (New York: D. Appleton, 1853), 625–33.

slightest degree evil. On the contrary, he argues that slavery is "indispensable to the peace and happiness of both" whites and blacks. Like other proslavery politicians, he makes claims for the constitutional protection of slavery while at the same time asserting that the racial inferiority of blacks requires that they be held as slaves. He asserts that "instead of an evil," slavery is "a good—a positive good." This argument helped characterize the entire debate over slavery until the Emancipation Proclamation, the realities of the Civil War, and the Thirteenth Amendment finally ended the institution.

Calhoun began this speech by reading two antislavery petitions. He then began speaking against them.

The peculiar institution of the South—that, on the maintenance of which the very existence of the slaveholding States depends, is pronounced to be sinful and odious, in the sight of God and man; and this with a systematic design of rendering us hateful in the eyes of the world—with a view to a general crusade against us and our institutions. This, too, in the legislative halls of the Union; created by these confederated States, for the better protection of their peace, their safety, and their respective institution;—and yet, we, the representatives of twelve of these sovereign States against whom this deadly war is waged, are expected to sit here in silence, hearing ourselves and our constituents day after day denounced, without uttering a word; for if we but open our lips, the charge of agitation is resounded on all sides, and we are held up as seeking to aggravate the evil which we resist. Every reflecting mind must see in all this a sate of things deeply and dangerously diseased.

I do not belong to the school which holds that aggression is to be met by concession. Mine is the opposite creed, which teaches that encroachments must be met at the beginning, and that those who act on the opposite principle are prepared to become slaves. In this case, in particular, I hold concession or compromise to be fatal. If we concede an inch, concession would follow concession—compromise would follow compromise, until our ranks would be so broken that effectual resistance would be impossible. We must meet the enemy on the frontier, with a fixed determination of maintaining our position at every hazard. Consent to receive these insulting petitions, and the next demand will be that they be referred to a committee in order that they may be deliberated and acted upon. At the last session we were modestly asked to receive them, simply to lay them on the table, without any view to ulterior action. I then told the Senator from Pennsylvania (Mr. Buchanan), who so strongly urged that course in the Senate, that it was a position that could not be maintained; as the argument in favor of acting on the petitions if we were bound to receive, could not be resisted. I then said, that the next step would be to refer the petition to a committee, and I already see indications that such is now the intention. If we yield, that will be followed by another, and we will thus proceed, step by step, to the final consummation of the object of these petitions. We are now told that the most effectual mode of arresting the progress of abolition is, to reason it down; and with this view it is urged that the petitions ought to be referred to a committee. That is the very ground which was taken at the last session in the other House, but instead of arresting its progress it has since advanced more rapidly than ever. The most unquestionable right may be rendered doubtful, if one admitted to be a subject of controversy, and that would be the case in the present instance. The subject is beyond the jurisdiction of Congress—they have no right to touch it in any shape or form, or to make it the subject of deliberation or discussion.

In opposition to this view it is urged that Congress is bound by the constitution to receive petitions in every case and on every subject, whether within its constitutional competency or not. I hold the doctrine to be absurd, and do solemnly believe, that it would be as easy to prove that it has the right to abolish slavery, as that it is bound to receive petitions for that purpose. The very existence of the rule that requires a question to be put on the reception of petitions, is conclusive to show that there is no such obligation. It has been a standing rule from the commencement of the Government, and clearly shows the sense of those who formed the constitution on this point. The question on the reception would be absurd, if, as is contended, we are bound to receive; but I do not intend to argue the question; I discussed it fully at the last session, and the arguments then advanced neither have been nor can be answered.

As widely as this incendiary spirit has spread, it has not yet infected this body, or the great mass of the intelligent and business portion of the North; but unless it be speedily stopped, it will spread and work upwards till it brings the two great sections of the Union into deadly conflict. This is not a new impression with me. Several years since, in a discussion with one of the Senators from Massachusetts (Mr. Webster), before this fell spirit had showed itself, I then predicted that the doctrine of the proclamation and the Force Bill,— that this Government had a right, in the last resort, to determine the extent of its own powers, and enforce its decision at the point of the bayonet, which was so warmly maintained by that Senator, would at no distant day arouse the dormant spirit of abolitionism. I told him that the doctrine was tantamount to the assumption of unlimited power on the part of the Government, and that such would be the impression on the public mind in a large portion of the Union. The consequence would be inevitable. A large portion of the Northern States believed slavery to be a sin, and would consider it as an obligation of conscience to abolish it if they should feel themselves in any degree responsible for its continuance,—and that this doctrine would necessarily lead to the belief of such responsibility. I then predicted that it would commence as it has with this fanatical portion of society, and that they would begin their operations on the ignorant, the weak, the young, and the thoughtless,—and gradually extend upwards till they would become strong enough to obtain political control, when he and others holding the highest stations in society, would, however reluctant, be compelled to yield to their doctrines, or be driven into obscurity. But four years have since elapsed, and all this is already in a course of regular fulfillment.

Standing at the point of time at which we have now arrived, it will not be more difficult to trace the course of future events now than it was then. They who imagine that the spirit now abroad in the North, will die away of itself without a shock or convulsion, have formed a very inadequate conception of its real character; it will continue to rise and spread, unless prompt and efficient measures to stay its progress be adopted. Already it has taken possession of the pulpit, of the schools, and, to a considerable extent, of the press; those great instruments by which the mind of the rising generation will be formed.

However sound the great body of the non-slaveholding States are at present, in the course of a few years they will be succeeded by those who will have been taught to hate the people and institutions of nearly one-half of this Union, with a hatred more deadly than one hostile nation ever entertained towards another. It is easy to see the end. By the necessary course of events, if left to themselves, we must become, finally, two people. It is impossible under the deadly hatred which must spring up between the two great sections, if the present causes are permitted to operate unchecked, that we should continue under the same political system. The conflicting elements would burst the Union asunder, powerful as are the links which hold it together. Abolition and the Union cannot co-exist. As the friend of the Union I openly proclaim it,—and the sooner it is known the better. The former may now be controlled, but in a short time it will be beyond the power of man to arrest the course of events. We of the South will not, cannot surrender our institutions. To maintain the existing relations between the two races, inhabiting that section of the Union, is indispensable to the peace and happiness of both. It cannot be subverted without drenching the country in blood, and extirpating one or the other of the races. Be it good or bad, it has grown up with our society and institutions, and is so interwoven with them, that to destroy it would be to destroy us as a people. But let me not be understood as admitting, even by implication, that the existing relations between the two races in the slaveholding States is an evil:—far otherwise; I hold it to be a good, as it has thus far proved itself to be to both, and will continue to prove so if not disturbed by the fell spirit of abolition. I appeal to facts. Never before has the black race of Central Africa, from the dawn of history to the present day, attained a condition so civilized and so improved, not only physically, but morally and intellectually. It came among us in a low, degraded, and savage condition, and in the course of a few generations it has grown up under the fostering care of our institutions, reviled as they have been, to its present comparatively civilized condition. This, with the rapid increase of numbers, is conclusive proof of the general happiness of the race, in spite of all the exaggerated tales to the contrary.

In the mean time, the white or European race has not degenerated. It has kept pace with its brethren in other sections of the Union where slavery does not exist. It is odious to make comparison; but I appeal to all sides whether the South is not equal in virtue, intelligence, patriotism, courage, disinterestedness, and all the high qualities which adorn our nature. I ask whether we have not contributed our full share of talents and political wisdom in forming and sustaining this political fabric; and whether we have not constantly inclined most strongly to the side of liberty, and been the first to see and first to resist the encroachments of power. In one thing only are we inferior—the arts of gain; we acknowledge that we are less wealthy than the Northern section of this Union, but I trace this mainly to the fiscal action of this Government, which has extracted much from, and spent little among us. Had it been the reverse,—if the exaction had been from the other section, and the expenditure with us, this point of superiority would not be against us now, as it was not at the formation of this Government.

But I take higher ground. I hold that in the present state of civilization, where two races of different origin, and distinguished by color, and other physical differences, as well as intellectual, are brought together, the relation now existing in the slaveholding States between the two, is, instead of an evil, a good—a positive good. I feel myself called upon to speak freely upon the subject where the honor and interests of those I represent are involved. I hold then, that there never has yet existed a wealthy and civilized society in which one portion of the community did not, in point of fact, live on the labor of the other. Broad and general as is this assertion, it is fully borne out by history. This is not the proper occasion, but if it were, it would not be difficult to trace the various devices by which the wealth of all civilized communities has been so unequally divided, and to show by what means so small a share has been allotted to those by whose labor it was produced, and so large a share given to the nonproducing classes. The devices are almost innumerable, from the brute force and gross superstition of ancient times, to the subtle and artful fiscal contrivances of modern. I might well challenge a comparison between them and the more direct, simple, and patriarchal mode by which the labor of the African race is, among us, commanded by the European. I may say with truth, that in few countries so much is left to the share of the laborer, and so little exacted from him, or where there is more kind attention paid to him in sickness or infirmities of age. Compare his condition with the tenants of the poor houses in the more civilized portions of Europe—look at the sick, and the old and infirm slave, on one hand, in the midst of his family and friends, under the kind superintending care of his master and mistress, and compare it with the forlorn and wretched condition of the pauper in the poor house. But I will not dwell on this aspect of the question; I turn to the political; and here I fearlessly assert that the existing relation between the two races in the South, against which these blind fanatics are waging war, forms the most solid and durable foundation on which to rear free and stable political institutions. It is useless to disguise the fact. There is and always has been in an advanced stage of wealth and civilization, a conflict between labor and capital. The condition of society in the South exempts us from the disorders and dangers resulting from this conflict; and which explains why it is that the political condition of the slaveholding States has been so much more stable and quiet than that of the North. The advantages of the former, in this respect, will become more and more manifest if left undisturbed by interference from without, as the country advances in wealth and numbers. We have, in fact, but just entered that condition of society where the strength and durability of our political institutions are to be tested; and

I venture nothing in predicting that the experience of the next generation will fully test how vastly more favorable our condition of society is to that of other sections for free and stable institutions, provided we are not disturbed by the interference of others, or shall have sufficient intelligence and spirit to resist promptly and successfully such interference. It rests with ourselves to meet and repel them. I look not for aid to this Government, or to the other States; not but there are kind feelings towards us on the part of the great body of the non-slaveholding States; but as kind as their feelings may be, we may rest assured that no political party in those States will risk their ascendency for our safety. If we do not defend ourselves none will defend us; if we yield we will be more and more pressed as we recede; and if we submit we will be trampled under foot. Be assured that emancipation itself would not satisfy these fanatics:—that gained, the next step would be to raise the negroes to a social and political equality with the whites; and that being effected, we would soon find the present condition of the two races reversed. They and their northern allies would be the masters, and we the slaves; the condition of the white race in the British West India Islands, bad as it is, would be happiness to ours. There the mother country is interested in sustaining the supremacy of the European race. It is true that the authority of the former master is destroyed, but the African will there still be a slave, not to individuals but to the community,—forced to labor, not by the authority of the overseer, but by the bayonet of the soldiery and the rod of the civil magistrate.

Surrounded as the slaveholding States are with such imminent perils, I rejoice to think that our means of defence are ample, if we shall prove to have the intelligence and spirit to see and apply them before it is too late. All we want is concert, to lay aside all party differences, and unite with zeal and energy in repelling approaching dangers. Let there be concert of action, and we shall find ample means of security without resorting to secession or disunion. I speak with full knowledge and a thorough examination of the subject, and for one, see my way clearly. One thing alarms me—the eager pursuit of gain which overspreads the land, and which absorbs every faculty of the mind and every feeling of the heart. Of all passions avarice is the most blind and compromising—the last to see and the first to yield to danger. I dare not hope that any thing I can say will arouse the South to a due sense of danger; I fear it is beyond the power of mortal voice to awaken it in time from the fatal security into which it has fallen.

3

EDMUND RUFFIN

The Political Economy of Slavery

1853

Edmund Ruffin (1794–1865) was one of the most fanatic proslavery theorists of the late antebellum period. In 1859, the sixty-five-year-old Ruffin enrolled in a militia company so he could attend the execution of John Brown. Two years later, he moved to South Carolina when his home state of Virginia did not immediately secede. Shortly thereafter, this long-time advocate of secession was given the honor of igniting a fuse to fire the first shot on Fort Sumter. When the war ended with the Confederacy in ashes, Ruffin shot himself in the head with a pistol, preferring death to the prospect of living in a reconstructed Union where slavery was illegal.

In this famous essay, Ruffin defends slavery on a variety of grounds, arguing that it is better for workers than free labor but also that it is more profitable. Like most Southern defenders of the institution, he also roots his arguments in theories of race.

SLAVERY GENERAL IN ANCIENT TIMES—CAUSES OF SLAVERY—AVERSION
TO LABOR OF DEGRADED CLASSES AND OF BARBAROUS COMMUNITIES

Slavery has existed from as early time as historical records furnish any information of the social and political condition of mankind. There was no country, in the most ancient time of its history, of which the people had made any considerable advances in industry or refinement, in which slavery had not been previously and long established, and in general use. The reasons for this universal early existence of slavery, and of domestic or individual slavery, (except among the most ignorant and savage tribes,) can be readily deduced from the early conditions of society.

Whether in savage or civilized life, the lower that individuals are degraded by poverty and want, and the fewer are their means for

Edmund Ruffin, *The Political Economy of Slavery; or, The Institution Considered in Regard to Its Influence on Public Wealth and the General Welfare* (Washington, D.C.: Lemuel Towers, 1853).

Edmund Ruffin in a photograph taken around the time of the start of the Civil War.

Culver Pictures.

comfort, and the enjoyment of either intellectual or physical pleasures, or of relief from physical sufferings, the lower do they descend in their appreciation of actual and even natural wants; and the more do they magnify and dread the efforts and labors necessary to protect themselves against the occurrence of the privations and sufferings with which they are threatened. When man sinks so low as not to feel artificial wants, or utterly to dispair of gratifying any such wants, he becomes brutishly careless and indolent, even in providing for natural and physical wants, upon which provision even life is dependent. All such persons soon learn to regard present and continuous labor as an evil greater than the probable but uncertain future occurrence of extreme privation, or even famine, and consequent death from want. Hence the most savage tribes of tropical regions are content to rely for sustenance almost entirely on the natural productions of a fertile and bounteous soil. The savage inhabitants of less fruitful lands, and under more rigorous climates, depend on hunting and fishing for a precarious support and with irregular alternations of abundance and lavish waste, with destitution and hunger and famine. And in every civilized and plentiful, and even generally industrious country, there are to be found, in the lowest grade of free inhabitants, many individuals, families, and communities of many families, who live in the most abject condition of poverty and privation in which life can be preserved, (and is not always preserved,) and prefer such wretched existence to the alternative of steady labor, by which they might greatly improve their condition, if not relieve all wants for the necessaries of life. Even in countries, and among a general population, in which the highest rewards are held out for labor and industry—where some intellectual, and also moral and religious instruction, are within the reach of all who will seek and accept such benefits, there are numerous cases of men who not only forego all intellectual and moral improvement for themselves and their families, and the attempt to gratify all artificial wants, but who also neglect the relief of the most humble comforts and even necessaries of life, rather than resort to that regular course of labor which would furnish the means for comfortable subsistence. In all such cases—whether in civilized or in savage society, or whether in regard to individuals, families in successive generations, or to more extended communities—a good and proper remedy for this evil, if it could be applied, would be the enslaving of these reckless, wretched drones and cumberers of the earth, and thereby compelling them to habits of labor, and in return satisfying their wants for necessaries, and raising them and their progeny in the scale of humanity, not only physically, but morally and intellectually. Such a measure would be the most beneficial in young or rude communities, where labor is scarce and dear, and the means for subsistance easy to obtain. For even among a barbarous people, where the aversion to labor is universal, those who could not be induced to labor with their own hands, and in person, if they became slaveholders, would be ready enough to compel the labor of their slaves, and also would soon learn to economize and accumulate the products of their labor. Hence, among any savage people, the introduction and establishment of domestic slavery is necessarily an improvement of the condition and wealth and well-being of the community in general, and also of the comfort of the enslaved class, if it had consisted of such persons as were lowest in the social scale—and is beneficial in every such case to the master class, and to the community in general.

INDOLENCE OF FREE LABORERS AT HIGH WAGES—DIFFERENT
INCENTIVES TO FREE AND SLAVE LABOR—COMPARATIVE VALUES

But the disposition to indulge indolence (even at great sacrifices of benefit which might be secured by industrious labor) is not peculiar to the lowest and most degraded classes of civilized communities. It is notorious that, whenever the demand for labor is much greater than the supply, or the wages of labor are much higher than the expenses of living, very many, even of the ordinary laboring class, are remarkable for indolence, and work no more than compelled by necessity. The greater the demand, and the higher the rewards, for labor, the less will be performed, as a general rule, by each individual laborer. If the wages of work for one day will support the laborer or mechanic and his family for three, it will be very likely that he will be idle two-thirds of his time.

Slave labor, in each individual case, and for each small measure of time, is more slow and inefficient than the labor of a free man. The latter knows that the more work he performs in a short time, the greater will be his reward in earnings. Hence, he has every inducement to exert himself while at work for himself, even though he may be idle for a longer time afterwards. The slave receives the same support, in food, clothing, and other allowances, whether he works much or little; and hence he has every inducement to spare himself as much as possible, and to do as little work as he can, without drawing on himself punishment, which is the only incentive to slave labor. It is, then, an unquestionable general truth, that the labor of a free man, for any stated time, is more than the labor of a slave, and if at the same cost, would be cheaper to the employer. Hence it has been inferred, and asserted by all who argue against slavery, and is often admitted even by those who would defend its expediency, that, as a general rule, and for whole communities, free labor is cheaper than slave labor. The rule is false, and the exceptions only are true. Suppose it admitted that the labor of slaves, for each hour or day, will amount to but two-thirds of what hired free laborers would perform in the same time. But the slave labor is continuous, and every day at least it returns to the employers and to the community, this two-thirds of full labor. Free laborers, if to be hired for the like duties, would require at least double the amount of wages to perform one-third more labor in each day, and in general, would be idle and earning nothing, more length of time than that spent in labor. Then, on these premises and supposi- tions, it is manifest that slave labor, with its admitted defect in this respect, will be cheapest and most profitable to the employer, and to the whole community, and will yield more towards the general increase of production and public wealth; and that the free laborer who is idle two days out of three, even if receiving double wages for his days of labor, is less laborious, and less productive for himself, and for the community, and the public wealth, than the slave.

The mistake of those who maintain, or admit, this generally as- serted proposition, that "free labor is cheaper than slave labor," is caused by assuming as true, that self-interest induces free hirelings to labor continuously and regularly. This is never the case in general, except where daily and continuous labor is required to obtain a bare daily subsistence. . . .

THE GREATEST WORKS OF ANCIENT NATIONS DUE TO SLAVERY,
AND IN ITS WORST FORM

Still, even this worst and least profitable kind of slavery (the subjec- tion of equals, and men of the same race with their masters) served as the foundation and the essential first cause of all the civilization and refinement, and improvement of arts and learning, that distinguished the oldest nations. Except where the special Providence and care of God may have interposed to guard a particular family and its descen- dants, there was nothing but the existence of slavery to prevent any race or society in a state of nature from sinking into the rudest bar- barism. And no people could ever have been raised from that low con- dition without the aid and operation of slavery, either by some individuals of the community being made slaves to others, or the whole community being enslaved, by conquest and subjugation, in some form, to a foreign and more enlightened people. The very ancient and wonderful works of construction and sculpture in Egypt and Hindostan could never have been executed, nor even the desire to possess them conceived, except where compulsory labor had long been in use, and could be applied to such great works. And to the same cause was due, not only the later and far more perfect and admirable works of art in Greece and Rome, but also the marvellous triumphs of intellect among these successive masters of the then known world. And not only were great works of utility and ornament so produced, nations enriched and strengthened, and empires established and maintained, but also there were moral results, in private and social life, of far more value. In much earlier time, it was on this institution of domestic slavery that was erected the admirable and beneficent mastership and government of the patriarch Abraham, who owned so many domestic slaves that he could suddenly call out and lead three hundred and eighteen of them, able to bear arms, to repel and punish the invasion of foreign hostile tribes. The like system of domestic slavery then, and for many ages after, subsisted in every part of the world in which any considerable moral or mental progress or economical improvement was to be seen.

EVILS OF ANCIENT SLAVERY, AND ITS GREAT EXTENSION AND ABUSE,
AND RELIEF OFFERED BY ANOTHER KIND

The institution of slavery in ancient times, with its great benefits, had also its great evils, and not only in its first establishment, but in its latest incidents. The ease and cheapness with which slaves could be acquired in the latter times of the Roman Empire induced their being held in great and unnecessary numbers, and no small proportion of them were of captive barbarian and warlike enemies. These conditions were necessary causes of weakness of the master class, and of the general community, and helped to invite and to aid the success of the hordes of barbarian invaders that swept over the then civilized world like a deluge, and, for ages afterwards, buried Europe under dark ignorance and barbarian rule. Still, slow-growing, yet complete, final relief, sprang from the same cause—slavery—that had produced the former civilization. In one or other form, whether of the general and political slavery of a people, (as of the conquered to their conquerors,) or of class to class, or of serfdom, villenage, or slavery to the soil, or of personal slavery, this institution was universal during the dark and semi-barbarous middle ages of Europe. And in the beginning it was from the slaves made of the enlightened refined, but effeminate and cowardly former masters of the lands, that the latter civilization first began, and was communicated to their barbarous conquerors and their masters. Thus, and contrary to the general order of things in this case, the enslaved, and not the master class, was the source of improvement to the other. To this cause it was owing that the revival of civilization and learning in Europe occurred centuries earlier than would have been the case if the slaves, after the complete conquests made by barbarians, had been as ignorant as their masters.

THE EXTINCTION OF INDIVIDUAL SLAVERY THE NECESSARY RESULT
OF AN EXCESS OF FREE LABOR—THE COMPETITION OF FREE LABORERS,
AND THEIR GREATEST SUFFERINGS, PRODUCE THE GREATEST PROFITS
OF CAPITAL

But in every country, when covered by a dense population, and when subsistence to free laborers becomes difficult to be obtained, the competition for employment will tend to depress the price of labor, gradually, to the lowest rate at which a bare subsistence can be purchased. The indolence natural to man, and especially in his lowest and most degraded state, can then no longer be indulged; because to be idle would not be to suffer privation only, and to incur risks of greater suffering, but absolutely and speedily to starve and die of want. If domestic slavery could have continued to exist so long, the slaves then would be in a very much better condition than the free laborers, because possessing assured means for support, and that for much less labor and hardship. For sharp want, hunger and cold, are more effective incentives to labor than the slaveowner's whip, even if its use is not restrained by any feeling of justice or mercy. But under such conditions of free labor, domestic or individual slavery could not exist. For whenever want and competition shall reduce the wages of free labor below the cost of slave labor, then it will be more profitable for the slaveowner and employer to hire free labor (both cheapened and driven by hunger and misery) than to maintain slaves, and compel their labor less effectually and at greater expense. Under such conditions, slaves (if they could not be sold and removed to some other country, where needed) would be readily emancipated by masters to whom they had become burdensome. Soon, under the operating influence of self-interest alone on the master class, domestic slavery would come to an end of itself—give place to the far more stringent and oppressive rule of want, as a compeller of labor, and be substituted by class-slavery, or the absolute subjection of the whole class of laborers to the whole class of employers—or of labor to capital. Then, in the progress of society, first begins to be true, and soon becomes entirely true, the hackneyed proposition that "free labor is cheaper than slave labor;" and it is only true under these circumstances, when the supply of labor is regularly or generally greater than the demand. Then the surplus hands must be left without employment, and therefore without means for subsistence. They can obtain employment only by under-bidding the rate of wages then received by the laborers employed, and so be engaged by throwing as many other laborers out of work. These must, in like manner, submit to the same reduction of wages, to be enabled again to obtain employment by getting the places of as many others. Finally, all are compelled to work for the reduced wages. But, after this general reduction, still, as before, the supply of hands will exceed (and more and more with the increase of population) the demand for their labor; as many therefore as are surplus must be always out of employment, and struggling to obtain it—and by the same process, competition, urged by extreme want, will tend still more to lower wages. Thus want and competition will continue to compel the superfluous and unemployed hands to submit to more and more reduction of wages, until the amount generally obtained is very much less than what is needed for the comfortable subsistence and healthy support of the laborer. And during all the time of this long continued competition and struggle for subsistence, while the rate of wages is being gradually lowered, the amount of toil of each laborer is increased—or at least as long as the human frame can bear increased exertion. *When the greatest possible amount of labor is thus obtained for the lowest amount of wages that can barely sustain life and strength for labor, there has been attained the most perfect and profitable condition of industrial operations for the class of capitalists and employers, and also for the most rapid increase of general and national wealth.* But these benefits (so much lauded and deemed so desirable for every country, and by almost every writer,) are purchased only by the greatest possible amount of toil, privation, and misery of the class of laborers under which they can live and work. It is readily admitted that slave labor could never yield anything like such large net returns—and that it would not only produce less, but would cost more. Slaves could not be subjected to such extreme privation and misery, because they must be fed and clothed, and cannot generally be greatly over-worked, (and never to the profit of the master,) as is caused continually by the pressure of extreme want, and through competition, on free laborers. If the political and economical problem to be worked out is the production of the greatest amount of profit to capitalists, and of wealth to the nation, in a country of dense population and advanced industrial operations, without regard to the sufferings of the laboring class, it is certain that the laborers must not be slaves, but free from all masters except extreme want. England, after the general abolition of slavery, was more than two centuries approaching this condition, which was finally reached, and has now been fully enjoyed for many years. Since then, England has been, of all the countries of the world, the most prosperous in manufactures, commerce, and all industrial employments of capital and labor—and the laboring and poorest classes have been among the most destitute and miserable. That they have not been sunk, by competition for food, to still greater misery, and that many more numerous and frequent deaths have not occurred from absolute starvation, is owing to this introduction and protection of another kind of slavery—pauper slavery—which is the certain consequence of, and the partial remedy for, the evils and sufferings produced by the competition of free labor.

PAUPER SLAVERY

Though, after the supply of labor in any country has long exceeded the demand, competition for employment will, necessarily, reduce wages to as little as will serve to maintain life under great suffering—yet wages cannot be reduced any lower, at least to the further profit of the whole class of capitalists or employers. For, when laborers can no longer subsist on their wages, the deficiency must in some way be supplied by the property owners. In lawless or badly governed countries, beggary and theft may be the irregular means of drawing that support from property which was denied in wages. In better regulated communities, the supply is furnished by the "poor law," or a compulsory provision for the laboring poor who cannot subsist on their wages, as well as for the infirm poor, incapable of labor. This system is most extensive and complete in England, and is the necessary result of the competition for employment of free laborers—of England's great and boasted success in all industrial pursuits and profitable employment of labor by capital. And thus it is, that the cruel oppression by capital, in reducing wages to the lowest rate, is avenged by the tax levied by and for the poor, equal to the deficiency of wages for the amount necessary for bare subsistence. And to this relief, which the poor law promises and affords, every day-laborer in England looks forward as the almost certain destiny and last resource of himself and his family. There are but few of that class who do not, at some time, have to resort to support by the parish; and every English laborer has more reason to expect to die a parish-supported pauper, than otherwise.

But this aid held out to pauperism, wretched as it is, serves to encourage improvidence, and to increase, as much as to relieve extreme want. The pauper laborer, supported by the compulsory and reluctant charity of his parish, is but a little better off than those who perish elsewhere for want of such provision. But it is not my purpose to consider the system in either of these aspects, but in another. The pauper, whether laborer or otherwise, receiving support from the parish, is neither more nor less than a slave to the administrators of the law and dispensers of the public charity. The pauper ceases to be a free agent in any respect. If at work far from the place of his birth, (in England,) he is remanded and transported to his own or native parish, there to obtain support. If either this forced exile from his long previous place of residence and labor, or other reasons of expediency require it, husband and wife, and parents and children, are separated, and severally disposed of at the will of the overseers of the poor. The able-bodied laborer, who at his agricultural or other work can earn but six shillings a week, and cannot support his family for less than ten, may, indeed, obtain the deficient four shillings from the parish. But to do so, he is subject to be forced to take any service that the authorities may direct. And as the employer receives the pauper laborer against his will, and only because he thereby pays so much of his share of the poor tax, he not only has the pauper as an involuntary slave, but he has not even the inducement of self-interest to treat the pauper slave well, or to care to preserve his health or life. The death of the pauper laborer is no loss to his temporary employer, and is a clear gain to the parish. Hence, while all of the millions of pauper population of England are truly slaves, and as much under constraint as if each one and his family belonged to an individual master, or as negro slaves are here, they have not the family comforts, or the care for the preservation of their health and lives, enjoyed by every negro slave in Virginia or Mississippi. The negro slaves in the United States have increased from 300,000, the number originally imported from Africa, to nearly 4,000,000, or more than twelve for one. This is a sufficient evidence of their general good treatment, induced by the self-interest of the owners. If it were possible to designate, separately, the whole class of poor laborers in England, and to trace them and their descendants for two hundred years, it is most probable that the original number would be found diminished in as great proportion as that in which our negro slaves have increased—or reduced to less than one-twelfth part. Yet this widespread, miserable, and life-destroying hunger slavery and pauper slavery in England is there called freedom by the fanatics and so-called philanthropists, who abhor, and call incessantly for God's vengeance upon, the negro slavery of this country! . . .

GENERAL AND EXTREME SUFFERING FROM WANT IMPOSSIBLE
IN A SLAVE-HOLDING COMMUNITY

So long as domestic slavery is general in any country, and for the most part supplies the labor of the country, there is no possibility of the occurrence of the sufferings of the laboring class, such as were described above. There, the evils which are caused by extreme want and destitution, the competition for sustenance, class slavery of labor to capital, and lastly pauper slavery, are all the incidents and necessary results of free society, and "free labor." Before such evils can visit any laboring class of personal slaves, they must have first been emancipated, and personal slavery abolished. This abolition of slavery is indeed like to occur in every country in the progress of society, and where the increasing population has no sufficient and advantageous outlet. But so long as domestic slavery remains, and is the main supply of labor, among any civilized people, it is a certain indication, and the most unquestionable evidence, that extensive and long continued suffering from want or hunger have as yet had no existence in that country. The first great effect of such distress will be to reduce (by competition) the wages of free labor below the cost of maintaining slaves—and this effect would next cause the extinction of slavery, by the mode of sale and exportation, or otherwise the emancipation of all the slaves. After this step has been made, of course, in due time, the want and suffering, which are the necessary incidents and consequences of free society, are to be expected to follow in after times.

When temporary evils, great loss, and distress, fall upon slaveholding countries, it is not the laboring class (as in free society) that feels the first and heaviest infliction, but the masters and employers. If a slaveholding country is visited by dearth, ravaged by war, or by pestilence—or suffers under any other causes of wide-spread calamity—every domestic slave is as much as before assured of his customary food and other allowances, and of a master's care in sickness and infirmity, even though the master class, and the country at large, have but half the previously existing profits, or value of capital. A striking proof of this was afforded by the recent (and still continuing) general suspension of payments of the banks in this country, and the consequent universal pecuniary loss and distress. Payments of debts could not be obtained, commodities could not be sold, and all manufacturing and some other great industrial operations either had to be continued for greatly reduced prices and wages, or to be entirely suspended, if of such kind as could be suspended. In consequence, in the Northern States, the free hired laborers were thrown out of employment, or employed only at much reduced wages. Hence all such persons were greatly damaged or distressed, and thousands of the most destitute were ready to starve. Hence hunger mobs were menacing the city of New York with pillage, and the last evils of a vicious and unbridled and starving populace, excited to insurrection and defiance of legal authority. Universal loss from this cause also visited the slaveholding States, and every property holder, and also, to some extent, every other free man therein. But not a slave has lost a meal, or a comfort; and as a class, the slaves scarcely know of the occurrence of this great national calamity which has so universally damaged their masters, and the capitalists and employers of labor. Nor was the difference of effect owing to the slaves being generally engaged in agricultural labors. The very large business of manufacturing tobacco, in Virginia, is carried on almost exclusively by the labor of slaves, and those mostly hired by the year. The late bank suspension serving to suspend all payments of debts to, and income of, their great establishments, they were generally compelled to suspend work, even though still obliged to feed and support their hired slave laborers, who, for some time, thus received their full allowance and support, while remaining perfectly idle, and returning no compensation whatever to their employers who had hired them for the year.

THE "ASSOCIATED LABOR" DOCTRINE OF THE SOCIALISTS TRUE—BUT
DEFICIENT IN THE MAIN AGENCY, WHICH SLAVERY ONLY CAN SUPPLY

The socialists of Europe, and of the Northern States of this Union, (there are none existing in our Southern States,) of every sect, and however differing on other points, have all advocated the *association of labor,* in some form or other, as the great means for reforming the evils of society arising from starving competition for labor. The founders and preachers of socialism had all observed and earnestly appreciated these evils. They saw that, in advanced society, labor was the slave of capital, and that the more capital was enriched by the employment of labor, the less was acquired and retained by the individual laborers, and the more their wants and sufferings were increased. They also saw, and correctly, that there was great loss of time and labor in the domestic operations of every poor family, and most in the poorest families—and also, that the productive labors of all, if associated, and thus aiding each other, might be made much more productive. And if by laborers being associated in large numbers, and directed by their combined knowledge to the most profitable purposes and ends, all unnecessary waste (as occurs in isolated families) was prevented, and all the actual efforts of labor utilized—the net profits and economy of such associated labor would be much increased, and thus, the laborers might secure and retain a sufficient subsistence, out of the larger share of the profits of their labors, which now goes to the share of employers and capitalists. Their views and doctrines are true in the main, and are altogether so plausible, and so applicable to the wretched condition of labor in the most advanced conditions of society in Europe, that the teachers have found numerous believers and zealous disciples. Sundry associations have been originated in Europe, and established in America, (as a new country only offered the needed facilities,) to carry out, in different modes, the great object of associating and combining labor, for the common and general profit and benefit. But every such attempt has met with signal, and also speedy, failure; except a few, of religious associations, which were under the guidance and direction of a single despotic head. In all other cases, no matter how benevolent and intelligent the leaders—and though one hour of labor, in each day, in this cheap and fertile country, would yield more food than fifteen hours' labor in Europe—still these associations soon failed in their every aim and purpose, and were severally broken up as soon as their inherent defects were made manifest, and seen to be inevitable and incurable incidents of the system.

Yet, so far as their facts and reasoning go, and in their main doctrines, the socialists are right. Associated labor can be much more productive, and be conducted more economically, than the labors of individual persons or families. The socialist theorists reasoned correctly, and in their practical experiments they devised good but defective plans. They constructed admirable and complex machinery to produce certain final results, in which every wheel and other operating agent was well adjusted as a secondary cause, or effect of another preceding cause. But in all these great and complicated works, the artificers had omitted to supply the first and great motive power, which is to be found only in one directing mind, and one controlling will. Supply the one supreme head and governing power to the association of labor, (for the suitable conditions of society,) and the scheme and its operation will become as perfect as can be expected of any human institution. But in supplying this single ruling power, the association is thereby converted to the condition of *domestic slavery*. And our system of domestic slavery offers in use, and to the greatest profit for all parties in the association, the realization of all that is sound and valuable in the socialists' theories and doctrines, and supplies the great and fatal defect of all their plans for practically associating labor. A few illustrative views will be submitted, which will apply to both the theoretical free associated labor, and to the practical domestic slave labor.

Suppose that some extensive industrial operation, as the tillage of a great farm, the working of a mine, or a cotton factory, is carried on by the labor of fifty men, with that of such other few members of their families as can be spared from home. These men, as usual, generally, are married, and have one or more young children. But whether single and without children, or husbands, or widowers with children, every man is the head of an isolated family, for which separate services are indispensable. Each home or family requires, and has, its separate purchasing of food, (and at retail and highest prices,) its separate cooking, washing, fires, lights, nursing of children, and of the sick, &c., &c. Such duties, in an ordinary or average family, fully occupy the time of the wife and mother. If there is no wife, or the mother is dead, the single man, or the father, is more or less required to perform the like household and woman's duties. Thus, of the supposed fifty households, probably including not less than from 150 to 200 persons, there may be but the fifty men to labor for wages. All the many others capable of labor, are fully employed as menial servants and nurses for their respective families. This is necessarily the condition of free laborers, each working for himself and his family.

Now suppose, instead of this free population, that all the laborers and their families were slaves to the employer. Then, with proper and convenient arrangement of buildings, &c., instead of there being fifty women cooking, washing, and nursing the sick or the helpless of so many different small households, four or five might even better (with the better means and facilities afforded by the master) perform these services for all. This would dispense with some forty-five women, or other hands fit for labor, previously engaged in these household duties, and which would nearly double the number previously working for production and profit. This great increase of numbers would fully compensate for the general lessening of each individual's labor, which is certain of domestic slaves compared to free laborers driven by hunger. This abatement of toil, together with the allowances indispensable to the profitable existence of slavery, would render certain the comfortable subsistence of the slaves, which, if it could have been for free laborers, would ultimately have given way to the sufferings from competition and slavery, to want, and next to the pauper slavery now so general in England. Further, in this form of associated labor, there would be secured many of the savings in expenses which the socialists correctly counted upon, besides those already mentioned. By the single head and master providing all the necessaries for the maintenance and comfort of the laboring class, the contracts and purchases would be few and on a large scale, and at wholesale prices. There would not, at any time, be a deficiency of food, nor any necessary deficiency of medical or nursing attendance on the sick. When required by economy, fire and light could be supplied to all at half the cost that would be required separately for each family. Thus, in the institution of domestic slavery, and in that only, are most completely realized the dreams and sanguine hopes of the socialist school of philanthropists. Yet the socialists are all arrayed among the most fanatical and intolerant denouncers of domestic slavery, and the most malignant enemies of slaveholders. . . .

THE INTELLECTUAL INFERIORITY OF THE BLACK RACE,
TESTED BY FACTS, IN THE UNITED STATES

Hundreds of thousands of individual cases of emancipated negro slaves, and their descendants, have existed in this country in the last two centuries. This class has now increased, in Virginia alone, to more than 50,000 in number. In the non-slaveholding States, also, there are numerous free negroes. It is true, that when thus interspersed among the much more numerous and dominant class of white inhabitants, the free negroes are subjected to some depressing and injurious influences, from which they would be relieved if forming a separate community. But, on the other hand, they have derived more than compensating benefits from their position, in the protection of government to person and property, and the security of both, and exemption from the evils of war, and from great oppression by any stronger power. Yet, in all this long time, and among such great numbers of free negroes, everywhere protected in person and property, and in the facilities to acquire property—and in some of the Northern States, endowed with political, as well as civil rights and power, equal with the white citizens—still to this day, and with but few individual exceptions, the free negroes in every State of this Confederacy, are noted for igno- rance, indolence, improvidence, and poverty—and very generally, also, for vicious habits, and numerous violations of the criminal laws. In this plentiful country, where the only great want is for labor, and where every free laborer may easily earn a comfortable support, this free negro class is so little self-sustaining, that it now scarcely increases, in general, by procreation, and would annually decrease throughout the United States, if not continually recruited by new emancipations, and by fugitives from slavery. . . . A very few have acquired considerable amounts of property. But these rare qualities were not hereditary—and the children of these superior individuals would be as like as others to fall back to the ordinary condition of their class. In short, taken throughout, and with but few exceptions, the free negro class, in every part of this country, is a nuisance, and noted for ignorance, laziness, improvidence, and vicious habits.

4

THOMAS R. R. COBB

Effects of Abolition in the United States

1858

Thomas Reade Rootes Cobb (1823–1862) was a Georgia lawyer, a legal scholar, and, until the late 1850s, a strong Unionist. By the end of the decade, however, he had become a confirmed secessionist. He was a lead- ing figure at the Montgomery Convention, which set up the Confederacy, and was the primary drafter of the Confederate Constitution. His brother, Howell Cobb, had been governor of Georgia, Speaker of the U.S. House of Representatives, and secretary of the treasury in the 1850s. When the

Thomas R. R. Cobb, *An Inquiry into the Law of Negro Slavery in the United States of America, to Which is Prefixed an Historical Sketch of Slavery* (Philadelphia: T. & J. W. Johnson; Savannah: W. Thorne Williams, 1858), cxcvii.

Civil War began, Thomas R. R. Cobb served in the Confederate legislature and then became a colonel and organized Cobb's Legion. He was promoted to brigadier general shortly before he was killed at the battle of Fredericksburg in 1862.

Before the war, Cobb wrote a massive tome, An Inquiry into the Law of Negro Slavery in the United States of America, to Which Is Prefixed an Historical Sketch of Slavery *(1858), the only legal treatise on slavery written by a Southerner. The selection presented here is from that "Historical Sketch" and focuses on the United States. Document 13 contains an excerpt from the "Inquiry."*

One key argument in favor of slavery was the failure of free blacks to prosper. In the previous chapter, Cobb considered the condition of blacks in the West Indies, Africa, and elsewhere in the world. In this chapter, he discusses what he calls "the savage barbarity, the miserable idleness, the continual outbreaks, the ruined cities, the abandoned agriculture" of Haiti, where, he asserts, "the dark mantle of heathenism" has "settled upon this once beautiful and fertile island." Cobb, of course, predicted that emancipation in the United States would lead to similar results.

Part of Cobb's argument in this section is circular. He notes that blacks have not been able to succeed at the same rate as whites but also notes that they face various forms of legal discrimination. Cobb, however, would no doubt have denied the circularity of this argument by asserting that no state gives blacks equal rights because they are in fact racially inferior to whites.

Chapter XV

EFFECTS OF ABOLITION IN THE UNITED STATES

The number of negroes emancipated in the United States was comparatively small, but the effects do not vary materially as to their condition, from those already noticed. The fact of their limited number, as well as the additional facts, that previous to their emancipation they were employed but little in agricultural pursuits, and that the nature of the agriculture of the Northern States of the Union was illy suited to this species of labor, protected the prosperity of those States from the depressing influences experienced elsewhere from the abolition of slavery. That their physical condition does not compare favorably with that of the slaves of the South is evident from the decennial census of the United States, showing a much larger increase in the latter than in the former. No surer test can be applied.*

Notwithstanding the very labored efforts made for their intellectual improvement, taken as a body they have made no advancement. Averse to physical labor, they are equally averse to intellectual effort. The young negro acquires readily the first rudiments of education, where memory and imitation are chiefly brought into action, but for

---

*In order to obtain accurate information, I sent a circular to the Governors and leading politicians of the non-slaveholding States. I received answers as follows:

Maine Hon. I. J. D. Fuller.
Vermont, Hon. J. Meacham.
Connecticut, Gov. Pond, and Hon. O. S. Seymour.
Rhode Island, Hon. B. B. Thurston.
New Jersey, Gov. Foot.
New York, Hon. S. G. Haven.
Pennsylvania, Hon. E. D. Ingraham.
Indiana, Gov. Wright.
Illinois, Gov. Matteson, Hon. W. A. Richardson.
Iowa, Judge Mason, Hon. Mr. Hern.
Michigan, Gov. Parsons.

I extract from their answers:

Maine. — "The condition of the negro population varies; but is very far below the whites."

Vermont. — "Their condition and character have great varieties. They are not in as good condition as the whites."

Connecticut. — Gov. Pond says: "The condition of the negro population, as a class, is not thrifty, and does not compare favorably with the whites. There are many, comparatively speaking, who are industrious."

Rhode Island. — "They are, generally, industrious and frugal."

New Jersey. — "Their condition is debased; with few exceptions very poor; generally indolent."

New York. — "The condition of the negro population is diversified, — some prosperous, some industrious. They have no social relations with the whites. Generally on about the same level that whites would occupy with like antecedents."

Pennsylvania. — "I deem the condition of the negro population, in this State, to be that of a degraded class, much deteriorated by freedom. They are not industrious."

Indiana. — "They are not prosperous. The majority of them are not doing well. We have sent off thirty or forty this year to Liberia, and hope to send off one hundred or more, next year, and finally to get rid of all we have in the State, and do not intend to have another negro or mulatto come into the State."

Illinois. — "As a class, they are thriftless and idle. Their condition far inferior to that of the whites." (Gov.) "About the towns and cities, idle and dissolute, with exceptions. In the rural districts, many are industrious and prosperous." (Mr. Richardson.)

Iowa. — "Very few negroes in Iowa. Far above the condition of those met with in our Eastern cities."

Michigan. — "Tolerably prosperous. Far behind the white population."

any higher effort of reason and judgment he is, as a general rule, utterly incapable.*

His moral condition compares unfavorably with that of the slave of the South. He seeks the cities and towns, and indulges freely in those vices to which his nature inclines him. His friends inveigh against "the prejudice of color," but he rises no higher in Mexico, Central America, New Grenada, or Brazil, where no such prejudice exists. The cause lies deeper: in the nature and constitution of the negro race.*

The emancipated negroes do not enjoy full and equal civil and political rights in any State in the Union, except the State of Vermont. In several of the States they are not permitted to vote, in some under peculiar restrictions. In almost every State where the matter has been

---

*Maine. — "Admitted into the public schools with the whites. Very far below them in education."

Vermont. — "Generally able to read and write; a few are liberally educated; not like the whites."

Connecticut. — "Fall much below the whites in education."

Rhode Island. — "Some are educated in the district schools. Compare well with the whites of their condition."

New Jersey. — "Generally ignorant. Far below the whites in intelligence."

New York. — "Generally very poorly, or but little educated."

Pennsylvania. — "Not educated. It is remarkable, that almost all of the decent and respectable negroes we have, have been household slaves in some Southern State."

Indiana. — "Not educated."

Illinois. — "Ignorant." (Gov.)

Michigan. — "Not generally educated. Far below the whites."

*Maine. — "Far below the whites."

Vermont. — "Not as good as the whites."

Connecticut. — "Does not compare favorably with the whites." (Gov.) "They are, with us, an inferior caste; and in morality fall much below the whites." (Seymour.)

New Jersey. — "Immoral; vicious animal propensities; drunkenness, theft, and promiscuous sexual intercourse quite common. One-fourth of the criminals in the State prison are colored persons; while they constitute only one twenty-fifth of the population."

New York. — "Diversified; some moral."

Pennsylvania. — "Immoral. I am satisfied, from forty years' attention to the subject, that the removal of the wholesome restraint of slavery, and the consequent absence of the stimulus of the coercion to labor of that condition, have materially affected their condition for the worse. They exhibit all the characteristics of an inferior race, to whose personal comfort, happiness, and morality, the supervision, restraint, and coercion of a superior race seem absolutely necessary."

Indiana. — "In many instances very immoral."

Illinois. — "Thriftless, idle, ignorant, and vicious." (Gov.) "In towns and cities dissolute, with exceptions." (Richardson.)

Iowa. — "Of a fair character."

Michigan. — "Tolerably moral. Far below the whites."

made a subject of legislation, intermarriages with the whites are forbidden. In none are such marriages at all common. In many they are forbidden to serve as jurors, or to be sworn as witnesses against a white person, or hold any elective office.

The criminal statistics of the slaveholding and non-slaveholding states show that the proportion of crime committed by negroes in the former does not reach the ratio of this population as compared with the whites, while in the latter the ratio is much greater. The same is true of the statistics of mortality and disease. The apparent disproportion in the former case is greater than the truth, as many petty crimes by slaves do not reach the courts; and in the latter, it may be truly said that the southern climate is more favorable to the health and longevity of the negro. But making due allowances in both cases for these causes, it is still true, that the negroes are less addicted to crime, and are more healthy and longlived, in a state of slavery than of freedom.

5

JAMES HENRY HAMMOND

The Mudsill Speech

1858

James Henry Hammond (1807–1864) was a lawyer, planter, man of letters, and South Carolina politician. He was governor of the state (1842–44) and served as a U.S. senator from 1857 until he resigned in 1860 when South Carolina seceded. He was fiercely proslavery and an early advocate of secession. This excerpt is from Hammond's "Speech on the Admission of Kansas, under the Lecompton Constitution," which he gave in the Senate on March 4, 1858. In this speech, Hammond defends the proposed Kansas constitution written by the proslavery state constitutional convention that met at Lecompton, Kansas, in 1857. Almost all Northerners at the time believed—and all scholars today agree—that

James H. Hammond, "Speech on the Admission of Kansas, under the Lecompton Constitution, Delivered in the Senate of the United States, March 4, 1858," in *Selections from the Letters and Speeches of the Hon. James H. Hammond of South Carolina* (New York: John F. Trow, 1866), 301–22.

this convention was fraudulently elected and that the overwhelming majority of settlers in Kansas did not want slavery in their territory or state. After defending the Kansas constitutional process, Hammond turns to the defense of slavery. The speech was not only Hammond's greatest, but also the most memorable defense of slavery on the floor of the Senate.

This speech is often referred to as the "mudsill speech" because in it Hammond argues that blacks provide a natural floor, or mudsill, for American society. It is also famous for his thundering assertions that the cotton-producing South was immune from the forces of politics or markets and that no state, nation, or economy would dare "make war on cotton." Hammond asserts that Southern cotton controlled and dictated the world economy. This belief, which turned out to be quite wrong, helped lead Southerners to believe that they could create their own slave-based nation. In fact, the U.S. government was able to wage war successfully against "cotton," and England found other sources of cotton in Egypt and India. But without the benefit of this hindsight, Hammond's ideological analysis led the Confederate States of America to its disastrous policy of placing an embargo on cotton, both to drive up the world price and to force England to intervene on behalf of the putative Southern nation. The policy failed, and no European nation came to the support of the Confederacy.

The whole history of Kansas is a disgusting one, from the beginning to the end. I have avoided reading it as much as I could. Had I been a Senator before, I should have felt it my duty, perhaps, to have done so; but not expecting to be one, I am ignorant, fortunately, in a great measure, of details. . . .

I hear, on the other side of the Chamber, a great deal said about "gigantic and stupendous frauds;" and the Senator from New York [William H. Seward], in portraying the character of his party and the opposite one, laid the whole of those frauds upon the pro-slavery party. To listen to him, you would have supposed that the regiments of immigrants recruited in the purlieus of the great cities of the North, and sent out, armed and equipped with Sharpe's rifle and bowie knives and revolvers, to conquer freedom for Kansas, stood by, meek saints, innocent as doves, and harmless as lambs brought up to the sacrifice. . . . I presume that there were frauds; and that if there were frauds, they were equally great on all sides; and that any investigation into them on this floor, or by a commission, would end in nothing but disgrace to the United States.

But, sir, the true object of the discussion on the other side of the Chamber, is to agitate the question of slavery. I have very great doubts whether the leaders on the other side really wish to defeat this bill. I think they would consider it a vastly greater victory to crush out the Democratic party in the North, and destroy the authors of the Kansas-Nebraska bill; and I am not sure that they have not brought about this imbroglio for the very purpose. They tell us that year after year the majority in Kansas was beaten at the polls! They have always had a majority, but they always get beaten! How could that be? It does seem, from the most reliable sources of information, that they have a majority, and have had a majority for some time. Why has not this majority come forward and taken possession of the government, and made a free-State constitution and brought it here? We should all have voted for its admission cheerfully. There can be but one reason: if they had brought, as was generally supposed at the time the Kansas-Nebraska act was passed would be the case, a free-State constitution here, there would have been no difficulty among the northern Democrats; they would have been sustained by their people. The statement made by some of them, as I understood, that that act as a good free-State act, would have been verified, and the northern Democratic party would have been sustained. But Kansas coming here a slave State, it is hoped will kill that party, and that is the reason they have refrained from going to the polls; that is the reason they have refrained from making it a free State when they had the power. They intend to make it a free State as soon as they have effected their purpose of destroying by it the Democratic party at the North, and now their chief object here is, to agitate slavery. For one, I am not disposed to discuss that question here in any abstract form. I think the time has gone by for that. Our minds are all made up. I may be willing to discuss it—and that is the way it should be and must be discussed—as a *practical thing,* as a thing that *is,* and *is to be;* and to discuss its effect upon our political institutions, and ascertain how long those institutions will hold together with slavery *ineradicable.* . . .

If we never acquire another foot of territory for the South, look at her. Eight hundred and fifty thousand square miles. As large as Great Britain, France, Austria, Prussia and Spain. Is not that territory enough to make an empire that shall rule the world? With the finest soil, the most delightful climate, whose staple productions none of those great countries can grow, we have three thousand miles of continental sea-shore line so indented with bays and crowded with islands, that, when their shore lines are added, we have twelve thousand miles. Through the heart of our country runs the great Mississippi, the father of waters, into whose bosom are poured thirty-six thousand miles of tributary rivers; and beyond we have the desert prairie wastes to protect us in our rear. Can you hem in such a territory as that? You talk of putting up a wall of fire around eight hundred and fifty thousand square miles so situated! How absurd.

But, in this territory lies the great valley of the Mississippi, now the real, and soon to be the acknowledged seat of the empirc of the world. The sway of that valley will be as great as ever the Nile new in the earlier ages of mankind. We own the most of it. The most valuable part of it belongs to us now; and although those who have settled above us are now opposed to us, another generation will tell a different tale. They are ours by all the laws of nature; slave-labor will go over every foot of this great valley where it will be found profitable to use it, and some of those who may not use it are soon to be united with us by such ties as will make us one and inseparable. The iron horse will soon be clattering over the sunny plains of the South to bear the products of its upper tributaries of the valley to our Atlantic ports, as it now does through the ice-bound North. And there is the great Mississippi, a bond of union made by Nature herself. She will maintain it forever.

On this fine territory we have a population four times as large as that with which these colonies separated from the mother country, and a hundred, I might say a thousand fold stronger. Our population is now sixty per cent. greater than that of the whole United States when we entered into the second war of independence [the War of 1812]. It is as large as the whole population of the United States was ten years after the conclusion of that war, and our own exports are three times as great as those of the whole United States then. Upon our muster-rolls we have a million of men. In a defensive war, upon an emergency, every one of them would be available. At any time, the South can raise, equip, and maintain in the field, a larger army than any Power of the earth can send against her, and an army of soldiers—men brought up on horseback, with guns in their hands.

If we take the North, even when the two large States of Kansas and Minnesota shall be admitted, her territory will be one hundred thousand square miles less than ours. I do not speak of California and Oregon; there is no antagonism between the South and those countries, and never will be. The population of the North is fifty per cent. greater than ours. I have nothing to say in disparagement either of the soil of the North, or the people of the North, who are a brave and energetic race, full of intellect. But they produce no great staple that the South does not produce; while we produce two or three, and these the very greatest, that she can never produce. As to her men, I may be allowed to say, they have never proved themselves to be superior to those of the South, either in the field or in the Senate.

But the strength of a nation depends in a great measure upon its wealth, and the wealth of a nation, like that of a man, is to be estimated by its surplus production. You may go to your trashy census books, full of falsehood and nonsense—they tell you, for example, that in the State of Tennessee, the whole number of house-servants is not equal to that of those in my own house, and such things as that. You may estimate what is made throughout the country from these census books, but it is no matter how much is made if it is all consumed. If a man possess millions of dollars and consumes his income, is he rich? Is he competent to embark in any new enterprise? Can he long build ships or railroads? And could a people in that condition build ships and roads or go to war without a fatal strain on capital? All the enterprises of peace and war depend upon the surplus productions of a people. They may be happy, they may be comfortable, they may enjoy themselves in consuming what they make; but they are not rich, they are not strong. It appears, by going to the reports of the Secretary of the Treasury, which are authentic, that last year the United States exported in round numbers $279,000,000 worth of domestic produce, excluding gold and foreign merchandise re-exported. Of this amount $158,000,000 worth is the clear produce of the South; articles that are not and cannot be made at the North. There are then $80,000,000 worth of exports of products of the forest, provisions and breadstuffs. If we assume that the South made but one third of these, and I think that is a low calculation, our exports were $185,000,000, leaving to the North less than $95,000,000.

In addition to this, we sent to the North $30,000,000 worth of cotton, which is not counted in the exports. We sent to her $7 or $8,000,000 worth of tobacco, which is not counted in the exports. We sent naval stores, lumber, rice, and many other minor articles. There is no doubt that we sent to the North $40,000,000 in addition; but suppose the amount to be $35,000,000, it will give us a surplus production of $220,000,000. But the *recorded* exports of the South now are greater than the whole exports of the United States in any year before 1856. They are greater than the whole average exports of the United States for the last twelve year, including the two extraordinary years of 1856 and 1857. They are nearly double the amount of the average exports of the twelve preceding years. If I am right in my calculations as to $220,000,000 of surplus produce, there is not a nation on the face of the earth, with any numerous population, that can compete with us in produce *per capita*. It amounts to $16 66 per head, supposing that we have twelve millions of people. England with all her accumulated wealth, with her concentrated and educated energy, makes but sixteen and a half dollars of surplus production per head. . . .

With an export of $220,000,000 under the present tariff, the South organized separately would have $40,000,000 of revenue. With one-fourth the present tariff, she would have a revenue with the present tariff adequate to all her wants, for the South would never go to war; she would never need an army or a navy, beyond a few garrisons on the frontiers and a few revenue cutters. It is commerce that breeds war. It is manufactures that require to be hawked about the world, and that give rise to navies and commerce. But we have nothing to do but to take off restrictions on foreign merchandise and open our ports, and the whole world will come to us to trade. They will be too glad to bring and carry us, and we never shall dream of a war. Why the South has never yet had a just cause of war except with the North. Every time she has drawn her sword it has been on the point of honor, and that point of honor has been mainly loyalty to her sister colonies and sister States, who have ever since plundered and calumniated her.

But if there were no other reason why we should never have war, would any sane nation make war on cotton? Without firing a gun, without drawing a sword, should they make war on us we could bring the whole world to our feet. The South is perfectly competent to go on, one, two or three years without planting a seed of cotton. I believe that if she was to plant but half her cotton, for three years to come, it would be an immense advantage to her. I am not so sure but that after three years' entire abstinence she would come out stronger than ever she was before, and better prepared to enter afresh upon her great career of enterprise. What would happen if no cotton was furnished for three years? I will not stop to depict what every one can imagine, but this is certain: England would topple headlong and carry the whole civilized world with her, save the South. No, you dare not make war on cotton. No power on earth dares to make war upon it. Cotton *is* king. Until lately the Bank of England was king; but she tried to put her screws as usual, the fall before the last, upon the cotton crop, and was utterly vanquished. The last power has been conquered. Who can doubt, that has looked at recent events, that cotton is supreme? When the abuse of credit had destroyed credit and annihilated confidence; when thousands of the strongest commercial houses in the world were coming down, and hundreds of millions of dollars of supposed property evaporating in thin air; when you came to a dead lock, and revolutions were threatened, what brought you up? Fortunately for you it was the commencement of the cotton season, and we have poured in upon you one million six hundred thousand bales of cotton just at the crisis to save you from destruction. That cotton, but for the bursting of your speculative bubbles in the North, which produced the whole of this convulsion, would have brought us $100,000,000. We have sold it for $65,000,000, and saved you. Thirty-five million dollars we, the slaveholders of the South, have put into the charity box for your magnificent financiers, your "cotton lords," your "merchant princes."

But, sir, the greatest strength of the South arises from the harmony of her political and social institutions. This harmony gives her a frame of society, the best in the world, and an extent of political freedom, combined with entire security, such as no other people ever enjoyed upon the face of the earth. Society precedes government; creates it, and ought to control it; but as far as we can look back in historic times we find the case different; for government is no sooner created than it becomes too strong for society, and shapes and moulds, as well as controls it. In later centuries the progress of civilization and of intelligence has made the divergence so great as to produce civil wars and revolutions; and it is nothing now but the want of harmony between governments and societies which occasions all the uneasiness and trouble and terror that we see abroad. It was this that brought on the American Revolution. We threw off a Government not adapted to our social system, and made one for ourselves. The question is, how far have we succeeded? The South, so far as that is concerned, is satisfied, harmonious, and prosperous, but demands to be let alone.

In all social systems there must be a class to do the menial duties, to perform the drudgery of life. That is, a class requiring but a low order of intellect and but little skill. Its requisites are vigor, docility, fidelity. Such a class you must have, or you would not have that other class which leads progress, civilization, and refinement. It constitutes the very mud-sill of society and of political government; and you might as well attempt to build a house in the air, as to build either the one or the other, except on this mud-sill. Fortunately for the South, she found a race adapted to that purpose to her hand. A race inferior to her own, but eminently qualified in temper, in vigor, in docility, in capacity to stand the climate, to answer all her purposes. We use them for our purpose, and call them slaves. We found them slaves by the common "consent of mankind," which, according to Cicero, *"lex naturae est."* The highest proof of what is Nature's law. We are old-fashioned at the South yet; slave is a word discarded now by "ears polite;" I will not characterize that class at the North by that term; but you have it; it is there; it is everywhere; it is eternal.

The Senator from New York said yesterday that the whole world had abolished slavery. Aye, the *name,* but not the *thing;* all the powers of the earth cannot abolish that. God only can do it when he repeals the *fiat,* "the poor ye always have with you;" for the man who lives by daily labor, and scarcely lives at that, and who has to put out his labor in the market, and take the best he can get for it; in short, your whole hireling class of manual laborers and "operatives," as you call them, are essentially slaves. The difference between us is, that our slaves are hired for life and well compensated; there is no starvation, no begging, no want of employment among our people, and not too much employment either. Yours are hired by the day, not cared for, and scantily compensated, which may be proved in the most painful manner, at any hour in any street in any of your large towns. Why, you meet more beggars in one day, in any single street of the city of New York, than you would meet in a lifetime in the whole South. We do not think that whites should be slaves either by law or necessity. Our slaves are black, of another and inferior race. The *status* in which we have placed them is an elevation. They are elevated from the condition in which God first created them, by being made our slaves. None of that race on the whole face of the globe can be compared with the slaves of the South. They are happy, content, unaspiring, and utterly incapable, from intellectual weakness, ever to give us any trouble by their aspirations. Yours are white, of your own race; you are brothers of one blood. They are your equals in natural endowment of intellect, and they feel galled by their degradation. Our slaves do not vote. We give them no political power. Yours do vote, and, being the majority, they are the depositaries of all your political power. If they knew the tremendous secret, that the ballot-box is stronger than "an army with banners," and could combine, where would you be? Your society would be reconstructed, your government overthrown, your property divided, not as they have mistakenly attempted to initiate such proceedings by meeting in parks, with arms in their hands, but by the quiet process of the ballot-box. You have been making war upon us to our very hearthstones. How would you like for us to send lecturers and agitators North, to teach these people this, to aid in combining, and to lead them?

. . . Your people are awaking. They are coming here. They are thundering at our doors for homesteads, one hundred and sixty acres of land for nothing, and Southern Senators are supporting them. Nay, they are assembling, as I have said, with arms in their hands, and demanding work at $1,000 a year for six hours a day. Have you heard that the ghosts of Mendoza and Torquemada[1] are stalking in the streets of your great cities? That the inquisition is at hand? . . .

Transient and temporary causes have thus far been your preservation. The great West has been open to your surplus population, and your hordes of semi-barbarian immigrants, who are crowding in year by year. They make a great movement, and you call it progress. . . . The South have sustained you in a great measure. You are our factors. You fetch and carry for us. One hundred and fifty million dollars of our money passes annually through your hands. Much of it sticks; all of it assists to keep your machinery together and in motion. Suppose we were to discharge you; suppose we were to take our business out of your hands;—we should consign you to anarchy and poverty. You complain of the rule of the South; that has been another cause that has preserved you. We have kept the Government conservative to the great purposes of the Constitution. We have placed it, and kept it, upon the Constitution; and that has been the cause of your peace and prosperity. The Senator from New York says that that is about to be at an end; that you intend to take the Government from us; that it will pass from our hands into yours. Perhaps what he says is true; it may be; but do not forget—it can never be forgotten—it is written on the brightest page of human history—that we, the slaveholders of the South, took our country in her infancy, and, after ruling her for sixty out of the seventy years of her existence, we surrendered her to you without a stain upon her honor, boundless in prosperity, incalculable in her strength, the wonder and the admiration of the world. Time will show what you will make of her; but no time can diminish our glory or your responsibility.

---

[1]*Mendoza and Torquemada:* leaders of the Spanish Inquisition.

6

ALEXANDER STEPHENS

The Cornerstone Speech

1861

---

*Alexander Hamilton Stephens (1812–1870) gave this speech extempora-
neously on March 21, 1861, in Savannah, Georgia. The text was then
printed in the* Savannah Republican. *Stephens, a congressman from
Georgia, had been a national leader of the Whig party. In 1850, he was
a leader of the Unionist movement in Georgia, which helped elect Howell
Cobb governor in the face of an early secessionist movement. In 1855,
after the collapse of the Whigs, Stephens became a Democrat. In 1860,
he supported Stephen A. Douglas for president and was a Union delegate
to Georgia's secession convention. Indeed, he was the most important
opponent of secession in the Deep South. But when the Georgia convention voted to leave the Union, Stephens signed the Ordinance of Secession. A leading conservative within the Confederacy, he was chosen as
vice president to balance the radicalism of the Confederate president, Jefferson Davis of Mississippi. Stephens remained the Confederate vice president throughout the Civil War.*

*Stephens was brutally honest in this, his most famous speech, known
as the "Cornerstone Speech." In fact, Jefferson Davis thought the speech
harmed the Confederacy because Stephens so openly proclaimed the new
nation to be built on slavery. But for Stephens, this made sense. Although
the speech might offend Britain or the North, he hoped it would help
bring the remaining slave states, especially Virginia, into the Confederacy. Once the Civil War began, Virginia, Tennessee, North Carolina,
and Arkansas did in fact join the Confederacy. Abolitionist papers in the
North reprinted the speech and used it to agitate for a strong response to
secession. Although a strong advocate of states' rights, Stephens here
boldly lays out what nearly everyone at the time knew: Slavery was the
ultimate reason for secession, and it was indeed the "cornerstone" of
Southern society and of the Confederacy.*

Henry Cleveland, *Alexander H. Stephens, in Public and Private: With Letters and
Speeches, Before, During, and Since the War* (Philadelphia and Chicago: National Publishing Co., 1866), 717–29.

We are passing through one of the greatest revolutions in the annals of the world. Seven States have within the last three months thrown off an old government and formed a new. This revolution has been signally marked, up to this time, by the fact of its having been accomplished without the loss of a single drop of blood.

This new constitution, or form of government, constitutes the subject to which your attention will be partly invited. In reference to it, I make this first general remark. It amply secures all our ancient rights, franchises, and liberties. All the great principles of Magna Charta are retained in it. No citizen is deprived of life, liberty, or property, but by the judgment of his peers under the laws of the land. The great principle of religious liberty, which was the honor and pride of the old constitution, is still maintained and secured. All the essentials of the old constitution, which have endeared it to the hearts of the American people, have been preserved and perpetuated. Some changes have been made. Of these I shall speak presently. Some of these I should have preferred not to have seen made; but these, perhaps, meet the cordial approbation of a majority of this audience, if not an overwhelming majority of the people of the Confederacy. Of them, therefore, I will not speak. But other important changes do meet my cordial approbation. They form great improvements upon the old constitution. So, taking the whole new constitution, I have no hesitancy in giving it as my judgment that it is decidedly better than the old. . . .

The new constitution has put at rest, *forever,* all the agitating questions relating to our peculiar institution—African slavery as it exists amongst us—the proper *status* of the negro in our form of civilization. This was the immediate cause of the late rupture and present revolution. Jefferson in his forecast, had anticipated this, as the "rock upon which the old Union would split." He was right. What was conjecture with him, is now a realized fact. But whether he fully comprehended the great truth upon which that rock *stood* and *stands,* may be doubted. The prevailing ideas entertained by him and most of the leading statesmen at the time of the formation of the old constitution, were that the enslavement of the African was in violation of the laws of nature; that it was wrong in *principle,* socially, morally, and politically. It was an evil they knew not well how to deal with, but the general opinion of the men of that day was that, somehow or other in the order of Providence, the institution would be evanescent and pass away. This idea, though not incorporated in the constitution, was the prevailing idea at that time. The constitution, it is true, secured every essential guarantee to the institution while it should last, and hence no argument can be justly urged against the constitutional guarantees thus secured, because of the common sentiment of the day. Those ideas, however, were fundamentally wrong. They rested upon the assumption of the equality of races. This was an error. It was a sandy foundation, and the government built upon it fell when the "storm came and the wind blew."

Our new government is founded upon exactly the opposite idea; its foundations are laid, its corner-stone rests upon the great truth, that the negro is not equal to the white man; that slavery—subordination to the superior race—is his natural and normal condition. This, our new government, is the first, in the history of the world, based upon this great physical, philosophical, and moral truth. This truth has been slow in the process of its development, like all other truths in the various departments of science. It has been so even amongst us. Many who hear me, perhaps, can recollect well, that this truth was not generally admitted, even within their day. The errors of the past generation still clung to many as late as twenty years ago. Those at the North, who still cling to these errors, with a zeal above knowledge, we justly denominate fanatics. All fanaticism springs from an aberration of the mind—from a defect in reasoning. It is a species of insanity. One of the most striking characteristics of insanity, in many instances, is forming correct conclusions from fancied or erroneous premises; so with the anti-slavery fanatics; their conclusions are right if their premises were. They assume that the negro is equal, and hence conclude that he is entitled to equal privileges and rights with the white man. If their premises were correct, their conclusions would be logical and just—but their premise being wrong, their whole argument fails. I recollect once of having heard a gentleman from one of the northern States, of great power and ability, announce in the House of Representatives, with imposing effect, that we of the South would be compelled, ultimately, to yield upon this subject of slavery, that it was as impossible to war successfully against a principle in politics, as it was in physics or mechanics. That the principle would ultimately prevail. That we, in maintaining slavery as it exists with us, were warring against a principle, a principle founded in nature, the principle of the equality of men. The reply I made to him was, that upon his own grounds, we should, ultimately, succeed, and that he and his associates, in this crusade against our institutions, would ultimately fail. The truth announced, that it was as impossible to war successfully against a principle in politics as it was in physics and mechanics, I admitted; but told him that it was he, and those acting with him, who were warring against a principle. They were attempting to make things equal which the Creator had made unequal.

In the conflict thus far, success has been on our side, complete throughout the length and breadth of the Confederate States. It is upon this, as I have stated, our social fabric is firmly planted; and I cannot permit myself to doubt the ultimate success of a full recognition of this principle throughout the civilized and enlightened world.

As I have stated, the truth of this principle may be slow in development, as all truths are and ever have been, in the various branches of science. It was so with the principles announced by Galileo—it was so with Adam Smith and his principles of political economy. It was so with Harvey, and his theory of the circulation of the blood. It is stated that not a single one of the medical profession, living at the time of the announcement of the truths made by him, admitted them. Now, they are universally acknowledged. May we not, therefore, look with confidence to the ultimate universal acknowledgment of the truths upon which our system rests? It is the first government ever instituted upon the principles in strict conformity to nature, and the ordination of Providence, in furnishing the materials of human society. Many governments have been founded upon the principle of the subordination and serfdom of certain classes of the same race; such were and are in violation of the laws of nature. Our system commits no such violation of nature's laws. With us, all of the white race, however high or low, rich or poor, are equal in the eye of the law. Not so with the negro. Subordination is his place. He, by nature, or by the curse against Canaan, is fitted for that condition which he occupies in our system. The architect, in the construction of buildings, lays the foundation with the proper material—the granite; then comes the brick or the marble. The substratum of our society is made of the material fitted by nature for it, and by experience we know that it is best, not only for the superior, but for the inferior race, that it should be so. It is, indeed, in conformity with the ordinance of the Creator. It is not for us to inquire into the wisdom of his ordinances, or to question them. For his own purposes, he has made one race to differ from another, as he has made "one star to differ from another star in glory."

The great objects of humanity are best attained when there is conformity to his laws and decrees, in the formation of governments as well as in all things else. Our confederacy is founded upon principles in strict conformity with these laws. This stone which was rejected by the first builders "is become the chief of the corner"—the real "corner-stone"—in our new edifice.

I have been asked, what of the future? It has been apprehended by some that we would have arrayed against us the civilized world. I care not who or how many they may be against us, when we stand upon the eternal principles of truth, *if we are true to ourselves and the principles for which we contend,* we are obliged to, and must triumph.

Thousands of people who begin to understand these truths are not yet completely out of the shell; they do not see them in their length and breadth. We hear much of the civilization and christianization of the barbarous tribes of Africa. In my judgment, those ends will never be attained, but by first teaching them the lesson taught to Adam, that "in the sweat of his brow he should eat his bread," and teaching them to work, and feed, and clothe themselves.

But to pass on: Some have propounded the inquiry whether it is practicable for us to go on with the confederacy without further accessions? Have we the means and ability to maintain nationality among the powers of the earth? On this point I would barely say, that as anxiously as we all have been, and are, for the border States, with institutions similar to ours, to join us, still we are abundantly able to maintain our position, even if they should ultimately make up their minds not to cast their destiny with us. That they ultimately will join us—be compelled to do it—is my confident belief; but we can get on very well without them, even if they should not. . . .

It is true, I believe I state but the common sentiment, when I declare my earnest desire that the border States should join us. The differences of opinion that existed among us anterior to secession, related more to the policy in securing that result by co-operation than from any difference upon the ultimate security we all looked to in common.

These differences of opinion were more in reference to policy than principle, and as Mr. Jefferson said in his inaugural, in 1801, after the heated contest preceding his election, there might be differences of opinion without differences on principle, and that all, to some extent, had been federalists and all republicans; so it may now be said of us, that whatever differences of opinion as to the best policy in having a co-operation with our border sister slave States, if the worst came to the worst, that as we were all co-co-operationists, we are now all for independence, whether they come or not.

But to return to the question of the future. What is to be the result of this revolution?

Will every thing, commenced so well, continue as it has begun? In reply to this anxious inquiry, I can only say it all depends upon ourselves. A young man starting out in life on his majority, with health, talent, and ability, under a favoring Providence, may be said to be the architect of his own fortunes. His destinies are in his own hands. He may make for himself a name, of honor or dishonor, according to his own acts. If he plants himself upon truth, integrity, honor and uprightness, with industry, patience and energy, he cannot fail of success. So it is with us. We are a young republic, just entering upon the arena of nations; we will be the architects of our own fortunes. Our destiny, under Providence, is in our own hands. With wisdom, prudence, and statesmanship on the part of our public men, and intelligence, virtue and patriotism on the part of the people, success, to the full measures of our most sanguine hopes, may be looked for. . . .

We have intelligence, and virtue, and patriotism. All that is required is to cultivate and perpetuate these. Intelligence will not do without virtue. France was a nation of philosophers. These philosophers become Jacobins. They lacked that virtue, that devotion to moral principle, and that patriotism which is essential to good government. Organized upon principles of perfect justice and right-seeking amity and friendship with all other powers—I see no obstacle in the way of our upward and onward progress. Our growth, by accessions from other States, will depend greatly upon whether we present to the world, as I trust we shall, a better government than that to which neighboring States belong. If we do this, North Carolina, Tennessee, and Arkansas cannot hesitate long; neither can Virginia, Kentucky, and Missouri. They will necessarily gravitate to us by an imperious law. We made ample provision in our constitution for the admission of other States; it is more guarded, and wisely so, I think, than the old constitution on the same subject, but not too guarded to receive them as fast as it may be proper. Looking to the distant future, and, perhaps, not very far distant either, it is not beyond the range of possibility, and even probability, that all the great States of the north-west will gravitate this way, as well as Tennessee, Kentucky, Missouri, Arkansas, etc. Should they do so, our doors are wide enough to receive them, but not until they are ready to assimilate with us in principle.

The process of disintegration in the old Union may be expected to go on with almost absolute certainty if we pursue the right course. We are now the nucleus of a growing power which, if we are true to ourselves, our destiny, and high mission, will become the controlling power on this continent. To what extent accessions will go on in the process of time, or where it will end, the future will determine. So far as it concerns States of the old Union, this process will be upon no such principles of *reconstruction* as now spoken of, but upon *reorgani-*

zation and new assimilation. Such are some of the glimpses of the future as I catch them. . . .

The prospect of war is, at least, not so threatening as it has been. The idea of coercion, shadowed forth in President Lincoln's inaugural, seems not to be followed up thus far so vigorously as was expected. . . . Our object is *peace,* not only with the North, but with the world. All matters relating to the public property, public liabilities of the Union when we were members of it, we are ready and willing to adjust and settle upon the principles of right, equity, and good faith. War can be of no more benefit to the North than to us. Whether the intention of evacuating Fort Sumter is to be received as an evidence of a desire for a peaceful solution of our difficulties with the United States, or the result of necessity, I will not undertake to say. I would fain hope the former. Rumors are afloat, however, that it is the result of necessity. All I can say to you, therefore, on that point is, keep your armor bright and your powder dry.

The surest way to secure peace, is to show your ability to maintain your rights. The principles and position of the present administration of the United States—the republican party—present some puzzling questions. While it is a fixed principle with them never to allow the increase of a foot of slave territory, they seem to be equally determined not to part with an inch "of the accursed soil." Notwithstanding their clamor against the institution, they seemed to be equally opposed to getting more, or letting go what they have got. They were ready to fight on the accession of Texas, and are equally ready to fight now on her secession. Why is this? How can this strange paradox be accounted for? There seems to be but one rational solution—and that is, notwithstanding their professions of humanity, they are disinclined to give up the benefits they derive from slave labor. Their philanthropy yields to their interest. The idea of enforcing the laws, has but one object, and that is a collection of the taxes, raised by slave labor to swell the fund, necessary to meet their heavy appropriations. The spoils is what they are after—though they come from the labor of the slave. . . .

In olden times the olive branch was considered the emblem of peace; we will send to the nations of the earth another and far more potential emblem of the same, the cotton plant. . . .

If, we are true to ourselves, true to our cause, true to our destiny, true to our high mission, in presenting to the world the highest type of civilization ever exhibited by man—there will be found in our lexicon no such word as fail.

Religion and Slavery

7

REVEREND A. T. HOLMES

The Duties of Christian Masters

1851

*In 1849, the Alabama Baptist State Convention offered a prize of $200
for the best essay on "the Duties of Christian Masters to Their Servants."
The following, by Reverend A. T. Holmes of Hayneville, Georgia, was one
of the three winning entries. On its face, this essay is directed at masters
and is designed to persuade them to treat their slaves better and to provide them with access to religion. The essay is also, however, an argument for the legitimacy of slavery.*

*This legitimacy stems from three sources. First, the essay implicitly
argues that slavery is a vehicle for bringing religion to blacks who might
otherwise remain ignorant of the Gospels. Second, the essay contains the
notion that the Bible supports slavery and that slaveholding is not inconsistent with being a devout Christian. This dovetails with the third part
of the proslavery argument: that masters are themselves good people and
that slaveholders should not be condemned by other Christians. On the
contrary, those slaveowners who accepted the "duties of Christian masters" should be praised for their devotion to religion and their fulfillment
of their Christian duty to accept their God-given role as masters of an
inferior race.*

A. T. Holmes, "The Duties of Christian Masters," reprinted in Holland N. Mctyeire, ed.,
Duties of Masters to Servants (Charleston, S.C.: Southern Baptist Publication Society,
1851).

When, at the formation of Eve, the God of the Universe declared, that it was not good for man to be alone, the importance of the social principle was fully recognized, and man became a social being. Founded upon the union thus originally instituted, certain relations are discovered to exist, in which are involved certain duties, each relation urging its claim respectively. Thus, the husband sustains a relation to his wife, the parent to his child, the citizen to his country, in each of which distinctive duties are to be discharged, growing out of the particular relation thus sustained. Among other relations which he sustains, *man is master;* and in this, as in all others, certain duties are involved. These relations are, all, of Divine appointment, (that between master and servant as positively as any other,) and, therefore, the duties which are involved, are all of Divine requirement. Every duty is a command, and God must be regarded as commanding the master to perform those duties to his servants, which the relation he bears to them involves and imposes.

If the position assumed in the preceding proposition is correct, and, surely, the proposition itself may be regarded as self-evident, then is it of great moment, that all the duties involved should be ascertained, as far as practicable, with special reference to their proper observance and their faithful discharge. Our present purpose is to inquire into the duties of *masters,* and, especially, of *Christian masters,* according to the word of God.

The Apostle, Paul, in writing to the Ephesian Church, (Eph. vi., 5–8,) exhorts servants to obedience. They are admonished, that *cheerful* obedience is the will of God, and are assured that He, himself, will secure the recompense, in regard to whatsoever good thing a man doeth, whether bond or free, it being done as unto the Lord, and not unto men. An act performed, whether by master or servant, from a sense of duty, God's authority and God's favor being properly recognized, cannot fail of its reward. Having been thus explicit in his direction and encouragement to servants, the Apostle calls upon masters to "do the same things (v. 9) unto them, forbearing threatening, knowing that their master, also, is in Heaven, and that there is no respect of persons with him." To do the same things, may be understood to cherish the same spirit of kindness and fidelity, to act in the same conscientious manner, and to have respect to the same recompense of reward. To forbear threatening, is to guard against a fretful, dissatisfied temper, and to resist a disposition to govern by terror rather than by love. The mutual obligations, here enjoined, seem limited by the law of Christ, and the law of Christ is the law of kindness and good will. Such a spirit should be cultivated between master and servant, but, especially, on the part of the master, in view of the distinction, in his favor, which exists. But the law of Christ contemplates a wise and judicious exercise of kindness, and imposes the necessity of that wholesome discipline, which secures, in its result, the happiness of all concerned. Now, as the servant's obedience, if rendered in a sullen, reluctant spirit, and prompted only by the fear of punishment, cannot be *good-will* service, as to the Lord, so the exercise of right and authority, on the part of the master, with reference only to his interest, uninfluenced by kindness to his servant, and desire for his good, must incur the displeasure of Him with whom there is no respect of persons. A master *may* move among his servants, as a father among his children. He *can* impress the conviction upon them that he is concerned for their comfort and welfare, and that he aims to secure their confidence and affection. His presence need not be a terror, but to them that do evil, because he has it in his power to satisfy them that his domestic policy is based upon the principle, that virtue must be encouraged and vice restrained. The necessary amount of labor can be, consistently, required, and all insubordination discountenanced, because labor is requisite to the support of all, and strict discipline essential to the peace and well-being of all. Such a spirit moves to action, not from passion or impulse, but from principle, and requires service and subordination from the servant, as from a *fellow being,* sustaining an humble relation to the master, but presenting claims upon his kindness and faithfulness which he may not disregard. The Christian master, in pursuing such a course, acts in the fear of God, discharges his trust in singleness of heart, and contemplates the end, as one who, knowing that he has a master in Heaven, would be prepared to render a satisfactory account of his stewardship. Not so with him who disregards the Divine instruction, and does not realize the obligation which his station imposes. Threatening, abuse, avowed suspicion, hasty and unjust charges, and, too often, severe punishment, in anger, or prompted by vindictive motives, mark the intercourse between master and servant. No regard is manifested for the feelings of the servant, and no effort is made to induce his confidence and affection. The look of kindness never beams in the master's eye, the note of kindness is never heard in his voice, and the mortifying conviction is forced upon him, that the master entertains no feeling for him but such as may be excited by his interest in him as his property. True, he feeds him, shelters him, and attends to him in sickness; but all this he does to his mule or his ox, and, seemingly, influenced by no better motives in the one case than in the other. Can it be rung too loudly in the ears of such, ye, also, have a master in Heaven, and there is no respect of persons with him?

The same Apostle, in another letter, (Col. iv. 1,) calls upon masters to give unto their servants that which is *"just* and *equal,"* the consideration being urged, that they have a master in heaven. In pursuing the investigation, as to the Christian master's duty, we may learn something from the use of the terms, *"just* and *equal,"* as we find them in the Scripture referred to. Justice, in a restricted, legal sense, is almost universally observed among masters; but when a master has given that which is *"just"* to his servant, has he done his duty? Has he met the Divine requirement? Or, is there something more required than what the law simply specifies? The answer is plain—equity, as well as justice, should regulate all our intercourse with others, nor does the relation of master and servant constitute an exception. Masters, give unto your *servants* that which is "just and equal," for God hath shewed you what is good; and what doth the Lord require of you but to do justly, and to *love mercy,* and to walk humbly with thy God? (Micah, vi, 8.) As justice and equity appear to be the Divine requirement in the master's conduct towards his servant, (and concurrence in this interpretation is almost universal,) we shall be much assisted in determining what is the Christian master's duty, by ascertaining what is to be understood by these respective terms. Let the distinction be noticed. *The laws of society* constitute the foundation of justice. That is right, which those laws recognize as right, and therefore the decisions of justice must be according to them. Equity has for its foundation *the laws of nature.* The law of justice is a written rule of life, binding its subjects to strict conformity in all their conclusions:—the law of equity dwells in the heart, is regulated by circumstances, and determines according to its convictions of right and wrong. The decisions of justice respect the rights of property;—the decisions of equity, those of humanity. The obligations of justice are imperative; civil jurisdiction enforces the observance of its laws, and inflicts punishment upon the transgressor:—the obligations of equity are moral in their character, conscience dictates the observance of its laws, and the Divine displeasure attends their violation. Now, let the distinction be applied. Masters, in *"giving to servants,"* are to be governed by the laws of justice, but they are to be governed, also, by the laws of equity. Justice recognizes the master's right in his servant as property, and prescribes certain laws to which he must conform in his use of that property; and the master is just, according as he respects those laws. Equity pleads the right of humanity, is not limited by the strict requirement of the law, and, in the conscientious discharge of duty, prompts the master to such treatment of his servant as would be desired, on his part, were their positions reversed. The master gives that which is *"just"* to his servant, when he acts towards him in strict accordance with legal requirement; he respects that law, the penalty of which is enforced at some civil tribunal; but he gives him that which is *"equal,"* when his conduct is directed by his consciousness of right and wrong; when he realizes the moral obligation imposed, and remembers, with humble reverence and with Godly fear, that he, also, has a master in Heaven.

Thus, in the eye of the law, the master may be *"just"* while he requires a certain amount of labor; but, in that requirement, conscience may be disregarded, right may be violated, and humanity may be outraged. Thus, also, in regard to food, and raiment, and rest. Justice feeds and clothes, according to law; but equity provides, according to the claims of nature, the suggestions of right, the impulses of kindness, and a proper regard for the Divine approbation. Masters, give unto your servants that which is "just and equal," and forget not that there is a tribunal before which master and servant must stand, when all earthly distinctions will have ceased forever. In full view of this solemn truth, when justice puts the servant to work, let equity prescribe the task; when justice would measure his meat or weigh his pork, let equity fill the measure and hold the scales; when justice would provide his clothing, let equity determine as to the quality and quantity: and when justice would build his house, let equity arrange for its comfort and convenience. It is true, that where the claims of equity are thus respected, the annual nett proceeds must be diminished to some inconsiderable extent; but, where is the master who will not feel himself amply compensated in the contentment, cheerfulness and comfortable condition of his servants, secured at a sacrifice so small, and in a manner so reasonable and consistent?

. . . The Christian master, therefore, should be known among his servants as frowning, uniformly upon vice, and smiling upon virtue; as approving that which is right, because it is right, and condemning that which is wrong, because it is wrong, and as exercising his authority, both in rewards and punishments, with that respect for right which will, directly, tend to improve the moral condition of his servants. This is the master's duty; it constitutes an important part of his personal responsibility, and, in the account which will be required of his stewardship, much of his *"joy"* or *"grief"* will be found connected with his faithfulness or neglect. How careful, then, should the master be, to convince his servant that while he will, certainly, be punished in some form, for neglect or carelessness in his daily work, for disregard of his authority, for theft, or for any thing else, which may affect his interest unfavorably, so, also, will he certainly be punished, in some proper form, for falsehood, profane language, Sabbath violation, or any thing else, which amounts to an act positively immoral, and, therefore, displeasing to God, and hurtful to the spiritual interest of the servant himself. I dread the self-condemnation of that Christian master, whose servants have never felt the force of his example and authority in encouraging moral propriety, and in reproving and suppressing that which was offensive in the sight of God. Masters, give unto your servants that which is *"just* and *equal,"* and, in order that this may be properly done, establish among them a mild and uniform system of discipline, having respect to impropriety of every sort. Be careful to satisfy them that motives of duty and benevolence prompt you to a strict observance of this system, and let it distinctly appear that your rewards and punishments have respect, not only to their increased value as *property,* but, also, to their improvement in moral worth. I know Abraham, said the Lord, that he will command his children and his *household* after him; and they shall keep the way of the Lord to do justice and judgment. That which in Abraham received the Divine favor, will obtain a similar acknowledgment in every other instance; and that which Abraham discharged, as a solemn duty, rests with equal force upon every Christian master. Let it not be forgotten, that we, also, have a master in Heaven, and that in regard to duties devolving upon us in the several relations which we sustain, He is no respecter of persons.

In connection with the Divine instruction which has been considered, may be noticed, here, Job's vindication of his integrity against the false charges of Eliphaz. "If I did despise the cause of my man servant, or of my maid servant, when they contended with me; what, then, shall I do, when God riseth up? And when he visiteth, what shall I answer him? Did not he that made me in the womb, make him? And did not one fashion us in the womb?" (Job, xxxi, 13–15.) In this just and necessary protest, Job evidently understands both the duty and responsibility involved in the relation which he sustained to his servants. A master himself, he remembered that he, also, had a master, with whom there was no respect of persons, and whose approbation was secured, not by the station occupied, but by the faithfulness of him who occupied that station, whether master or servant. Did not He that made me, make him?

When Job speaks of his servants contending with him, he is to be understood as referring to accusations made against them, which they denied; or to offences committed by them, which they attempted to excuse or justify; or to complaints which they urged, because of hardships imposed upon them. The "cause" of his servant, in either case specified, or in any case involving a just claim or an equitable demand, *he did not despise.* The servant was permitted to speak, and an opportunity afforded to prove the accusation false. His acknowledgment of the offence, his regret for it, and any palliating fact which he might urge in connection, were all heard with kindness, and received proper consideration. The cause of complaint was examined, and if found sufficient, proper measures were taken for its removal. He did not browbeat them, nor, in the haughty, tyrannical exercise of his power, refuse to hear their excuse or attend to their complaints, nor did he take their guilt *for granted,* without proper investigation. This he might have done, and have been regarded, in consequence, as a good manager, an excellent disciplinarian, a man who knew well how to keep his servants in subjection; but this he might *not* have done, with any hope of the favor of that God who made them both, and who requires of the master that he give to his servant that which is just and equal. For, let it be remembered, that Job was now repelling unjust charges; in defence of his character, he was pleading before the tribunal of a righteous God, and clearly intimates that a proper regard for the cause of his servant, as well as an upright conduct in other respects, was by him considered essential, in order that he might avoid that condemnation which he was supposed, justly, to have incurred. And, let it be further remembered, that among Job's numerous servants, many were rebellious, undutiful and unfaithful, and held both him and his cause in contempt. Yet *their* cause he did not despise, nor did he find any excuse for the neglect of duty, or any extenuation of his injustice and cruelty in the improper conduct of those who sustained to him the humble relation of servants, subject to his authority, and having no appeal from that authority but to Him who is no respecter of persons. How are masters, and especially Christian masters, admonished by this scrupulous adherence to right on the part of Job? While he was a law-abiding man, evidently, and respected the institutions of society and government, he regarded the requirement and approbation of God as paramount in their importance. Not satisfied to act as the law of the land directed, he was conscientious to observe the law of God.

Not content to render justice, where justice could be demanded, he was careful to obey its dictates, when naught but a sense of right prompted him to action; and when the case of the widow and fatherless was brought before him, the necessity of the poor, the claim of his neighbor, or *the cause of his servant,* he recognized but one law to govern his conduct. That law was the law of right, the *law of God.* To this he submitted every action, and by this was he regulated in every decision; and, in the spirit of the Apostle, "labored," in prosperity and adversity, in life and in death, to be "accepted" of God, believing, that in all nations, he that feareth God, and worketh the righteousness, is accepted of him.

Having, thus far, considered and urged the plain Scriptural direction respecting the duties of Christian masters, and, truly, a Christian master's duty is every master's duty, it is proposed to infer, from the views presented, some general and some special duties, which cannot be neglected, without doing violence to all the principles involved. These duties are, of course, more or less binding, according to the circumstances of the master, for God's requirements are according to what a man hath, and not according to what he hath not. In regard to this, Paul's rule is a good one: "Herein do I exercise myself, to have a conscience void of offence."

We infer, first, that the master should be the *friend* of his servant, and that the servant should know it. Friendship implies good will, kindness, a desire for the welfare of him for whom it is entertained. Thus should the master feel towards his servant, and in the cultivation of this spirit and its decided manifestation, there need be no compromise of authority, no undue familiarity. The servant, under such a master, knows his condition, and understands that, while he is restricted to certain privileges and required to perform certain duties, he is not held in subjection by an unfeeling tyrant, nor driven to his work by a heartless oppressor. A kind word, a pleasant look, a little arrangement for his comfort, assures him that there is one who cares for him; and, notwithstanding he goes forth to his daily labor, and toils at his daily task, his heart is light, his song is cheerful, and he seeks his humble couch at night, in the happy consciousness that his *master is his friend.* Such is the enviable lot of many servants in our *"sunny South,"* and on such plantations as feel the controlling influence of the master's friendship for his servants, it may be noticed, as a general fact, that order is observed, peace is cultivated, mutual confidence and good will are encouraged, as much work is done as ought to be done, the sound of the lash is but seldom heard, and the *runaway's* punishment is but rarely inflicted. And yet, the *friend* becomes not the *companion,* and the effort on the part of the master to secure confidence and affection, affords no warrant for improper familiarity. The kind word and the pleasant look, are still the word and look of the master, and the little arrangements which are made for the servant's comfort, are made in full recognition of the relative positions occupied, and produce, on his part, the grateful conviction that he is not regarded simply as property, but as a fellow being for whom feelings of kindness are cherished, and for whose happiness a proper desire is entertained.

Again, we infer, that the master should be the *protector* of his servant. The relation which they sustain to each other, is that of superior and inferior, and while occasional circumstances may require that the master defend or vindicate his servant, the obligations of every day call for his *protection.* The servant should *feel* that the superior wisdom, experience, power and authority of his master, constitute his abiding security. He should be encouraged to rely upon their certain and constant exercise, so that in regard to necessity, comfort, personal difficulty or danger, he may, confidently, look to his master for that protection which his particular case may demand. It is the master's duty that such an understanding be established between himself and his servant. In view of the servant's condition, it is both "*just* and *equal,*" and will contribute much towards securing that peace and mutual confidence which every good man loves to contemplate as the striking characteristic of his own family and household. Moreover, it will advance the master's interest, for, while no right is yielded, and no improper indulgence granted; while no authority is compromised, and no undue liberty allowed; at the same time, the servant learns to value his protection, loves his master, is attached to his home, and therefore less inclined to rove, dreads no separation from his family if he has one, and attends to his daily work, comparatively free from care and anxiety, and rejoicing in the assurance that, in his master, he has a kind, watchful and considerate protector.

Once more, we infer that the master should be the *guide* of his servant. In the duty here specified, reference is had, not only to the influence which the master is supposed to have over the movements or actions of his servant, but, also, to the superior intelligence of the master.

There is no relation, perhaps, unless it is that between father and son, in which a more decided influence is exerted, than that which exists between the master and his servant. Ordinary conduct and conversation are observed, manner is marked, habits are noticed, and, according as the master regulates his life by principles of right, his servant is influenced for good or for evil. The master may be a profane man, or a Sabbath breaker, or a drinker of ardent spirits — a licentious man in some positive sense — and, almost invariably, will his licentious course be acted out by those who are controlled, as well by his influence and example, as by his authority. That master speaks and acts thus, is not only a sufficient warrant with many servants, but, actually, a reason why they should speak and act thus themselves. And, are we accountable for the influence which we exert upon others? Will our common master in Heaven hold us responsible not only for the evil which we commit ourselves, but for that which we induce others to commit? Is there danger that I shall be confounded in the presence of the great Judge of all, and *doubly confounded,* because, daring myself to profane the name of God, my servant feels at liberty to do the same? Masters! Christian masters! what manner of persons ought ye to be! Twenty, fifty, perhaps an hundred immortal, accountable beings look up to you, respectively; they watch your movements, they note your example, and they, almost literally, follow your guidance, as the traveller follows his guide through some unknown region. Whither does your influence lead them? In following our example, what prospect have they for peace with God beyond the grave? To what extent are they encouraged to pursue the right and avoid the wrong, by their regard for your good opinion, and their conviction that it can only be obtained by a correct and upright course of conduct? How pleasant must be the consciousness of that master, who contemplating his relation to his servants, feels, that while they labor for his benefit, submit to his authority, and conform to his regulations, they, also, regard him as their friend, appeal to him as their protector, and trust to his superior intelligence for direction? and, that while they follow his example, and live under his influence, they are preparing for the joys and employments of that better world, where master and servant will find that with God there is no respect of persons, and that he only distinguishes between "him that serves him and him that serves him not."

We infer, lastly, that the master should be the *teacher* of his servant. Ignorance, in a peculiar sense, attaches to the negro, and ignorance ... is one principal cause of the want of virtue, and of the immoralities which abound in the world. The law of the land, sustained by public opinion, and justified in view of the causes which require its existence and enforcement, denies to the servant the opportunity for instruction which might, otherwise, be afforded. As a very natural consequence, the servant, independent of his constitutional tendency is, more or less, credulous and superstitious. He is constantly exposed to error, and especially error in regard to religious matters. It devolves, therefore, upon the master, in the discharge of his duty, to have respect to the ignorant condition of his servant, for ignorant, credulous and superstitious as he is, at the same time he is an immortal and accountable being. Sooner or later, he must die, and be judged with righteous judgment. In that judgment will the master have no interest? Will he be allowed to witness it, and feel that its retributions, in no manner, concern him? Will his servants be destroyed for "lack of knowledge," and conscience not remind him that he had neglected to teach them the way of truth? Will he not quail before the glance of that eye, which, in the ignorance of the servant, detects the indifference and unfaithfulness of the master? Alas! in that awful, fearful hour, no longer affected by the false sanctions of worldly policy, common usages, and popular prejudice, and no longer influenced by the false suggestions of worldly interest, how will some masters speak aloud their self-condemnation, when they remember how little they did, if they did any thing at all, that their servants might receive that instruction which would make them wise unto eternal life! It is urged, therefore, as an imperious duty, that the master, the Christian master, be the teacher of his servant. But teach him what, it may be asked? Teach him how to read and write? Instruct him in those branches of learning taught in our schools and colleges? Make him acquainted with those matters of general interest which agitate and disturb the political world? We answer, no; but teach him that he is a *sinner,* and that the Lord Jesus Christ is the sinner's friend. Teach him the absolute necessity of repentance toward God, and faith in the crucified Redeemer. Teach him that he must deny himself all ungodliness and worldly lusts, and live soberly, and righteously, and godly, in this present world. Let the light of your superior knowledge shine upon the darkness of his ignorance, and let his credulity and superstition yield to that simplicity and godly sincerity, which the holy religion of the Son of God secures to all, masters and servants, who are brought to feel its sanctifying and saving power. Christian master, enter the dark cabin of thy servant, and with the lamp of truth in thy hand, light up his yet darker soul with the knowledge of him, whom to know is life eternal. . . .

The effort made to instruct our servants, should be *appropriate.* Some plan should be adopted suited to their capacity. *"Understandest thou what thou readest,"* is as important a question to the negro now, as it was to the Ethiopian eighteen hundred years ago. Questions should be asked, which will lead them to *think,* and encourage them to remember what they hear. Short portions of Divine truth should be read and explained, and their particular application to them urged with kindness and faithfulness. Let the master exercise his judgment, that his servants may be benefited by his wise arrangements for their spiritual well-being.

The effort should be a *persevering* one. So long as the relation shall continue, so long will the duty be binding upon us. Besides, perseverance is necessary to success. Many things, doubtless, will occur to discourage us, but let us not be "weary in well doing, for in due season we shall reap, if we faint not." In no one particular is this exhortation of the Apostle more worthy of solemn consideration than in that which now occupies our attention. In this case, as in all others, the path of duty is the path of peace, of interest, and of safety, for He who has a right thus to speak, has promised that if we are faithful unto death, we shall receive a crown of life. The effort should be a prayerful one. The Divine blessing is essential to our success in every thing that we undertake. In praying with our servants and for them, we shall understand our duty more correctly; we shall be aided in making the most appropriate arrangements for the performance of that duty; we shall find our perseverance and self-denial encouraged and sustained in carrying out those arrangements, and shall be able, with humble confidence, to submit all to Him, whose prerogative it is to say, *"Well done, good and faithful servant."*

And now, Christian masters, suffer the word of exhortation from one, who, like yourselves, sustains this important relation. Lift your eyes to the judgment seat of Christ, remember your stewardship, consider the eternal welfare of your servants, and determine for yourselves, whether it is the part of wisdom to neglect this duty, or to make the proper effort, in order that it may be properly discharged. Anticipate that trying hour, when the smile or frown of your Maker and your Judge will depend upon the developments of that "Book of Remembrance," wherein is registered your faithfulness or your neglect. Stand with your servants before His righteous throne, and let the convictions of that honest hour fix your purpose to meet the claims which your relation, as masters, imposes upon you. "Whatsoever thy hand findeth to do, do it with thy might; for there is no work, nor device, nor knowledge, nor wisdom, in the grave, whither thou goest." Ecc. ix, 10.

8

DE BOW'S REVIEW

Slavery and the Bible

1850

The following essay appeared in the September 1850 issue of De Bow's Review, which was one of the most important antebellum journals in the South. The timing of the article is significant; it appeared just as Congress was finishing off the last pieces of legislation that are collectively known as the Compromise of 1850. Many Southerners at the time felt that they were under siege from the North and indeed the rest of the world. Thus a reiteration of the biblical defense of slavery seemed appropriate.

The essay is anonymous, but as the editor, James D. B. De Bow, notes, it is a "summary of the Bible argument for slavery." Most likely it was either compiled by De Bow himself or by a well-known Southern minister. The author apparently did not want to be associated with such a straightforward summary of the proslavery argument but at the same time felt that the fall of 1850 was an appropriate time for its publication.

This essay begins with Abraham and thus ignores the story of Noah and the argument that God decreed that the children of Ham should be the slaves of the children of Noah's other sons. The essay also ignores the book of Job, which provided important arguments in favor of the religious legitimacy of slavery. Nevertheless, as De Bow noted, although "hacknied," this was a valuable summary of how the Bible could be used to defend slavery.

A very large party in the United States believe that holding slaves is morally wrong; this party founds its belief upon precepts taught in the Bible, and takes that book as the standard of morality and religion. We, also, look to the same book as our guide in the same matters; yet, we think it right to hold slaves—do hold them, and have held and used them from childhood.

"Slavery and the Bible," *De Bow's Review* 9 (Sept. 1850): 281–86.

As we come to such opposite conclusions from the same foundation, it may be well to consider, whether the Bible teaches us anything whatever, in regard to slavery; if so, what is it and how is it taught.

The anti-slavery party maintain, that the Bible teaches nothing *directly* upon the subject, but, that it establishes rules and principles of action, from which they infer, that, in holding slaves, we are guilty of a moral wrong. This mode of reasoning would be perfectly fair, if the Bible really taught nothing directly upon the subject of slavery: but when that book applies the principles it lays down to the particular subject in controversy, we must take the application to be correct. We think we can show, that the Bible teaches clearly and conclusively that the holding of slaves is right; and if so, no deduction from general principles can make it wrong, if that book is true.

From the earliest period of time down to the present moment, slavery has existed in some form or under some name, in almost every country of the globe. It existed in every country known, even by name, to any one of the sacred writers, at the time of his writing; yet no one of them condemns it in the slightest degree. Would this have been the case had it been wrong in itself? would not some one of the host of sacred writers have spoken of this alleged crime, in such terms as to show, in a manner not to be misunderstood, that God wished all men to be equal?

Abraham, the chosen servant of God, had his bond servants, whose condition was similar to, or worse than, that of our slaves. He considered them as his property, to be bought and sold as any other property which he owned. In Genesis xvii, 13, 23, 27, we are told that God commanded Abraham to circumcise all his bond-servants, *"bought with his money,"* and that Abraham obeyed God's commandment on that same day. In Genesis xx, 14, we are told that Abimelech took sheep and oxen, and *men servants* and *women servants,* and gave them to Abraham. In chapter xii, verse 14, we are told that Abraham possessed sheep and oxen, and he asses, and men servants and maid servants, and she asses, and camels. Also, in Genesis xxvi, 14, Isaac is said to have had possessions of flocks and herds, and a great store of servants. In other places in Genesis, they are spoken of, but always as property.

Jacob's sons sold Joseph, their brother, to the Ishmaelites for twenty pieces of silver. They agreed with each other that they would sell him, when the Ishmaelites were afar off, and before they could have known that the Ishmaelites would buy him; only they knew, that such sales were common in the country at the time. The narrative of Joseph's life in Egypt, shows that the sale of slaves was common there.

No one can doubt, that Abraham regarded his servants as his property, and that they were so regarded in the country in which he lived. Not only was the bond-servant of Abraham considered his property, but the condition of the bond-servant was hereditary, or his child was a servant. In Genesis xvii, 13, God not only commanded Abraham to circumcise his servants, bought with his money, but also, those born in his house, and those which, at any future time, should be born in his house, or in that of any of his descendants; and in the twenty-third and twenty-seventh verses of the same chapter, we are told that Abraham did circumcise all his male servants, born in his house, on the same day. In chapter xiv of Genesis we are told, that Abraham took three hundred and eighteen trained servants, which had been born in his house, and pursued the kings who had carried off Lot. These three hundred and eighteen servants were born servants.

Let us now see what control Abraham exercised over these servants born in his house and bought with his money. God commanded Abraham to circumcise all his male servants—those born in his house were so numerous, that he had of them three hundred and eighteen men fit for battle. The command was, not that Abraham should use his influence over them and persuade them to be circumcised, but he and all his descendants are commanded to circumcise them—the crime and punishment for a disobedience to this command, were to fall on him or his descendants. Now, in order that God could have required this from Abraham, with any degree of justice, it was necessary that Abraham should have had both the power over his servants, which was necessary to enable him to do this, and also, that he should have had the legal and moral right to exercise that power.

Circumcision was a requirement, until then, totally unknown. Abraham's servants must have regarded it as a foolish whim of his own. Nothing else could have been considered more degrading to them, or more absurd in him. Yet, no one of all the immense number of his servants, refused to permit the circumcision to be performed. We may well suppose, that Abraham might have required anything else which his fancy dictated, and equally have enforced obedience, if it were not more absurd, painful or degrading.

When Sarai, Abraham's wife, complained to him of the conduct of Hagar, her maid servant, he answered, "thy maid is in thy hand, do to her as it pleaseth thee," showing that she only wanted her husband's consent to punish Hagar as she pleased. We are then told, that, when Sarai dealt hardly with her, she fled from her face into the wilderness—there the angel of the Lord found her; but, instead of relieving her distresses, and sending her to some free country, he told her to return and submit herself to her mistress.

When Abraham pursued Chederlaomer, the king of Elam, he took his three hundred and eighteen servants, and his three friends, Aner, Eschol and Mamre, and recaptured a large amount of property which had been carried away from Sodom. But when the king of Sodom offered him all the property which he had taken, he refused everything, except what his servants had eaten and the portion of his three friends—answering immediately for himself and his servants, and refusing everything, but reserving the right to his friends to answer for themselves.

From the passages which I have recited and referred to, we can obtain some idea of the condition of Abraham's servants. They were property bought and sold for money; their services belonged to him, and was disposed of without their consent. Their condition was hereditary—the master could punish or chastise the slave, and even maim him, at his pleasure. He exercised rights which no southern planter would dare to exercise, and which a southern negro would not submit to.

Abraham was a worshiper of God; he had direct and immediate communication with him. He showed his willingness to obey God's commands, even in offering his only son a sacrifice to God. He is spoken of by all the sacred writers, as one who was selected, from the whole human race, as the father of the faithful. God would not have so highly honored him, had he been living in constant and habitual violation of his laws: nor would he have required from him the performance of immaterial ceremonies, or of painful things not required by the moral law, and left him ignorantly to continue to violate his duties to his fellow men. Had our abolition friends been in God's stead, they would have certainly acted in a very different manner. Is there one of them who will dare to say, he would have done better than God did?

But God, instead of teaching Abraham, his chosen servant, that it was immoral to use and buy his slaves, demanded from him the performance of certain things, which required that the relation of master and slave should be kept up, not only during Abraham's time, but in all future ages. And when the angel of the Lord interfered between Sarai and Hagar, it was to cause the slave to submit to the punishment inflicted by her mistress. Under like circumstances, our slaves are persuaded to go to Canada.

From what I have written, if it stood alone, I would infer that the holding of slaves was right, in some cases. But this is, by no means, all that is found in the Bible upon the subject. After the Israelites had been a long time in Egypt, they became servants to the Egyptians. At this time, God sent Moses, as a messenger, to bring them out of Egypt. Through Moses, God gave them laws by which they were to be governed. No law which came directly from him *(the fountain of morality)*, can be considered morally wrong; it might be imperfect, in not providing for circumstances not then existing—but, so far as it does provide, its provisions are correct. Nothing which God ordained can be a crime, and nothing for which he gave express permission can be considered wrong.

In Leviticus xxv, we are told, that the Lord spake to Moses, saying: "Speak unto the children of Israel, and say unto them"—after various provisions of the law, the 39th verse reads as follows, in regard to servitude: "If thy brother that dwelleth by thee be waxen poor, and be sold unto thee, then shalt not compel him to serve as a bond-servant, but as an hired servant," &c.—clearly showing that there was a distinction between bond-servant and hired-servant. After providing for the case of a Hebrew servant, verses 44, 45 and 46, of the same law, read as follows: "Both thy bondmen, and thy bondmaids, which thou shalt have, shall be of the heathen that are round about you; of them shall ye buy bondmen and bondmaids. Moreover, of the children of the strangers that do sojourn among you, of them shall ye buy, and of their families that are with you, which they begat in your land: and they shall be your possession. And ye shall take them as an inheritance for your children after you, to inherit them for a possession; they shall be your bondmen *for ever.*"

In Exodus xxi, 20, 21, we find this law: "And if a man smite his servant, or his maid, with a rod, and he die under his hand, he shall be surely punished. Notwithstanding, if he continue a day or two, he shall not be punished: for he is his money."

The 26th and 27th verses of the same chapter provide, that if the servant have lost an eye or a tooth, by a blow from the master, the servant should go free.

The 29th, 30th, 31st and 32d verses provide, that if an ox was known to be vicious and killed a freeman, the ox and his owner were both put to death; but if he gored a bond-servant, the ox should be killed and the master should pay thirty shekels of silver: showing the distinction between bond and freemen.

The law given to the Israelites, in regard to circumcision, required the master to circumcise his male servant, bought with his money or born in his house; and, of course, it presupposes the right and power to enforce the circumcision.

Thus, we see that at a time when the Israelites had no slaves, but were themselves, in a manner, fugitive slaves, and when they had no use for slaves, being wanderers in a wilderness, and fed by God's own hand, he provided laws for bringing in, buying, inheriting and governing, slaves, in the land unto which they were to be brought at the end of forty years. He made laws recognizing the right of property, in man and in his descendants, forever—the right to trade in that property, without any limit, except that the Israelites could not buy each other; and the right to punish the slave, with no limitation, except that if the slave should die under his master's hand, the master should be punished—and if maimed, in certain ways, he had a right to freedom. These laws are worse, for the slave, than the laws of any southern State. They were provided, by God himself, for his chosen people. To any man, who admits that the Bible is given by inspiration from God, they prove that, in buying, selling, holding and using slaves, there is no moral guilt. Like all the institutions of the Deity, the holding of slaves may become criminal, by abuse of the slave; but the relation, in itself, is good and moral.

In the New Testament I find frequent mention of master and servant, and of their duties. Paul and Timothy, in writing to the Colossians, in the third chapter and twenty-second to twenty-fifth verses, exhort servants to obey their masters in all things, and not with eye-service; and in the fourth chapter and first verse, they exhort masters to give their servants what is just and equal.

Paul, in writing to Timothy, tells him to teach the same doctrines; and says, if any man teach otherwise, he is proud, knowing nothing, but doting about questions and strifes of words: see 1 Timothy vi, 1–6. Peter, also (1 Peter ii, 18–24), exhorts servants to be obedient to their masters, not only to the good and gentle, but to the froward.

Now, we all know, that the condition of the servant of the Roman empire, was much less free than that of the southern negro. His master had a more unlimited control over him; yet, the apostles say to servants, to submit to their masters—not only to the good and gentle, but to the froward; and to masters to give to their servants what is just and equal. Now, had they considered the relation of master and slave, one criminal or immoral, in itself, they must either have omitted to speak of it at all, or have condemned the relation altogether.

Paul wrote an epistle to Philemon, a Christian, a disciple of his, and a slaveholder. He sent it to him by Onesimus, also a convert, a slave of

Philemon, who was a fugitive. In it, he prays Philemon to charge the fault of Onesimus to him, saying, he would repay it, unless Philemon forgave it for his sake.

Now, had the holding of slaves been a crime, Paul's duty to Philemon would have required him to instruct Philemon, that he had no rights over Onesimus, but that the attempt to hold him in servitude, was criminal; and his duty to Onesimus would have been, in such case, to send him to some foreign free country, whereby he might have escaped from oppression. But Paul sent him back. Our northern friends think that they manage these matters better than Paul did.

We find, then, that both the Old and New Testaments speak of slavery—that they do not condemn the relation, but, on the contrary, expressly allow it or create it; and they give commands and exhortations, which are based upon its legality and propriety. It can not, then, be wrong.

What we have written is founded solely upon the Bible, and can have no force, unless it is taken for truth. If that book is of divine origin, the holding of slaves is right: as that which God permitted, recognized and commanded, cannot be inconsistent with his will.

9

PROTESTANT EPISCOPAL CONVENTION OF SOUTH CAROLINA

Duty of Clergymen in Relation to the Marriage of Slaves

1859

A persistent criticism of slavery was that it deprived slaves of the sanctity of marriage. Southerners had no real answer to this because, in fact, slaves could never be "legally" married in the South, and masters were free to break up families for whatever reason they wished. This report from the Protestant Episcopal Convention of South Carolina attempts to address this problem by urging masters to respect slave marriages and by

Report of the Special Committee Appointed by the Protestant Episcopal Convention, at Its Session in 1858, to Report on the Duty of Clergymen in Relation to the Marriage of Slaves (Charleston, S.C.: Walker, Evans, 1859).

asserting that the destruction of a slave marriage through the acts of a master should be regarded as the de facto death of one of the partners, thus allowing remarriage. The report does not apologize for slavery; on the contrary, it is fully supportive of it. Here churchmen find a theological way out of the dilemma of slave marriages and the power of the master to separate slave partners.

The first question which naturally presents itself is, whether as a Church founded upon the apostles and prophets, with Jesus Christ as the corner-stone, we can see any difference in the marriage institution as affecting the master and as affecting the slave.

We have the authority of the Great Head of the Church for declaring that the marriage relation is part of the original constitution of man, when God made them at the beginning, male and female. For this cause, He declares "that a man shall leave father and mother, and shall cleave to his wife, and they twain shall be one flesh. Wherefore" he expressly enjoins "that what God has thus joined together, man shall not put asunder." Every descendant of the first pair of human beings is evidently included in this statement, and it follows that the marriage relation between slaves has the same direct obligation, as that between masters and mistresses. It follows with equal clearness, that the injunction, that no man shall put asunder husband and wife, is as universal in extent as the marriage relation itself. The duty of every Christian master is thus ascertained with the certainty which attaches to divine precepts. He is bound to preserve inviolate the marriage tie between his slaves, and to prevent, as far as in him lies, the separation of husband and wife.

Your Committee believe that the Christian community in this Diocese recognizes this obligation, and endeavors to fulfill it; and that the separations which occur are either sought by the married parties themselves, or are brought about by circumstances beyond the control of the master or the slave.

The State has deemed it wise and expedient to vest in the master absolute authority over the slave. Other relations demand a similar delegation of power, because of the impossibility of defining precisely its limits. The child is subjected to the discretionary power of the parent; the wife is under the authority of the husband; and in the case of the slave, it would be still more inexpedient and unwise to attempt to define the modes in which the master's discretion should be exercised. A Christian master will, of course, exercise his authority in conformity to the law of God. But among masters who do not recognize the force of Christian obligation, there will be abuses in this, as in other social relations. From these abuses, as well as from other causes, separations of husband and wife will occur; and these separations give rise to questions, the solution of which require grave and prayerful consideration.

An obvious and wide distinction exists between separations produced by the voluntary action of a party to the contract, and those which are produced by some external power controlling the parties, and separating them against their will. The first class of separations may occur both among masters and among slaves. But those which are produced by a controlling authority acting against the will of the married parties are generally confined to slaves. With this distinction before us, we proceed to examine the texts of Scripture which bear upon the subject, and to ascertain the rules which they prescribe.

The first is to be found in our Saviour's Sermon on the Mount, in 5th St. Matthew, v. 32. There it is declared by the Saviour himself, that "whosoever shall put away his wife, saving for the cause of fornication, causeth her to commit adultery; and whosoever shall marry her, that is divorced, committeth adultery." This passage evidently embraces only the case of voluntary action, on the part of the husband. The expression used is "put away." At first sight it might seem that inasmuch as the wife put away, is an involuntary sufferer, and still is not permitted to marry again, that the precept might include both the classes of separations which we have distinguished. But upon further examination, it will appear that the denial of another marriage to the wife, is included in the assertion, that she is unlawfully put away by her husband. The husband who puts away is said to cause her to commit adultery. This can only be, because she remains his wife, notwithstanding the putting away. And if she continues to be his wife, then whosoever shall marry her, committeth adultery. The marriage contract is thus declared by the Saviour to remain in full force, notwithstanding the attempt by the husband, to dissolve it; and all the consequences must ensue, which would attach to a valid continuing marriage. Neither husband nor wife can undertake a new obligation.

The same propositions are still more distinctly announced in the 19th St. Matthew. There the question is propounded to our Saviour, by the Pharisees: "Whether it is lawful for a man to put away his wife for every cause." The voluntary action of the husband is the subject matter, and the enquiry is, as to its lawfulness and extent. Our Saviour distinctly answers as to both points, by saying "whosoever shall put away his wife, except it be for fornication, and shall marry another, committeth adultery; and whosoever marrieth her, which is put away, doth commit adultery." In other words, the attempted divorce is declared to be unlawful; the marriage continues valid; the husband committeth adultery if he marry again; the wife remains his wife, in spite of the divorce, and any one marrying her, commits adultery.

St. Mark's Gospel, Chap. 10, records the reply of our Saviour to the same question of the Pharisees—"Is it lawful for a man to put away his wife." In concluding his reply, our Saviour says: "Whosoever shall put away his wife, and marry another, committeth adultery against her; and if a woman shall put away her husband, and be married to another, she committeth adultery." In this passage, the alternative proposition is for the first time presented, of the wife putting away her husband. It meets with the same condemnation. Both parties are declared guilty of sin if they marry again—that sin is called adultery, both in the husband and in the wife; and thus includes the assertion that the marriage continues valid, notwithstanding the attempt of either party to set it aside.

In St. Luke's Gospel, chapter 16, verse 18, our Saviour announces the same rule in general terms, without noticing the exception stated in the former texts. He says: "Whosoever putteth away his wife, and marrieth another, commiteth adultery, and whosoever marrieth her, that is put away from her husband, committeth adultery." Here again the divorce is attempted by the voluntary action of one of the parties to the contract; the same rule is repeated for such cases: but none is yet announced for cases of separation produced by an external controlling power, acting against the will, and without the fault of the married parties.

The other Evangelist, St. John, is silent upon this subject; and we next find it considered by St. Paul, in the 7th chapter of 1 Cor., verse 10. This Apostle, in considering the obligation of believers to continue their social relations with unbelievers, says: "Unto the married I command, yet not I, but the Lord; let not the wife depart from her husband; but, and if she depart, let her remain unmarried, or be reconciled to her husband, and let not the husband put away his wife." Here again we have a distinct prohibition of voluntary separation, and an equally distinct prohibition of a second marriage, in case the wife voluntarily depart from her husband.

The Apostle goes on to consider the case of a wife abandoned by her husband because of her becoming a Christian. He seems to give judgment with some hesitation. He is careful to inform us that he gives his individual judgment, not the Lord's; and while he advises the woman who has an unbelieving husband not to leave her husband, he goes on to say, "but if the unbelieving depart, let him depart. A brother or a sister is not under bondage in such cases."

The precise meaning of the word bondage here used by the Apostle, has been the subject of controversy. If the word be construed to apply to the marriage bond, (which in the case under the Apostle's consideration might be justly called a bondage,) then in the judgment of the Apostle, the abandoned party is released from the obligation of the marriage contract, and a second marriage by that party is sanctioned. This construction, however, does not consist with the previous declaration of our Saviour, that the wife put away by her husband commits adultery in marrying again. There is no substantial difference between the words "put away and depart," used in the different passages; it follows, therefore, that this construction cannot be sustained. The remark of the Apostle nevertheless opens to our view a distinction between the party who abandons, and the innocent sufferer who is abandoned. It draws a line between the voluntary agent, and the involuntary subject of the separation. The latter is released from the obligation of her marriage vow, and although not free to contract another marriage, she is no longer under bondage to her husband.

Thus far we have been guided by Scripture; all the cases decided in the texts quoted are cases of separation by the voluntary act of one of the married parties. Nothing has been said as to the case of separation in which they have no agency, and which has been effected by a lawful authority to which they are bound to submit.

The State, for wise and sufficient reasons, has committed to the master a discretionary power to dispose of his slave. The mode of exercising that power is left to the conscience of the master. If that master should disregard the commands of God, and be led by caprice or self-interest to separate those who are lawfully joined together in marriage, he incurs all the consequences of his act, and must answer for it to the Final Judge. But the innocent parties who have been separated, stand upon a different footing, and are objects of sympathy and not of censure. They are deprived by an external authority, of all the benefits of the marriage relation; they can no longer fulfill its obligations, and if the separation be continued and final, they are virtually dead to each other. Under such circumstances, the marriage no longer subsists but in name.

To require persons thus separated to remain unmarried, would involve consequences injurious to themselves, and detrimental to the best interests of our social system. If it be commanded by the divine law, there is an end of all discussion; the parties must bear their burthen, and society must trust to the Providence of God for a remedy. But where, as we have already shown, the Scriptures are silent, we are left to the other guides given to us by God, and every Christian must follow the dictates of his own conscience and reason.

Upon a matter of so much practical importance, it would be inconvenient to find different rules prevailing in the same Diocese. It is, therefore, wise and proper to ascertain and set forth that which is most comformable to the judgment of the Church. This rule your Committee do not propose to clothe with the sanction of Law, but simply to announce as the opinion of the Convention.

Your Committee have opened a correspondence with many of the Clergy in our Diocese, and they find a general concurrence in the practice of allowing marriages, in cases where the parties have been separated in such a way, as to render impossible the fulfilment of the marriage obligations.

Our municipal law, although it gives no sanction to divorce, or to the marriage of divorced parties, yet furnishes some analogy to the case under consideration, in permitting the marriage of a party whose husband or wife has been absent for seven years. In such case, the law presumes the death of the absent party. In like manner a separation of married slaves, which as completely severs the married parties as though one were dead, should be entitled to the like relief; and ought to receive equal indulgence at the hands of the Clergy.

When the husband or wife have been removed by legal authority from the neighborhood of each other; when they have had no agency in the separation, and have done what they lawfully could do to avoid it; when they can no longer receive the benefits or fulfill the obligations of marriage, and this condition of things seems to be continued and final, then they are substantially in the same condition as though death had intervened, and the marriage really subsists but in name.

In what case a separation is to be considered final, and how great a distance is involved in the term separation, it is impossible to define. The sound judgment of the minister must be exercised in this, as in other cases. But it seems to your Committee that when exercised, it should be deemed final; and that the second marriage should stand, even in cases where another change of circumstances may bring back the separated husband or wife. Human judgment is necessarily finite, and no provision can be made for all contingencies. Cases of hardship will certainly exist. Separations will sometimes be considered temporary by the Ministers, where the parties will insist that they are final.

Distances will be regarded in different aspects. But, nevertheless, the general rule submitted is, upon the whole, the best, and the minister of the parish is the best arbiter to direct its application.

The Committee recommend to the Convention the adoption of the following resolutions:

1. *Resolved,* That the relation of husband and wife is of divine institution, and the duties which appertain to it, are of universal obligation, and bind with the same force the master and the slave.

2. That the injunction of our Saviour forbidding man to separate those whom God has joined together, is obligatory upon the conscience of every Christian master, and prohibits the separation of those who have been united in marriage.

3. That the power over the slave, which is conferred upon the master by the law of the land, should be exercised by every Christian, in conformity with the law of God; and, therefore, every Christian master should so regulate the sale or disposal of a married slave, as not to infringe the Divine injunction forbidding the separation of husband and wife.

4. That while this obligation is generally recognized by Christians, yet many cases arise in which separations among married slaves, occur from voluntary abandonment of duty by the parties themselves, or from circumstances beyond their control, and it is desirable that some judgment should be pronounced by the Church, which may establish for its members a uniform rule of conduct.

5. That the cases of separation produced by the voluntary action of either of the parties to the marriage contract, are expressly condemned by our Saviour; and this sentence, as already stated, embraces master and slave; but involuntary separation produced by causes over which the married parties have no control, do not appear to come within the scope of any direction recorded in the Scriptures.

6. That in the absence of such direction, the sound judgment of the Church, guided by the general principles of religion, and directed by the Great Head of the Church, must be exercised in devising the best rule for the action of its members.

7. That where an involuntary and final separation of married slaves has occurred, the case of the sufferers is to be distinguished from any human agency which has separated them; the latter is responsible to God for disregarding his commands; the former are entitled to sympathy and consideration.

8. That in such cases of separation, where neither party is in fault, and where the separation appears to be permanent and final, the

refusal to allow a second marriage would often produce much evil and hardship; and this Convention in giving its judgment in favor of such marriages, would do so in the qualified language applied by the Apostle to cases of self-restraint, "If they cannot contain, let them marry; for it is better to marry than to burn."
All which is respectfully submitted.

C. G. Memminger, *Chairman*

10

THORNTON STRINGFELLOW

The Bible Argument: Or, Slavery in the Light of Divine Revelation

1860

Thornton Stringfellow (1788–1869) was a Baptist minister and planter near Fredericksburg, Virginia. He wrote extensively on slavery and religion, believing that God had ordained slavery and that Christian masters should convert and baptize their slaves and treat them humanely. He believed that the role, or calling, of slaveowner was a duty Christians should accept and carry out with the highest level of morality and commitment to the Gospel.

The first version of this essay appeared in 1841 in the Religious Herald, *a Richmond publication. It was later reprinted as a pamphlet and then included in E. N. Elliott's compilation of proslavery thought,* Cotton Is King. *Part of the essay is designed to answer abolitionist ministers who attacked the morality of slavery. Abolitionists had argued that the use of the word* servants *in the Bible implied that slavery was not acceptable. Stringfellow devotes much of his essay to making a distinction between servants and bond-servants, or slaves. Most modern translations of the*

Thornton Stringfellow, "The Bible Argument: Or, Slavery in the Light of Divine Revelation," in E. N. Elliott, *Cotton Is King, and Pro-Slavery Arguments: Comprising the Writings of Hammond, Harper, Christy, Stringfellow, Hodge, Bledsoe, and Cartwright, on This Important Subject* (Augusta, Ga.: Pritchard, Abbott & Loomis, 1860), 461–521.

COTTON IS KING,

AND

PRO-SLAVERY ARGUMENTS:

COMPRISING THE WRITINGS OF

HAMMOND, HARPER, CHRISTY, STRINGFELLOW, HODGE,
BLEDSOE, AND CARTWRIGHT,

ON THIS IMPORTANT SUBJECT.

BY

E. N. ELLIOTT, L.L.D.,

PRESIDENT OF PLANTERS' COLLEGE, MISSISSIPPI.

WITH AN ESSAY ON SLAVERY IN THE LIGHT OF INTERNATIONAL LAW,
BY THE EDITOR.

PUBLISHED AND SOLD EXCLUSIVELY BY SUBSCRIPTION.

AUGUSTA, GA:
PRITCHARD, ABBOTT & LOOMIS.
1860.

The title page of *Cotton Is King,* an 1860 volume that
contained influential proslavery arguments by James
Hammond, Thornton Stringfellow, Samuel Cartwright, and others.
New York Public Library.

*Bible use the term slave in many of these instances. But Stringfellow,
trapped by the inaccurate King James translation, was forced instead to
develop arguments to explain why servants were really slaves. In addition, to answer the abolitionists, the essay also explores the many ways in
which both the Old and New Testaments allowed slavery and did not*

question its validity. Perhaps Stringfellow's most important argument is that God ordained slavery and established it on Earth after the flood.

If slavery be thus sinful, it behooves all Christians who are involved in the sin, to repent in dust and ashes, and wash their hands of it, without consulting with flesh and blood. Sin in the sight of God is something which God in his word makes known to be wrong, either by preceptive prohibition, by principles of moral fitness, or examples of inspired men, contained in the sacred volume. When these furnish no law to condemn human conduct, there is no transgression. Christians should produce a "thus saith the Lord," both for what they condemn as sinful, and for what they approve as lawful, in the sight of heaven.

It is to be hoped, that on a question of such vital importance as this to the peace and safety of our common country, as well as to the welfare of the church, we shall be seen cleaving to the Bible, and taking all our decisions about this matter, from its inspired pages. With men from the North, I have observed for many years a palpable ignorance of the Divine will, in reference to the institution of slavery. I have seen but a few who made the Bible their study, that had obtained a knowledge of what it did reveal on this subject. Of late their denunciation of slavery as a sin, is loud and long.

I propose, therefore, to examine the sacred volume briefly, and if I am not greatly mistaken, I shall be able to make it appear that the institution of slavery has received, in the first place,

1st. The sanction of the Almighty in the Patriarchal age.

2d. That it was incorporated into the only National Constitution which ever emanated from God.

3d. That its legality was recognized, and its relative duties regulated, by Jesus Christ in his kingdom; and

4th. That it is full of mercy.

. . . "Blessed be the Lord God of Shem; and Canaan shall be his servant." "God shall enlarge Japheth, and he shall dwell in the tents of Shem; and Canaan shall be his servant."—Gen. ix: 25, 26, 27. Here, language is used, showing the *favor* which God would exercise to the posterity of Shem and Japheth, while they were holding the posterity of Ham in a state of *abject bondage.* May it not be said in truth, that God decreed this institution before it existed; and has he not connected its *existence* with prophetic tokens of special favor, to those who should be slave owners or masters? He is the same God now, that he was when he gave these views of his moral character to the world; and unless the posterity of Shem and Japheth, from whom have sprung the Jews, and all the nations of Europe and America, and a great part of Asia, (the African race that is in them excepted,)—I say, unless they are all dead, as well as the Canaanites or Africans, who descended from Ham, then it is quite possible that his favor may now be found with one class of men who are holding another class in bondage. Be this as it may. God *decreed slavery*—and shows in that decree, tokens of good-will to the master. . . . Abraham was a native of Ur, of the Chaldees. From thence the Lord called him to go to a country which he would show him; and he obeyed, not knowing whither he went. He stopped for a time in Haran, where his father died. From thence he "took Sarai his wife, and Lot his brother's son, and all their substance that they had gathered, and the souls they had gotten in Haran, and they went forth to go into the land of Canaan."— Gen. xii: 5.

All the ancient Jewish writers of note, and Christian commentators agree, that by the "souls they had gotten in Haran," as our translators render it, are meant their slaves, or those persons they had bought with their money in Haran. In a few years after their arrival in Canaan, Lot with all he had was taken captive. So soon as Abraham heard it, he armed three hundred and eighteen slaves that were born in his house, and retook him. How great must have been the entire slave family, to produce at this period of Abraham's life, such a number of young slaves able to bear arms.—Gen. xiv: 14.

. . . When the famine drove Abraham to Egypt, he received the highest honors of the reigning sovereign. This honor at Pharaoh's court, was called forth by the visible tokens of immense wealth. In Genesis xii: 15, 16, we have the honor that was shown to him, mentioned, *with a list of his property,* which is given in these words, in the 16th verse: "He had sheep, and oxen, and he-asses, and men-servants, and maid-servants, and she-asses, and camels." The *amount* of his flocks may be inferred from the *number of slaves* employed in tending them. They were those he brought from Ur of the Chaldees, of whom the three hundred and eighteen were born; those gotten in Haran, where he dwelt for a short time, and those which he inherited from his father, who died in Haran. When Abraham *went up* from Egypt, it is stated in Genesis xiii: 2, that he was *"very rich,"* not only in *flocks* and *slaves,* but in *"silver* and *gold"* also. . . .

God had promised Abraham's seed the land of Canaan, and that in his seed all the nations of the earth should be blessed. He reached the age of eighty-five, and his wife the age of seventy-five, while as yet, they had no child. At this period, Sarah's anxiety for the promised seed, in connection with her age, induced her to propose a female slave of the Egyptian stock, as a secondary wife, from which to obtain the promised seed. This alliance soon puffed the slave with pride, and she became insolent to her mistress—the mistress complained to Abraham, the master. Abraham ordered Sarah to exercise her authority. Sarah did so, and pushed it to severity, and the slave absconded. The divine oracles inform us, that the angel of God found this runaway bond-woman in the wilderness; and if God had commissioned this angel to improve this opportunity of teaching the world how much he abhorred slavery, he took a bad plan to accomplish it. For, instead of repeating a homily upon doing to others as we "would they should do unto us," and heaping reproach upon Sarah, as a hypocrite, and Abraham as a tyrant, and giving Hagar direction how she might get into Egypt, from whence (according to abolitionism) she had been unrighteously sold into bondage, the angel addressed her as "Hagar, Sarah's maid," Gen. xvi: 1, 9; (thereby recognizing the relation of master and slave,) and asks her, "whither wilt thou go?" and she said "I flee from the face of my mistress." Quite a wonder she honored Sarah so much as to call her mistress; but she knew nothing of abolition, and God by his angel did not become her teacher.

We have now arrived at what may be called an *abuse* of the institution, in which one person is the property of another, and under their control, and subject to their authority without their consent; and if the Bible be the book, which proposes to furnish the case which leaves it without doubt that God abhors the institution, here we are to look for it. What, therefore, is the doctrine in relation to slavery, in a case in which a rigid exercise of its arbitrary authority is called forth upon a helpless female; who might use a strong plea for protection, upon the ground of being the master's wife. In the face of this case, which is hedged around with aggravations as if God designed by it to awaken all the sympathy and all the abhorrence of that portion of mankind, who claim to have more mercy than God himself—but I say, in view of this strong case, what is the doctrine taught? Is it that God abhors the institution of slavery; that it is a reproach to good men; that the evils of the institution can no longer be transmitted to posterity, with this stain upon it; that Sarah must no longer be allowed to live a stranger to the abhorrence God has for such conduct as she has been guilty of to this poor helpless female? I say, what is the doctrine taught? Is it so plain that it can be easily understood? and does God teach that she is a bond-woman or slave, and that she is to recognize

Sarah as her mistress, and not her equal—that she must return and submit herself unreservedly to Sarah's authority? Judge for yourself, reader, by the angel's answer: "And the angel of the Lord said unto her, Return unto thy mistress, and submit thyself under her hands."— Gen. xvi: 9. . . .

Having shown from the Scriptures, that slavery existed with Abraham and the patriarchs, with divine approbation, and having shown from the same source, that the Almighty incorporated it in the law, as an institution among Abraham's seed, until the coming of Christ, our precise object now is, to ascertain whether *Jesus Christ has abolished it,* or *recognized it* as a *lawful relation,* existing among men, and prescribed duties which belong to it, as he has other relative duties; such as those between husband and wife, parent and child, magistrate and subject. . . .

. . . I affirm then, first, (and no man denies,) that Jesus Christ has not abolished slavery by a prohibitory command: and second, I affirm, he has introduced no new moral principle which can work its destruction, under the gospel dispensation; and that the principle relied on for this purpose, is a fundamental principle of the Mosaic law, under which slavery was instituted by Jehovah himself: and third, with this absence of positive prohibition, and this absence of principle, to work its ruin, I affirm, that in all the Roman provinces, where churches were planted by the apostles, hereditary slavery existed, as it did among the Jews, and as it does now among us, (which admits of proof from history that no man will dispute who knows any thing of the matter,) and that in instructing such churches, the Holy Ghost by the apostles, has recognized the institution, as one *legally existing* among them, to be perpetuated in the church, and that its duties are prescribed.

Now for the proof: To the church planted at Ephesus the capital of the lesser Asia, Paul ordains by letter, subordination in the fear of God,—first between wife and husband; second, child and parent; third, servant and master; *all, as states, or conditions, existing among the members.*

The relative duties of each state are pointed out; those between the servant and master in these words: "Servants be obedient to them who are your masters, according to the flesh, with fear and trembling, in singleness of your heart as unto Christ; not with eye service as men pleasers, but as the servants of Christ, doing the will of God from the heart, with good-will, doing service, as to the Lord, and not to men, knowing that whatsoever good thing any man doeth, the same shall he receive of the Lord, whether he be bond or free. And ye masters do the same things to them, forbearing threatening, knowing that your master is also in heaven, neither is there respect of persons with him." Here, by the Roman law, the servant was property, and the control of the master unlimited, as we shall presently prove.

To the church at Colosse, a city of Phrygia, in the lesser Asia,— Paul in his letter to them, recognizes the three relations of wives and husbands, parents and children, servants and masters, as relations existing among the members; (here the Roman law was the same;) and to the servants and masters he thus writes: "Servants obey in all things your masters, according to the flesh: not with eye service, as men pleasers, but in singleness of heart, fearing God: and whatsoever you do, do it heartily, as to the Lord and not unto men; knowing that of the Lord ye shall receive the reward of the inheritance, for ye serve the Lord Christ. But he that doeth wrong shall receive for the wrong he has done; and there is no respect of persons with God. Masters give unto your servants that which is just and equal, knowing that you also have a master in heaven."

The same Apostle writes a letter to the church at Corinth; . . . Under the direction of the Holy Ghost, he instructs the church, that, on this particular subject, *one general principle* was ordained of God, applicable alike in all countries and at all stages of the church's future history, and that it was this: *"as the Lord has called every one, so let him walk."* "Let every man abide in the same calling wherein he is called." "Let every man wherein he is called, therein abide with God."—1 Cor. vii: 17, 20, 24. *"And so ordain I in all churches;"* vii: 17. The Apostle thus explains his meaning: . . .

"Art thou called, being a servant? Care not for it, but if thou mayest be made free, use it rather;" vii: 18, 21. Here, by the Roman law, slaves were property,—yet Paul ordains, in this, and all other churches, that Christianity gave them no title to freedom, but on the contrary, required them not to care for being slaves, or in other words, to be contented with their *state,* or *relation,* unless they could be *made free,* in a lawful way.

Again, we have a letter by Peter, . . . "Submit yourselves to every ordinance of man for the Lord's sake." "For so is the will of God." "Servants, be subject to your masters with all fear, not only to the good and gentle, but also to the froward."—1 Peter ii: 11, 13, 15, 18. What an important document is this! enjoining political subjection to *governments of every form,* and Christian subjection on the part of servants to their masters, whether good or bad; for the purpose of showing forth to advantage, the *glory of the gospel,* and putting to silence the ignorance of foolish men, who might think it seditious.

By "every ordinance of man," as the context will show, is meant governmental regulations or laws, as was that of the Romans for enslaving their prisoners taken in war, instead of destroying their lives.

When such enslaved persons came into the church of Christ let them (says Peter) "be subject to their masters with all fear," whether such masters be good or bad. It is worthy of remark, that he says much to secure civil subordination to the State, and hearty and cheerful obedience to the masters, on the part of servants; yet he says nothing to masters in the whole letter. It would seem from this, that danger to the cause of Christ was on the side of *insubordination among the servants,* and a *want of humility with inferiors,* rather than *haughtiness among superiors* in the church.

The Law in Defense of Slavery

11

NORTH CAROLINA SUPREME COURT

State v. Mann (Opinion of Thomas Ruffin)

1829

John Mann rented a slave named Lydia from her owner, Elizabeth Jones. When Mann tried to whip Lydia, she "ran off," presumably to avoid punishment rather than to escape from slavery. Mann then shot and wounded her. Jones complained to the authorities, who charged Mann with assault and battery. A jury convicted Mann, but the North Carolina Supreme Court reversed the conviction.

This opinion, written by North Carolina Chief Justice Thomas Ruffin, incorporates a number of traditional proslavery arguments. Ruffin does not appear to be a proslavery fanatic, although he was in fact a lifelong slaveowner. Indeed, much like Jefferson, he complains about the existence of slavery, even while defending it. This in itself is an aspect of proslavery thought.

The defendant was indicted for an assault and battery upon Lydia, the slave of one Elizabeth Jones.

On the trial it appeared that the defendant had hired the slave for a year; that during the term the slave had committed some small offence, for which the defendant undertook to chastise her; that while in the act of so doing the slave ran off, whereupon the defendant called upon her to stop, which being refused, he shot at and wounded her.

State v. Mann, 13 North Carolina Reports 263 (1829).

His Honor, Judge Daniel, charged the jury that if they believed the punishment inflicted by the defendant was cruel and unwarrantable, and disproportionate to the offence committed by the slave, that in law the defendant was guilty, as he had only a special property in the slave.

A verdict was returned for the State, and the defendant appealed.

. . .

Ruffin, Judge.—A judge cannot but lament when such cases as the present are brought into judgment. It is impossible that the reasons on which they go can be appreciated, but where institutions similar to our own exist and are thoroughly understood. The struggle, too, in the judge's own breast between the feelings of the man and the duty of the magistrate is a severe one, presenting strong temptation to put aside such questions, if it be possible. It is useless, however, to complain of things inherent in our political state. And it is criminal in a Court to avoid any responsibility which the laws impose. With whatever reluctance, therefore, it is done, the Court is compelled to express an opinion upon the extent of the dominion of the master over the slave in North Carolina.

. . . Our laws uniformly treat the master or other person having the possession and command of the slave as entitled to the same extent of authority. The object is the same—the services of the slave; and the same powers must be confided. . . . Upon the general question whether the owner is answerable *criminaliter* for a battery upon his own slave, or other exercise of authority or force not forbidden by statute, the Court entertains but little doubt. That he is so liable has never yet been decided; nor, as far as is known, been hitherto contended. There have been no prosecutions of the sort. The established habits and uniform practice of the country in this respect is the best evidence of the portion of power deemed by the whole community requisite to the preservation of the master's dominion. . . . This had indeed been assimilated at the bar to the other domestic relations; and arguments drawn from the well-established principles which confer and restrain the authority of the parent over the child, the tutor over the pupil, the master over the apprentice, have been pressed on us. The Court does not recognize their application. There is no likeness between the cases. They are in opposition to each other, and there is an impassable gulf between them. The difference is that which exists between freedom and slavery—and a greater cannot be imagined. In the one, the end in view is the happiness of the youth, born to equal rights with that governor, on whom the duty devolves of training the young to usefulness in a station which he is afterwards to assume among freemen. To such an end, and with such a subject, moral and intellectual instruction seem the natural means; and for the most part they are found to suffice. Moderate force is superadded only to make the others effectual. If that fail it is better to leave the party to his own headstrong passions and the ultimate correction of the law than to allow it to be immoderately inflicted by a private person. With slavery it is far otherwise. The end is the profit of the master, his security and the public safety; the subject, one doomed in his own person and his posterity, to live without knowledge and without the capacity to make anything his own, and to toil that another may reap the fruits. What moral considerations shall be addressed to such a being to convince him what it is impossible but that the most stupid must feel and know can never be true—that he is thus to labor upon a principle of natural duty, or for the sake of his own personal happiness, such services can only be expected from one who has no will of his own; who surrenders his will in implicit obedience to that of another. Such obedience is the consequence only of uncontrolled authority over the body. There is nothing else which can operate to produce the effect. The power of the master must be absolute to render the submission of the slave perfect. I most freely confess my sense of the harshness of this proposition; I feel it as deeply as any man can; and as a principal of moral right every person in his retirement must repudiate it. But in the actual condition of things it must be so. There is no remedy. This discipline belongs to the state of slavery. They cannot be disunited without abrogating at once the rights of the master and absolving the slave from his subjection. It constitutes the curse of slavery to both the bond and free portion of our population. But it is inherent in the relation of master and slave.

That there may be particular instances of cruelty and deliberate barbarity where, in conscience, the law might properly interfere, is most probable. The difficulty is to determine where a Court may properly begin. Merely in the abstract it may well be asked, which power of the master accords with right? The answer will probably sweep away all of them. But we cannot look at the matter in that light. The truth is that we are forbidden to enter upon a train of general reasoning on the subject. We cannot allow the right of the master to be brought into discussion in the courts of justice. The slave, to remain a slave, must be made sensible that there is no appeal from his master; that his power is in no instance usurped; but is conferred by the laws of man at least, if not by the law of God. The danger would be great, indeed, if the tribunals of justice should be called on to graduate the punishment appropriate to every temper and every dereliction of menial duty. No man can anticipate the many and aggravated provocations of the master which the slave would be constantly stimulated by his own passions or the instigation of others to give; or the consequent wrath of the master, prompting him to bloody vengeance upon the turbulent traitor—a vengeance generally practiced with impunity by reason of its privacy. The Court, therefore, disclaims the power of changing the relation in which these parts of our people stand to each other.

We are happy to see that there is daily less and less occasion for the interposition of the Courts. The protection already afforded by several statutes, that all-powerful motive, the private interest of the owner, the benevolences towards each other, seated in the hearts of those who have been born and bred together, the frowns and deep execrations of the community upon the barbarian who is guilty of excessive and brutal cruelty to his unprotected slave, all combined, have produced a mildness of treatment and attention to the comforts of the unfortunate class of slaves, greatly mitigating the rigors of servitude and ameliorating the condition of the slaves. The same causes are operating and will continue to operate with increased action until the disparity in numbers between the whites and blacks shall have rendered the latter in no degree dangerous to the former, when the police now existing may be further relaxed. This result, greatly to be desired, may be much more rationally expected from the events above alluded to, and now in progress, than from any rash expositions of abstract truths by a judiciary tainted with a false and fanatical philanthropy, seeking to redress an acknowledged evil by means still more wicked and appalling than even that evil.

I repeat that I would gladly have avoided this ungrateful question. But being brought to it the Court is compelled to declare that while slavery exists amongst us in its present state, or until it shall seem fit to the legislature to interpose express enactments to the contrary, it will be the imperative duty of the judges to recognize the full dominion of the owner over the slave, except where the exercise of it is forbidden by statute. And this we do upon the ground that this dominion is essential to the value of slaves as property, to the security of the master, and the public tranquility, greatly dependent upon their subordination; and, in fine, as most effectually securing the general protection and comfort of the slaves themselves.

Per Curiam.—Let the judgment below be reversed, and judgment entered for the defendant.

12

U.S. SUPREME COURT

Dred Scott v. Sandford
(Opinion of Roger B. Taney)

1857

Dred Scott v. Sandford *was the most important Supreme Court decision dealing with slavery. Scott, a Missouri slave, sued for his freedom based on his residence in what is today Minnesota, which was then federal territory made free of slavery by the Missouri Compromise of 1820. In his opinion for the Court, Chief Justice Roger B. Taney (1777–1864) struck down that portion of the Missouri Compromise that banned slavery in federal territories. This was based on his assertion that under the Fifth Amendment, Congress could not deprive citizens of their right to take property with them to the national territories. While helping slaveowners and undermining the platform of the Republican party, which called for a ban on slavery in all of the territories, this part of the decision might have been applied to any other kind of property or federal rights. However, in his opinion Taney also went to great lengths to show that slavery was particularly protected by the Constitution and that blacks, whether free or slave, could never be citizens of the United States. This was a profoundly proslavery result. Taney concluded that blacks were "an inferior order" and that at the time of the American founding, and forever after, "they had no rights which the white man was bound to respect." The Constitution, Taney declared, favored slavery and not freedom, and it was reasonable to presume that all black people were slaves or could be treated as slaves.*

Dred Scott came to symbolize the constitutional crisis over slavery while at the same time offering the South a powerful weapon in its struggle to secure slavery within the national Union. In effect, Taney declared that the Constitution was proslavery and that the American nation, from the beginning, was a slaveowners' nation. His use of the Founders to support his decision was an attempt to wrap his proslavery racism in the patriotic symbols of the nation.

Northerners who opposed the antislavery movement hoped that Taney's decision would end political agitation over slavery. Southerners cheered

---

60 U.S. (19 How.) 393 (1857).

Dred Scott and his wife, Harriet. Shortly after the Supreme Court rejected Scott's claim, Scott and his family did nevertheless gain their freedom. The family was purchased by the sons of Peter Blow, the man who had owned them many years earlier, and the Blow brothers freed the Scotts in May 1857. Library of Congress.

the decision, which put the force of the Constitution behind their institution. Opponents of slavery condemned the decision and effectively overturned it through the Thirteenth Amendment (1865), which ended slavery, and the Fourteenth Amendment (1868), which made all people born in the United States, including former slaves and their children, citizens of the nation and the state in which they lived.

Mr. Chief Justice Taney delivered the opinion of the court. . . .

The plaintiff [Dred Scott] . . . was, with his wife and children, held as slaves by the defendant [Sanford],[1] in the State of Missouri; and he brought this action in the Circuit Court of the United States for [Missouri], to assert the title of himself and his family to freedom.

The declaration is . . . that he and the defendant are citizens of different States; that . . . he is a citizen of Missouri, and the defendant a citizen of New York.

[1]The defendant's name was John Sanford, but the Supreme Court misspelled his name as Sandford in the official record of the case.

[Sanford countered with a plea in abatement, asserting that Scott was] not a citizen of the State of Missouri [because he was] a negro of African descent, whose ancestors were of pure African blood, and who were brought into this country and sold as slaves. . . .

The question is simply this: Can a negro, whose ancestors were imported into this country, and sold as slaves, become a member of the political community formed and brought into existence by the Constitution of the United States, and as such become entitled to all the rights, and privileges, and immunities, guarantied by that instrument to the citizen? One of which rights is the privilege of suing in a court of the United States in the cases specified in the Constitution. . . .

The words "people of the United States" and "citizens" are synonymous terms, and mean the same thing. They both describe the political body who . . . form the sovereignty, and who hold the power and conduct the Government through their representatives. . . . The question before us is, whether the class of persons described in the plea in abatement [people of African ancestry] compose a portion of this people, and are constituent members of this sovereignty? We think they are not, and that they are not included, and were not intended to be included, under the word "citizens" in the Constitution, and can therefore claim none of the rights and privileges which that instrument provides for and secures to citizens of the United States. On the contrary, they were at that time considered as a subordinate and inferior class of beings, who had been subjugated by the dominant race, and, whether emancipated or not, yet remained subject to their authority, and had no rights or privileges but such as those who held the power and the Government might choose to grant them. . . .

It is very clear, therefore, that no State can, by any act or law of its own . . . introduce a new member into the political community created by the Constitution of the United States. It cannot make him a member of this community by making him a member of its own. . . .

The question then arises, whether the provisions of the Constitution, in relation to the personal rights and privileges to which the citizen of a State should be entitled, embraced the negro African race . . . made free in any State; and to put it in the power of a single State to make him a citizen of the United States, and endue him with the full rights of citizenship in every other State without their consent? Does the Constitution of the United States act upon him whenever he shall be made free under the laws of a State, and raised there to the rank of a citizen, and immediately clothe him with all the privileges of a citizen in every other State, and in its own courts?

The court think the affirmative of these propositions cannot be maintained. And if it cannot, [Dred Scott] could not be a citizen of the State of Missouri, within the meaning of the Constitution of the United States, and, consequently, was not entitled to sue in its courts.

It is true, every person, and every class and description of persons, who were at the time of the adoption of the Constitution recognized as citizens in the several States, became also citizens of this new political body; but none other; it was formed by them, and for them and their posterity, but for no one else. And the personal rights and privileges guarantied to citizens of this new sovereignty were intended to embrace those only who were then members of the several State communities, or who should afterwards by birthright or otherwise become members, according to the provisions of the Constitution and the principles on which it was founded. . . .

It becomes necessary, therefore, to determine who were citizens of the several States when the Constitution was adopted. . . .

. . . [T]he legislation and histories of the times, and the language used in the Declaration of Independence, show, that neither the class of persons who had been imported as slaves, nor their descendants, whether they had become free or not, were then acknowledged as a part of the people, nor intended to be included in the general words used in that memorable instrument.

It is difficult at this day to realize the state of public opinion in relation to that unfortunate race, which prevailed in the civilized and enlightened portions of the world at the time of the Declaration of Independence, and when the Constitution of the United States was framed and adopted. . . .

They had for more than a century before been regarded as beings of an inferior order, and altogether unfit to associate with the white race, either in social or political relations; and so far inferior, that they had no rights which the white man was bound to respect; and that the negro might justly and lawfully be reduced to slavery. . . . He was bought and sold, and treated as an ordinary article of merchandise and traffic, whenever a profit could be made by it. This opinion was at that time fixed and universal in the civilized portion of the white race. It was regarded as an axiom in morals as well as in politics, which no one thought of disputing, or supposed to be open to dispute; and men in every grade and position in society daily and habitually acted upon it in their private pursuits, as well as in matters of public concern, without doubting for a moment the correctness of this opinion.

And in no nation was this opinion more firmly fixed or more uniformly acted upon than by the English Government and English people. They not only seized them on the coast of Africa, and sold them or held them in slavery for their own use; but they took them as ordinary articles of merchandise to every country where they could make a profit on them, and were far more extensively engaged in this commerce than any other nation in the world.

The opinion thus entertained and acted upon in England was naturally impressed upon the colonies they founded on this side of the Atlantic. And, accordingly, a negro of the African race was regarded by them as an article of property, and held, and bought and sold as such, in every one of the thirteen colonies which united in the Declaration of Independence, and afterwards formed the Constitution of the United States. The slaves were more or less numerous in the different colonies, as slave labor was found more or less profitable. But no one seems to have doubted the correctness of the prevailing opinion of the time.

The legislation of the different colonies furnishes positive and indisputable proof of this fact . . .

The province of Maryland, in 1717, passed a law declaring "that if any free negro or mulatto intermarry with any white woman, or if any white man shall intermarry with any negro or mulatto woman, such negro or mulatto shall become a slave during life, excepting mulattoes born of white women, who, for such intermarriage, shall only become servants for seven years. . . ."

The other colonial law to which we refer was passed by Massachusetts in 1705. It is entitled "An act for the better preventing of a spurious and mixed issue," &c.; and it provides, that "if any negro or mulatto shall presume to smite or strike any person of the English or other Christian nation, such negro or mulatto shall be severely whipped. . . ."

. . . [T]hese laws . . . show, too plainly to be misunderstood, the degraded condition of this unhappy race. They were still in force when the Revolution began, and are a faithful index to the state of feeling towards the class of persons of whom they speak, and of the position they occupied throughout the thirteen colonies, in the eyes and thoughts of the men who framed the Declaration of Independence and established the State Constitutions and Governments. They show that a perpetual and impassable barrier was intended to be erected between the white race and the one which they had reduced to slavery, and governed as subjects with absolute and despotic power, and which they then looked upon as so far below them in the scale of created beings, that intermarriages between white persons and negroes or mulattoes were regarded as unnatural and immoral, and punished as crimes, not only in the parties, but in the person who joined them in marriage. And no distinction in this respect was made between the free negro or mulatto and the slave, but this stigma, of the deepest degradation, was fixed upon the whole race.

We refer to these historical facts for the purpose of showing the fixed opinions concerning that race, upon which the statesmen of that day spoke and acted . . . in order to determine whether the general terms used in the Constitution of the United States, as to the rights of man and the rights of the people, was intended to include them, or to give to them or their posterity the benefit of any of its provisions.

The language of the Declaration of Independence is equally Conclusive: . . .

> We hold these truths to be self-evident: that all men are created equal; that they are endowed by their Creator with certain unalienable rights; that among them is life, liberty, and the pursuit of happiness; that to secure these rights, Governments are instituted, deriving their just powers from the consent of the governed.

The general words above quoted would seen to embrace the whole human family, and if they were used in a similar instrument at this day would be so understood. But it is too clear for dispute, that the enslaved African race were not intended to be included, and formed no part of the people who framed and adopted this declaration; for if the language, as understood in that day, would embrace them, the conduct of the distinguished men who framed the Declaration of Independence would have been utterly and flagrantly inconsistent with the principles they asserted; and instead of the sympathy of mankind, to which they so confidently appeared, they would have deserved and received universal rebuke and reprobation.

Yet the men who framed this declaration were great men—high in literary acquirements—high in their sense of honor, and incapable of asserting principles inconsistent with those on which they were acting. They perfectly understood the meaning of the language they used, and how it would be understood by others; and they knew that it would not in any part of the civilized world be supposed to embrace the negro race, which, by common consent, had been excluded from civilized Governments and the family of nations, and doomed to slavery. They spoke and acted according to the then established doctrines and principles, and in the ordinary language of the day, no one misunderstood them. The unhappy black race were separated from the white by indelible marks, and laws long before established, and were never thought of or spoken of except as property, and when the claims of the owner or the profit of the trader were supposed to need protection.

This state of public opinion had undergone no change when the Constitution was adopted, as is equally evident from its provisions and language....

[There] are two clauses in the Constitution which point directly and specifically to the negro race as a separate class of persons, and show clearly that they were not regarded as a portion of the people or citizens of the Government then formed.

One of these clauses reserves to each of the thirteen States the right to import slaves until the year 1808.... And by the other provision the States pledge themselves to each other to maintain the right of property of the master, by delivering up to him any slave who may have escaped from his service, and be found within their respective territories.... And these two provisions show, conclusively, that neither the description of persons therein referred to, nor their descendants, were embraced in any of the other provisions of the Constitution; for certainly these two clauses were not intended to confer on them or their posterity the blessings of liberty, or any of the personal rights so carefully provided for the citizen.

No one of that race had ever migrated to the United States voluntarily; all of them had been brought here as articles of merchandise. The number that had been emancipated at that time were but few in comparison with those held in slavery; and they were identified in the public mind with the race to which they belonged, and regarded as a part of the slave population rather than the free. It is obvious that they were not even in the minds of the framers of the Constitution when they were conferring special rights and privileges upon the citizens of a State in every other part of the Union.

Indeed, when we look to the condition of this race in the several States at the time, it is impossible to believe that these rights and privileges were intended to be extended to them.

It is very true, that in that portion of the Union where the labor of the negro race was found to be unsuited to the climate and unprofitable to the master, but few slaves were held at the time of the Declaration of Independence; and when the Constitution was adopted, it had entirely worn out in one of them, and measures had been taken for its gradual abolition in several others. But this change had not been produced by any change of opinion in relation to this race. . . .

And we may here again refer, in support of this proposition, to the plain and unequivocal language of the laws of the several States, some passed after the Declaration of Independence and before the Constitution was adopted, and some since the Government went into operation. [The] . . . laws of the present slaveholding States . . . are full of provisions in relation to this class [and] . . . have continued to treat them as an inferior class, and to subject them to strict police regulations, drawing a broad line of distinction between the citizen and the slave races, and legislating in relation to them upon the same principle which prevailed at the time of the Declaration of Independence. As related to these States, it is too plain for argument, that they have never been regarded as a part of the people or citizens of the State, nor supposed to possess any political rights which the dominant race might not withhold or grant at their pleasure. . . .

And if we turn to the legislation of the States where slavery had worn out, or measures taken for its speedy abolition, we shall find the same opinions and principles equally fixed and equally acted upon.

Thus, [a] Massachusetts . . . Law of 1786 . . . forbids the marriage of any white person with any negro, Indian, or mulatto . . . and declares all such marriages absolutely null and void, and degrades thus the unhappy issue of the marriage by fixing upon it the stain of bastardy. . . .

And again, in 1833, Connecticut passed another law, which made it penal to set up or establish any school in that State for the instruction of persons of the African race not inhabitants of the State, or to instruct or teach in any such school or institution, or board or harbor for that purpose, any such person, without the previous consent in writing of the civil authority of the town in which such school or institution might be. . . .

By the laws of New Hampshire . . . no one was permitted to be enrolled in the militia of the State, but free white citizens; and the same provision is found in a subsequent collection of the laws, made in 1855. Nothing could more strongly mark the entire repudiation of the African race. . . . [W]hy are the African race, born in the State, not permitted to share in one of the highest duties of the citizen? The answer is obvious; he is not, by the institutions and laws of the State, numbered among its people. He forms no part of the sovereignty of the State, and is not therefore called on to uphold and defend it. . . .

It would be impossible to enumerate . . . the various laws, marking the condition of this race, which were passed from time to time after the Revolution, and before and since the adoption of the Constitution of the United States. In addition to those already referred to, it is sufficient to say, that Chancellor Kent,* whose accuracy and research no one will question, states in . . . his Commentaries . . . that in no part of the country except Maine, did the African race, in point of fact, participate equally with the whites in the exercise of civil and political rights.

The legislation of the States therefore shows, in a manner not to be mistaken, the inferior and subject condition of that race at the time the Constitution was adopted, and long afterwards, . . . and it is hardly consistent with the respect due to these States, to suppose that they regarded at that time, as fellow-citizens and members of the sovereignty, a class of beings whom they had thus stigmatized; . . . and upon whom they had impressed such deep and enduring marks of inferiority and degradation; or, that when they met in convention to form the Constitution, they looked upon them as a portion of their constituents, or designed to include them in the provisions so carefully inserted for the security and protection of the liberties and rights of their citizens. It cannot be supposed that they intended to secure to them rights, and privileges, and rank, in the new political body throughout the Union, which every one of them denied within the limits of its own dominion. More especially, it cannot be believed that the large slaveholding States regarded them as included in the word citizens, or would have consented to a Constitution which might compel them to receive them in that character from another State. For if they were so received, and entitled to the privileges and immunities of citizens, it would exempt them from the operation of the special laws and from the police regulations which they considered to be necessary for

*James Kent (1763–1847) was a justice on the New York Supreme Court from 1798 to 1823, and he also served as chancellor of the state's court system from 1814 to 1823. He wrote the highly influential four-volume *Commentaries on American Law*. A forceful advocate of a strong judiciary, Kent was a Federalist in his politics and thus an advocate of a strong national government; he was a Northerner and at least a nominal opponent of slavery. Here Taney shrewdly uses Kent to support his position that blacks have no rights under the Constitution.

their own safety. It would give to persons of the negro race, who were recognized as citizens in any one State of the Union, the right to enter every other State whenever they pleased, singly or in companies, without pass or passport, and without obstruction, to sojourn there as long as they pleased, to go where they pleased at every hour of the day or night without molestation, unless they committed some violation of law for which a white man would be punished; and it would give them the full liberty of speech in public and in private upon all subjects upon which its own citizens might speak; to hold public meetings upon political affairs, and to keep and carry arms wherever they went. And all of this would be done in the face of the subject race of the same color, both free and slaves, and inevitably producing discontent and insubordination among them, and endangering the peace and safety of the State.

It is impossible, it would seem, to believe that the great men of the slaveholding States, who took so large a share in framing the Constitution of the United States, and exercised so much influence in procuring its adoption, could have been so forgetful or regardless of their own safety and the safety of those who trusted and confided in them. . . .

No one, we presume, supposes that any change in public opinion or feeling, in relation to this unfortunate race, in the civilized nations of Europe or in this country, should induce the court to give to the words of the Constitution a more liberal construction in their favor than they were intended to bear when the instrument was framed and adopted. Such an argument would be altogether inadmissible in any tribunal called on to interpret it. If any of its provisions are deemed unjust, there is a mode prescribed in the instrument itself by which it may be amended; but while it remains unaltered, it must be construed now as it was understood at the time of its adoption. It is not only the same in words, but the same in meaning, and delegates the same powers to the Government, and reserves and secures the same rights and privileges to the citizen; and as long as it continues to exist in its present form, it speaks not only in the same words, but with the same meaning and intent with which it spoke when it came from the hands of its framers, and was voted on and adopted by the people of the United States. Any other rule of construction would abrogate the judicial character of this court. and make it the mere reflex of the popular opinion or passion of the day. This court was not created by the Constitution for such purposes. Higher and graver trusts have been confided to it, and it must not falter in the path of duty.

13

THOMAS R. R. COBB

What Is Slavery, and Its Foundation in the Natural Law

1858

Thomas Reade Rootes Cobb (1823–1862) was one of the most brilliant lawyers in the antebellum South. He was a leader of the Georgia bar, the son-in-law of the state's first chief justice, the official reporter of the Georgia Supreme Court, and a cofounder of the Lumpkin School of Law, which later became the University of Georgia School of Law. Cobb, the key figure in drafting the Confederate Constitution, later died at the battle of Fredericksburg. His book, An Inquiry into the Law of Negro Slavery in the United States of America, to Which Is Prefixed an Historical Sketch of Slavery, *was the only treatise on the law of slavery published by a Southerner.*

The following excerpt is from Chapter 1 of this book. Here Cobb begins to set out the legal theory behind slavery. However, he quickly moves from law and philosophy to history and racial theories. Ultimately his defense of slavery, like so many others, is racial. Significantly, much of his defense of slavery ties into general legal notions. If blacks are incompetent and inferior, it is legitimate to have a different set of laws to govern them. Similarly, if blacks are naturally "thievish," special laws and legal rules must apply to them.

Cobb's piece is a high point of the defenses of slavery. He does not merely argue that slavery is legitimate or reasonable because blacks are inferior. Rather, he asserts that slavery is a positive good for blacks because slavery has "advanced the negro race" by aiding in their "mental and moral development."

§ 3. That slavery is contrary to the law of nature, has been so confidently and so often asserted, that slaveholders themselves have most

Thomas R. R. Cobb, *An Inquiry into the Law of Negro Slavery in the United States of America, to Which Is Prefixed an Historical Sketch of Slavery* (Philadelphia: T. & J. W. Johnson; Savannah: W. Thorne Williams, 1858), 3–52.

A portrait of Thomas R. R. Cobb in Confederate uniform.
University of Georgia, School of Law.

generally permitted their own minds to acknowledge its truth unques-
tioned. Hence, even learned judges in slaveholding States ... have
announced gravely, that slavery being contrary to the law of nature,
can exist only by force of positive law. The course of reasoning, by
which this conclusion is attained, is very much this: That in a state of
nature all men are free. That one man is at birth entitled by nature to
no higher rights or privileges than another, nor does nature specify

any particular time or circumstances under which the one shall begin to rule and the other to obey. Hence, by the law of nature, no man is the slave of another, and hence all slavery is contrary to the law of nature. . . .

§ 7. The expression "law of nature" is sometimes, though unphilosophically, used to express those deductions which may be drawn from a careful examination of the operations of the natural world. Hence, it is said that slavery is contrary to the law of nature, because we find no counterpart or analogous operation in the natural world. To this we may say, in the first place, that by such a definition of the law of nature, cannibalism and every other horrid crime of savage or natural man would be justified. Among lower animals, the destruction of their own species is of frequent occurrence. In the second place, that the fact does not exist as stated, for not only is slavery found to coexist with the human race, but even among the lower animals and insects, servitude, in every respect the counterpart of negro slavery, is found to exist. It is a fact, well known to entomologists, and too well established to admit of contradiction, that the red ant will issue in regular battle array, to conquer and subjugate the black or negro ant, as he is called by entomologists. And, that these negro slaves perform all the labor of the communities into which they are thus brought, with a patience and an aptitude almost incredible. These facts, originally noticed and published by Huber, have subsequently been verified by many observers. . . . Upon this definition, therefore, of the law of nature, negro slavery would seem to be perfectly consistent with that law. . . .

. . . From what has been said, it is evident that whatever definition we adopt, the nature of man enters as a very important element, and if that nature is subject to any variation, from race, or climate, or history, to that extent the consequences of the law of nature must vary when applied to him. To illustrate. The German student, immersed for years amid the ponderous tomes of some university library, finds nothing in his voluntary imprisonment uncongenial to his nature. But the American Indian submitting to the same fate, would do violence to the law of his nature, because his pursuit tends nothing to the great end of his existence, the greatest happiness of which he is susceptible. And hence slavery may be utterly inconsistent with the law of nature when applied to one race of men, and yet be perfectly consistent with the nature of others.

§ 11. Again. We must be careful to distinguish between the state of nature and the law of nature. Many things are contrary to the state of nature, which are not contrary to the law of nature. Marriage, government, all civilization is adverse to a state of nature, yet it would be hardly asserted, that thereby violence was done to the law of nature. A celebrated Scotch commentator applies this distinction clearly and philosophically to the subject of slavery: "It is indeed contrary to the state of nature, by which all men were equal and free; but it is not repugnant to the law of nature, which does not command men to remain in their native freedom, nor forbid the preserving persons at the expense of their liberty," &c. . . . "It may appear that slavery is repugnant to the law of nature; but that may be properly denied. For slavery in itself is nothing but an obligation for perpetual service. If it be not wrong to be bound to serve for a year, why not also for life?" . . . "This kind of slavery is not repugnant to the law of nature, but yet is not of natural right, which oftentimes authors confound." The admission therefore of the proposition that "all men are created free," or are free in a state of nature, does not carry with it as a consequence that slavery is inconsistent with the law of nature. . . .

§ 13. The same distinction was taken by the Fathers of the Church, on the subject of slavery. Bishop England, reviewing them at length, says: "Thus, a state of voluntary slavery is not prohibited by the law of nature." "All our theologians have, from the earliest epoch, sustained, that though in a state of pure nature all men are equal, yet the natural law does not prohibit one man from having dominion over the useful actions of another, as his slave." The following, quoted by him from St. Thomas of Aquin, makes the point clearly: "This man is a slave, absolutely speaking, rather a son, not by any natural cause, but by reason of the benefits which are produced; for it is more beneficial to this one to be governed by one who has more wisdom, and to the other to be helped by the labor of the former." Cassagnac, pursuing the same idea, gives us the views of other Fathers, to the same effect. Thus, Saint Basil says: "He who, by the weakness of the intellect, has not in him that which nature requires, finds it to his interest to become the slave of another, the experience of his master being to him what the pilot is to the vessel." . . .

§ 15. In this view, is Negro Slavery consistent with the Law of Nature? We confine the inquiry to negro slavery, because, upon the principles already established, it is undoubtedly true, that the enslavement, by one man or one race, of another man or another race, physically, intellectually, and morally, their equals, is contrary to the law of nature, because it promotes not their happiness, and tends not to their perfection. Much of the confusion upon this subject has arisen from a failure to notice this very palpable distinction. The ancient Greeks were so far the superiors of their contemporaries, that it did no violence to the existing state of things for their philosophers to declare their preeminence, and draw thence the conclusions which legitimately followed. Hence, Aristotle declared that some men were slaves by nature, and that slavery was absolutely necessary to a perfect society. . . .

§ 18. Resuming then the inquiry as to the consistency of negro slavery with the law of nature, the first question which demands our attention, and necessarily is preliminary to all other investigation, is, what is the nature of the negro? Were this question asked of a mere animal, our inquiry would be confined to his physical nature alone, and could we show that, like the horse and the cow, the domestication and subjection to service did not impair, but on the contrary improved his physical condition, the conclusion would be inevitable, that such subjection was consistent with his natural development, and therefore not contrary to his nature. But we recognize in the negro a man, endowed with reason, will, and accountability, and in order to justify his subjection we must inquire of his intellectual and moral nature, and must be satisfied that its development is thereby promoted. If this be true, if the physical, intellectual, and moral development of the African race are promoted by a state of slavery, and their happiness secured to a greater extent than if left at liberty, then their enslavement is consistent with the law of nature, and violative of none of its provisions. Is the negro's own happiness thereby best promoted? Is he therein most useful to his fellow-man? Is he thereby more surely led to the discharge of his duty to God? These, as we have seen, are the great objects of the law of nature, "God, our neighbor, and ourselves."

§ 19. In this investigation, we should understand distinctly the meaning to be attached to "Negro." The black color alone does not constitute the negro, nor does the fact of a residence and origin in Africa. Agassiz very properly remarks, that "in Africa, we have the Hottentot and Negro races in the south and central portions respectively, while the people of Northern Africa are allied to their neighbors in Europe, just as we have seen to be the case with the zoological fauna in general." The language and history of the nations of Northern Africa show them to have a different and Asiatic origin. The people we are inquiring of are thus described by Cuvier: "The negro race is marked by a black complexion, crisped or woolly hair, compressed cranium, and a flat nose. The projection of the lower parts of the face and the thick lips evidently approximate it to the monkey tribe. The hordes of which it consists have always remained in the most complete state of utter barbarism." And even of this very extensive negro race, there are a great number of tribes, differing not so much in their physical as moral nature, and adapting them more or less for a state of servitude. This difference was well known among the native tribes long before the Dutch, Portuguese, and English vied with each other in extending the slave-trade; and the Mandingo slave-dealer had determined this question long before a mart was opened for him by European enterprise. Our inquiry, therefore, is properly confined to those tribes of negroes who were in a state of servitude in their native land, viz.: the Fantis, Ashantis, Krumen, Quaquas, Congos, Ibos or Eboes, Whydah or Fidohs, Coromantines, Mandingoes, &c., and their descendents in America.

§ 20. *First* then is the inquiry as to the physical adaptation of the negro to a state of servitude. His black color peculiarly fits him for the endurance of the heat of long-continued summers. The arched leg and receding heel seem to indicate a natural preparation for strength and endurance. The absence of nervous irritability gives to him a complete exemption from those inflammatory diseases so destructive in hot and damp atmospheres, and hence the remarkable fact, that the ravages of that scourge of the tropics, the yellow fever, never reach the negro race. In other portions of the body, especially the formation of the pelvis, naturalists have discovered a well-defined deterioration in the negro which, a late learned observer, Vrolik, of Amsterdam, has declared, shows "a degradation in type, and an approach towards the lower form of animals." So the arched dome of the head and the perpendicularity of the vertebral column are said, by an observant writer, to be characteristic, and to fit the negro peculiarly for the bearing of burdens upon the head.

§ 21. As a connecting link between the physical and mental capacity of the negro, we may consider the osteological formation of his head, and comparative size of the brain. . . . Good, in describing the negro, says: "The head is narrow; the face narrow, projecting to the lower part. The countenance, in this variety, recedes farther than in any other from the European, and approaches much nearer than in any other that of the monkey." . . . Dr. Morton's experiments and observations seem to have led him to the conclusion that the brain of the negro was somewhat smaller. Without seeking to hold the balance between these authorities, we may remark, that it is too well settled now to be a matter of doubt, that the size of the brain is not the only criterion for deciding upon the mental capacity of the possessor; and philosophers least disposed to profess faith in phrenology as a science, are forced to admit that the arrangement and location of the brain, by some mysterious law, are, as a general rule, indicative of the mental power. The application of Camper's facial line and facial angle demonstrated the inferiority of the negro in this particular, and Prof. Tiedemann does not seek to deny the correctness of the result thus tested.

§ 22. *Second.* The mental inferiority of the negro has been often asserted and never successfully denied. An inviting field for digression is offered here, in the much-mooted question of the unity of the human race. It is unnecessary for our purposes to enter these lists. The law deals with men and things as they are, and whether the negro was originally a different species, or is a degeneration of the same, is a matter indifferent in the inquiry as to his proper status in his present condition. We deal with him as we find him, and according to the measure of his capacity, it is our duty to cultivate and improve him, leaving to time to solve the problem, whether he is capable of restoration to that pristine equality, from which his admirers maintain that he has fallen.

§ 23. Mentally inferior, now, certainly he is. Says Lawrence: "The mind of the negro is inferior to that of the European, and his organization also is less perfect." And this he proves, "not so much by the unfortunate beings who are degraded by slavery, as by every fact in the past history and present condition of Africa." Says Charles Hamilton Smith—whose opportunities for observing and judging, for ten years, on the Coast of Africa and in the West Indies (1797 to 1807), were unsurpassed, and whose sympathies he confesses are with the negro,—"The typical woolly-haired races have never invented a reasoned theological system, discovered an alphabet, framed a grammatical language, nor made the least step in science or art. They have never comprehended what they have learned, or retained a civilization taught them by contact with more refined nations, as soon as that contact had ceased. They have at no time formed great political states, nor commenced a self-evolving civilization; conquest with them has been confined to kindred tribes and produced only slaughter. Even Christianity, of more than three centuries duration in Congo, has scarcely excited a progressive civilization." Says Knox: "The grand qualities which distinguish men from the animal; the generalizing powers of pure reason; the love of perfectibility; the desire to know the unknown; and last and greatest, the ability to observe new phenomena and new relations,—these mental faculties are deficient or seem to be so in all dark races. But if it be so, how can they become civilized? What hopes for their progress?" These questions are answered by a most observant and intelligent French traveller in the West Indies: "The friends of useful and moral liberty should strive to maintain the supremacy of the white race, until the black race understands, loves, and practises the duties and obligations of civilized life."

§ 24. Carlyle places this question in an eccentric but plain view, addressing himself to the emancipated negroes of the West Indies: "You are not slaves now! nor do I wish, if it can be avoided, to see you slaves again; but decidedly you will have to be servants to those that are born wiser than you, that are born lords of you; servants to the whites if they are (as what mortal man can doubt they are?) born wiser than you. That, you may depend on it, my obscure black friends, is and was always the law of the world for you and for all men to be servants, the more foolish of us to the more wise. . . . Heaven's laws are not repealable by earth, however earth may try?"

§ 25. The intelligent, unprejudiced writers of the non-slaveholding States of America, are constrained to admit the inferiority of the negro mind. Paulding, speaking of amalgamation, says: "It is a scheme for lowering the standard of our nature, by approximating the highest grade of human beings to the lowest." And, "We have a right to conclude, from all history and experience, that there is an equal disparity of mental organization." "The experience of years stands arrayed against the principle of equality between the white man and the black." "All that the black man has ever done is to approach to the lowest scale of intellectual eminence, and the world has demonstrated its settled opinion of his inferiority by pronouncing even this a wonder." Dr. Morton, impartial and scientific as he is acknowledged to be, says: "It makes little difference whether the mental inferiority of the negro, the Samoyede, or the Indian, is natural or acquired; for if they ever possessed equal intelligence with the Caucasian, they have lost it, and if they never had it, they had nothing to lose. One party would arraign Providence for creating them originally different, another for placing them in circumstances by which they inevitably became so. Let us search out the truth, and reconcile it afterwards." Judge Conrad says: "The negro in the North has equal, if not superior, advantages to the mass of poor white men. . . . It cannot, however, be boasted that his intellectual character has been materially elevated, or his moral nature greatly improved." George H. Calvert says: "At one end of the human scale is the black man, at the other the white; between them the brown and the yellow. The white man never comes into contact and conflict with the others, that he does not conquer them." . . .

§ 27. In this opinion of the mental inferiority of the negro, every distinguished naturalist agrees. We have already seen that most of them agree as to their physical inferiority in the size of the brain. . . .

§ 28. Even the champions of the negro's freedom, who have distinguished themselves by their zeal, both in England and America, are forced to admit the apparent inferiority, and to ascribe the same to the degradation of slavery and other causes, which, in their opinion, if removed, would enable the negro to assert and prove his equality. Says Buxton: "I beg to call attention to certain indications, faint no doubt, but, considering the difficulties and impediments to improvement in Africa, encouraging indications, of a capability for better things." Says Armistead, in a late elaborate "Tribute for the Negro:" "The present apparent inferiority of the negro race is undoubtedly attributable, in a great measure, to the existence of the slave-traffic in Africa." Wilberforce admitted the same fact, and referred it to the same cause.

§ 29. The American philanthropists have been equally constrained to acknowledge the apparent inferiority, and equally industrious in accounting therefor. "The Caucasian," says Theodore Parker, differs from all other races. He is humane, he is civilized, he progresses. He conquers with his head as well as with his hand. It is intellect, after all, that conquers, not the strength of a man's arm. The Caucasian has often been the master of other races, never their slave. Republics are Caucasian. All the great sciences are of Caucasian origin. All inventions are Caucasian. Literature and romance come of the same stock." It will be noticed, that among these names, cited and quoted, no slaveholder appears, not even that of Mr. Jefferson, who is so often quoted as authority against the slaveholder. We might add the names of many men whose intellects were too bright to be dimmed by interest, and whose hearts were too pure to be closed to the claims of humanity. We refer to Dew, Harper, Campbell, Calhoun, Simms, Hammond, Fletcher, Priest, and others.

§ 30. Our conclusion from this investigation must be, that the negro race is inferior mentally to the Caucasian. Whether or not this inferiority is the result of centuries of barbarism or of the degrading effects of a state of slavery, we will presently briefly inquire. Certain it is that the negro, as we now find him, whether in a state of bondage or in his native wilds, exhibits such a weakness of intellect that, in the words of

Puffendorf, "when he has the fortune to live in subjection to a wise director, he is, without doubt, fixed in such a state of life as is most agreeable to his genius and capacity."

§ 31. The prominent defect in the mental organization of the negro, is a want of judgment. He forms no definite idea of effects from causes. He cannot comprehend, so as to execute the simplest orders, unless they refresh his memory as to some previous knowledge. He is imitative, sometimes eminently so, but his mind is never inventive or suggestive. Improvement never enters into his imagination. A trodden path, he will travel for years, without the idea ever suggesting itself to his brain, that a nearer and better way is present before him; what he has seen another do, he can do also, and practice will make him perfect in its execution, but the discovery of a better, easier, or cheaper process never engages his thoughts. . . . This mental defect, connected with the indolence and want of foresight of the negro, is the secret of his degradation. The imitative faculty makes the negro a good musician, yet he never originates a single air, nor invents a musical instrument. This faculty, combined with memory, sometimes might distinguish him in the acquisition of language, yet he never would originate an alphabet or distinguish the parts of speech. The earlier training of the child at school exercises largely and depends much upon memory and imitation. Hence negro children would learn with equal facility with the white, during the first essays in the schoolroom, but so soon as education reaches the point where reason and judgment and reflection are brought into action, the Caucasian leaves the negro groping hopelessly in the rear.

§ 32. Our next inquiry is as to the moral character of the negro race, and how far that character adapts them for a state of slavery. The degraded situation of the barbarous tribes of Africa is well attested by every observer. So debased is their condition generally, that their humanity has been even doubted. It is not of the negro in this state of barbarism alone, that we should inquire. The development of his moral character, when in contact with civilization, and under the fostering care of religious instruction, is also to be considered. Viewing him then in both these relations, we find, first, that the negro race are habitually indolent and indisposed to exertion, whether seen in their native country, according to the concurrent testimony of all travellers, or in the condition of slavery in America, or as free negroes after emancipation. With reference to the first fact, we are told that the hot climate and the free productions of the earth, on the one hand enervate, and on the other take away all stimulus for exertion. With reference to the second, that it is the degrading effect of slavery, leaving no hope to the slave. With reference to the third, that it is the prejudice of color that depresses the spirits of the free negro of America. We will not stop to inquire as to the truth of these apologies. One thing is certain, that the ingenuity of the philanthropist is severely taxed in behalf of the negro race, for wherever found they exhibit the same characteristics, and the reasons are obliged to be varied to suit the varying circumstances. Perhaps it is but right to remark, that this enervating effect of climate has never proved so powerful upon the white race, physically less prepared to withstand it; that slavery did not to this extent destroy the spirit of the Israelites in Egypt, nor of the villains in England, nor of the homines proprii of Germany. And that in Hayti, in Jamaica, in Brazil, and New Granada, no such prejudice of color exists, and yet notwithstanding the variant testimony of prejudiced observers, there can be no question that neither the enjoyment of liberty, nor the ingenuity of British statesmanship, has been sufficient to infuse energy and activity, where the Maker stamped indolence and sloth.

§ 33. In connection with this indolent disposition, may be mentioned the want of thrift and foresight in the negro race. When enslaved, there is no great necessity for the development of this faculty, and this may account for its absence, but unfortunately for the friends of negro equality, it displays itself more palpably in the free negro than in the slave. We speak of course of the general character, admitting the existence of individual exceptions. In their native wilds, with a most productive soil, they have recourse to the "most revolting food, as frogs, lizards, serpents, spiders, the larvæ of insects, &c. &c." In the free West India Islands, the same indolence appears, and is excused on account of climate, &c. And, even in the cold climate of the Northern States, where the apology fails to apply, the result of the labored effects of philanthropists, aided by the sympathies of the whole community, is "idleness, insolence, and profligacy."

§ 34. The negro is not malicious. His disposition is to forgive injuries, and to forget the past. His gratitude is sometimes enduring, and his fidelity often remarkable. His passions and affections are seldom very strong, and are never very lasting. The dance will allay his most poignant grief, and a few days blot out the memory of his most bitter bereavement. His natural affection is not strong, and consequently he is cruel to his own offspring, and suffers little by separation from them. He is superstitious and reverential, and consequently is very susceptible of religious impressions, exhibiting, in many individual instances, a degree of faith unsurpassed, and a Christian deportment free from blemish. He is passive and obedient, and consequently easily governed.

§ 35. The negro is naturally mendacious, and as a concomitant, thievish. His apologists have referred these traits to his bondage, and have instanced the Israelites borrowing the Egyptian gold, and the cases of Europeans enslaved by the barbarians in Africa, to show that such is the effect of slavery. Unfortunately, however, the prisons and court records of the non-slaveholding States show that enfranchisement has not taught the negro race honesty, nor caused them to cease from petty pilfering. And the census of Liberia shows the same disposition, as exhibited by their criminal court calendar.

§ 36. Another striking trait of negro character is lasciviousness. Lust is his strongest passion; and hence, rape is an offence of too frequent occurrence. Fidelity to the marriage relation they do not understand and do not expect, neither in their native country nor in a state of bondage. The latter, to some extent, is the fault of the law. Yet, colonized on their native shores, the same disregard for the marriage tie is noticed, and regretted by their friends. . . .

§ 44. This inquiry into the physical, mental, and moral development of the negro race, seems to point them clearly, as peculiarly fitted for a laborious class. Their physical frame is capable of great and long-continued exertion. Their mental capacity renders them incapable of successful self-development, and yet adapts them for the direction of a wiser race. Their moral character renders them happy, peaceful, contented, and cheerful in a status that would break the spirit and destroy the energies of the Caucasian or the native American.

§ 45. History and experience confirm this conclusion. Probably no better test could be adopted, to determine the adaptation of a system to a race, than their relative increase while living under it. Nature has so constituted the animal creation, that when any portion of it is placed in a position doing violence to the law of their nature, it dwindles and becomes extinct. Thus domestication is destruction to many animals *feroe naturoe,* while it perfects the development of the horse, the cow, and others. So bondage has ever proved annihilation to the American Indian, whether under the Spanish Hidalgo, or the New England Puritan, or the Virginia Cavalier. What has been its effect, in this respect, upon the negro? The answer to this question is, the voice of Nature, whether her law is violated in his enslavement.

§ 46. The census of the United States exhibits a steady and remarkable increase in the slave population. From a few hundred thousand, they now number more than four millions; and, making allowance for emigration and other causes, the ratio of increase is at least equal to that of the white population of the same States. On the contrary, the increase among the free black population of the Northern States, notwithstanding the element of fugitives from the South, and emancipated slaves, shows a ratio of increase very inferior. The Census of 1850 shows, also, the fact, that the duration of life is greater among the slaves of the South, than among the free negroes of the North. The same unerring testimony also shows, that there are three times as many deaf mutes, four times as many blind, more than three times as many idiots, and more than ten times as many insane, in proportion to numbers, among the free colored persons, than among the slaves. The same is true of the free blacks of Liberia. Notwithstanding the constant influx from America, the census of that colony shows no ratio of increase; but, on the contrary, for more than 12,000 emigrants, it contains now a civilized population of not exceeding 8000.

§ 47. From the same observation, we learn that the mere physical development of the negro is improved by his transport and enslavement. As an animal, in stature, in muscular energy, in activity, and strength, the negro has arrived at his greatest development while in slavery.

§ 48. In mental and moral development, slavery, so far from retarding, has advanced the negro race. The intelligence of the slaves of the South compares favorably with the negro race in any country, but more especially with their native tribes. While, by means of this institution, the knowledge of God and his religion has been brought home, with practical effect, to a greater number of heathens than by all the combined missionary efforts of the Christian world. But remove the restraining and controlling power of the master, and the negro becomes, at once, the slave of his lust, and the victim of his indolence, relapsing, with wonderful rapidity, into his pristine barbarism. Hayti and Jamaica are living witnesses to this truth; and Liberia would probably add her testimony, were it not for the fostering care of philanthropy, and the annual leaven of emancipated slaves.

§ 49. The history of Africa is too well known to require of us an argument or an extended notice, to show, that left to themselves, the negro races would never arrive at any high degree of civilization. . . .

While this fact may be admitted, we are told that after, by means of slavery and the slave-trade, the germs of civilization are implanted in the negro, if he is then admitted to the enjoyment of liberty, he is capable of arriving at a respectable degree of enlightenment. Charles

Hamilton Smith, an Englishman, and an acute observer, says, "They have never comprehended what they have learned, nor retained a civilization taught them by contact with more refined nations, as soon as that contact had ceased." The emancipated slaves of the French and English West Indies, have corroborated this statement. Hayti, once "la plus belle colonie" of France, despite the apologies made for her excesses is, to-day, fast retrograding to barbarism. Jamaica, and the other English islands, notwithstanding the care and deliberation to avoid the shock of too sudden liberty, have baffled the skill and ingenuity of the master minds of the British government. In a preliminary historical sketch, we have examined the facts in detail. The important truth is before us from history, that contact with the Caucasian is the only civilizer of the negro, and slavery the only condition on which that contact can be preserved.

§ 50. The history of the negro race then confirms the conclusion to which an inquiry into the negro character had brought us: that a state of bondage, so far from doing violence to the law of his nature, develops and perfects it; and that, in that state, he enjoys the greatest amount of happiness, and arrives at the greatest degree of perfection of which his nature is capable. And, consequently, that negro slavery, as it exists in the United States, is not contrary to the law of nature. Whenever the laws regulating their condition and relations enforce or allow a rigor, or withdraw a privilege without a corresponding necessity, so far they violate the natural law, and to removal of such evils should be directed the efforts of justice and philanthropy. Beyond this, philanthropy becomes fanaticism, and justice withdraws her shield.

That the system places the negro where his natural rights may be abused, is true; yet this is no reason why the system is in itself wrong. In the words of an enlightened contemporary, "It becomes us then to estimate the value of the declamations of those who oppose the institution of slavery in the Antilles and the United States, on account of the partial abuses which sometime happen. Judicial records are filled with processes for adultery; yet we should not, for that, destroy marriage. Every day our tribunals visit with severity parents who abuse their children, yet we would not, for that, abolish the paternal power. Every system has its abuses and its excesses. It becomes us to correct the excess, punish the abuse, and ameliorate the system. If we should deliberately compare the evils of colonial slavery, with its beneficial effect, in civilization, agriculture, and commerce, we would be quickly convinced upon which side the balances would fall."

Racial Theory and Slavery

14

SAMUEL A. CARTWRIGHT

Report on the Diseases of and Physical Peculiarities of the Negro Race

1851

Samuel Adolphus Cartwright was a leading physician in New Orleans who specialized in what were called "Negro diseases." In fact, he had a thriving practice treating slaves. Cartwright was also a prolific writer and scholar. He contributed to many antebellum medical journals, often writing about his practice and aspects of medicine or physiology that he observed. In addition to his medical scholarship, Cartwright wrote about anthropology and the origin of the races and about religion and biblical interpretation.

In 1851, Cartwright read a report to the Medical Association of Louisiana on "the diseases and physical peculiarities of the Negro race." The New Orleans Medical and Surgical Journal *promptly published the entire report, and* De Bow's Review *reprinted the report as installments. The report was ostensibly written for a scientific audience, concerned with medicine and health. However, much of what Cartwright wrote about focuses on religion, anthropology, plantation management, and politics—all geared toward defending slavery as a social and economic institution. Here Cartwright has used "science," as he understands it, to defend slavery and, more particularly, the enslavement of blacks.*

Samuel A. Cartwright, M.D., "Report on the Diseases and Physical Peculiarities of the Negro Race," *New Orleans Medical and Surgical Journal* 7 (May 1851): 691–715.

Before going into the peculiarities of their diseases, it is necessary to glance at the anatomical and physiological differences between the negro and the white man; otherwise their diseases cannot be understood. It is commonly taken for granted, that the color of the skin constitutes the main and essential difference between the black and the white race; but there are other differences more deep, durable and indelible, in their anatomy and physiology, than that of mere color. In the albino the skin is white, yet the organization is that of the negro. Besides, it is not only in the skin, that a difference of color exists between the negro and white man, but in the membranes, the muscles, the tendons and in all the fluids and secretions. Even the negro's brain and nerves, the chyle and all the humors, are tinctured with a shade of the pervading darkness. His bile is of a deeper color and his blood is blacker than the white man's. There is the same difference in the flesh of the white and black man, in regard to color, that exists between the flesh of the rabbit and the hare. His bones are whiter and harder than those of the white race, owing to their containing more phosphate of lime and less gelatine. His head is hung on the atlas differently from the white man; the face is thrown more upwards and the neck is shorter and less oblique; the spine more inwards, and the pelvis more obliquely outwards; the thigh-bones larger and flattened from before backwards; the bones more bent; the legs curved outwards or bowed; the feet flat; the gastrochemii muscles smaller; the heel so long, as to make the ankle appear as if planted in the middle of the foot; the gait, hopper-hipped, or what the French call *l'allure déhanchée,* not unlike that of a person carrying a burden. The projecting mouth, the retreating forehead, the broad, flat nose, thick lips and wooly hair, are peculiarities that strike every beholder. According to Soemmerring and other anatomists, who have dissected the negro, his brain is a ninth or tenth less than in other races of men, his facial angle smaller, and all the nerves going from the brain, as also the ganglionic system of nerves, are larger in proportion than in the white man. The nerves distributed to the muscles are an exception, being smaller than in the white race. Soemmerring remarks, that the negro's brain has in a great measure run into nerves. One of the most striking differences is found in the much greater size of the *foramen magnum* in the negro than the white man. The foramen, or orifice between the brain and the spinal marrow, is not only larger, but the medulla oblongata, and particularly the nerves supplying the abdominal and pelvic viscera. Although the nose is flat, the turbinated bones are more developed, and the pituitary membrane, lining the internal cavities of the nose, more extensive than in the white man, and causing the sense of smell to be more acute. The negro's hearing is better, his sight is stronger, and he seldom needs spectacles.

The field of vision is not so large in the negro's eye as in the white man's. He bears the rays of the sun better, because he is provided with an anatomical peculiarity in the inner canthus, contracting the field of vision, and excluding the sun's rays,—something like the membrana nictitans, formed by a preternatural development of the plica lunaris, like that which is observed in apes. His imitative powers are very great, and he can agitate every part of the body at the same time, or what he calls *dancing all over.* From the diffusion of the brain, as it were, into the various organs of the body, in the shape of nerves to minister to the senses, everything, from the necessity of such a conformation, partakes of sensuality, at the expense of intellectuality. Thus, music is a mere sensual pleasure with the negro. There is nothing in his music addressing the understanding; it has melody, but no harmony; his songs are mere sounds, without sense or meaning—pleasing the ear, without conveying a single idea to the mind; his ear is gratified by sound, as his stomach is by food. The great development of the nervous system, and the profuse distribution of nervous matter to the stomach, liver and genital organs, would make the Ethiopian race entirely unmanageable, if it were not that this excessive nervous development is associated with a deficiency of red blood in the pulmonary and arterial systems, from a defective atmospherization or arterialization of the blood in the lungs—constituting the best type of what is called the lymphatic temperament, in which lymph, phlegm, mucus, and other humors, predominate over the red blood. It is this defective hematosis, or atmospherization of the blood, conjoined with a deficiency of cerebral matter in the cranium, and an excess of nervous matter distributed to the organs of sensation and assimilation, that is the true cause of that debasement of mind, which has rendered the people of Africa unable to take care of themselves. It is the true cause of their indolence and apathy, and why they have chosen, through countless ages, idleness, misery and barbarism, to industry and frugality,—why social industry, or associated labor, so essential to all progress in civilisation and improvement, has never made any progress among them, or the arts and sciences taken root on any portion of African soil inhabited by them; as is proved by the fact that no letters, or even hieroglyphics—no buildings, roads or improvements, or monuments of any kind, are any where found, to indicate that they have ever been awakened from their apathy and sleepy indolence, to physical or mental exertion. To the same physiological causes, deeply rooted in the organization, we must look for an explanation of the strange facts, why none of the languages of the native tribes of Africa, as proved by ethnographical researches, have risen above common names, standing for things and actions, to abstract terms or generalizations;—why no form of government on abstract principles, with divisions of power into separate departments, has ever been instituted by them;—why they have always preferred, as more congenial to their nature, a government combining the legislative, judicial and executive powers in the same individual, in the person of a petty king, a chieftain or master;—why, in America, if let alone, they always prefer the same kind of government, which we call slavery, but which is actually an improvement on the government of their forefathers, as it gives them more tranquility and sensual enjoyment, expands the mind and improves the morals, by arousing them from that natural indolence so fatal to mental and moral progress. Even if they did not prefer slavery, tranquility and sensual enjoyment, to liberty, yet their organization of mind is such, that if they had their liberty, they have not the industry, the moral virtue, the courage and vigilance to maintain it, but would relapse into barbarism, or into slavery, as they have done in Hayti. The reason of this is founded in unalterable physiological laws. Under the compulsive power of the white man, they are made to labor or exercise, which makes the lungs perform the duty of vitalizing the blood more perfectly than is done when they are left free to indulge in idleness. It is the red, vital blood, sent to the brain, that liberates their mind when under the white man's control; and it is the want of a sufficiency of red, vital blood, that chains their mind to ignorance and barbarism, when in freedom.

The excess of organic nervous matter, and the deficiency of cerebral—the predominance of the humors over the red blood, from defective atmospherization of the blood in the lungs, impart to the negro a nature not unlike that of a new-born infant of the white race. . . .

Negroes, moreover, resemble children in the activity of the liver and in their strong assimilating powers, and in the predominance of the other systems over the sanguineous; hence they are difficult to bleed, owing to the smallness of their veins. On cording the arm of the stoutest negro, the veins will be found scarcely as large as a white boy's of ten years of age. They are liable to all the convulsive diseases, cramps, spasms, colics, etc., that children are so subject to.

Although their skin is very thick, it is as sensitive, when they are in perfect health, as that of children, and like them they fear the rod.

They resemble children in another very important particular; they are very easily governed by love combined with fear, and are ungovernable, vicious and rude under any form of government whatever, not resting on love and fear as a basis. Like children, it is not necessary that they be kept under the fear of the lash; it is sufficient that they be kept under the fear of offending those who have authority over them. Like children, they are constrained by unalterable physiological laws, to love those in authority over them, who minister to their wants and immediate necessities, and are not cruel or unmerciful. The defective hematosis, in both cases, and the want of courage and energy of mind as a consequence thereof, produces in both an instinctive feeling of dependence on others, to direct them and to take care of them. Hence, from a law of his nature, the negro can no more help loving a kind master, than the child can help loving her who gives it suck.

Like children, they require government in every thing; food, clothing, exercise, sleep—all require to be prescribed by rule, or they will run into excesses. Like children, they are apt to over-eat themselves or to confine their diet too much to one favorite article, unless restrained from doing so. They often gorge themselves with fat meat, as children do with sugar.

One of the greatest mysteries to those unacquainted with the negro character, is the facility with which an hundred, even two or three hundred, able-bodied and vigorous negroes are kept in subjection by one white man, who sleeps in perfect security among them, generally, in warm weather, with doors and windows open, with all his people, called slaves, at large around him. But a still greater mystery is the undoubted fact of the love they bear to their masters, similar in all respects to the love that children bear to their parents, which nothing but severity or cruelty in either case can alienate. The physiological laws on which this instinctive and most mysterious love is founded in the one case, are applicable to the other. Like children, when well-behaved and disposed to do their duty, it is not the arbitrary authority over them that they dread, but the petty tyranny and imposition of one another. The overseer among them, like the school-master among children, has only to be impartial, and to preserve order by strict justice to all, to gain their good will and affections, and to be viewed, not as an object of terror, but as a friend and protector to quiet their fears of one another.

... All negroes are not equally black—the blacker, the healthier and stronger; any deviation from the black color, in the pure race, is a mark of feebleness or ill health. When heated from exercise, the negro's skin is covered with an oily exudation that gives a dark color to white linen, and has a very strong odor. The odor is strongest in the most robust; children and the aged have very little of it.

I have thus hastily and imperfectly noticed some of the more striking anatomical and physiological peculiarities of the Negro race. The question may be asked, Does he belong to the same race as the white man? Is he a son of Adam? Does his peculiar physical conformation stand in opposition to the Bible, or does it prove its truth? These are important questions, both in a medical, historical and theological point of view. They can better be answered by a comparison of the facts derived from anatomy, physiology, history and theology, to see if they sustain one another. We learn from the Book of Genesis, that Noah had tree sons, Shem, Ham and Japheth, and that Canaan, the son of Ham, was doomed to be servant of servants unto his brethren. From history, we learn that the descendants of Canaan settled in Africa, and are the present Ethiopians, or black race of men; that Shem occupied Asia, and Japheth the north of Europe. In the 9th chapter and the 27th verse of Genesis, one of the most authentic books of the Bible, is the remarkable prophecy: God shall enlarge Japheth and he shall dwell in the tents of Shem, and Canaan shall be his servant. Japheth has been greatly enlarged by the discovery of a new world, the continent of America. He found in it the Indians, whom natural history declares to be of Asiatic origin, in other words, the descendants of Shem: he drove out Shem, and occupied his tents: and now the remaining part of the prophecy is in the process of fulfillment, from the facts every where before us, of Canaan having become his servant. The question arises, is the Canaanite, or Ethiopian, qualified for the trying duties of servitude, and unfitted for the enjoyment of freedom? If he be, there is both wisdom, mercy and justice in the decree dooming him to be servant of servants, as the decree is in conformity to his nature. Anatomy and physiology have been interrogated, and the response is, that the Ethiopian, or Canaanite, is unfitted, from his organization and physiological laws predicated on that organization, for the responsible duties of a free man, but, like the child, is only fitted for a state of dependence and subordination. When history is interrogated, the response is, that the only government under which the negro has made any improvement in mind, morals, religion, and the only government under which he has led a happy, quiet and contented life, is that under which he is subjected to the arbitrary power of Japheth in obedience to the Divine decree. When the original Hebrew of the Bible is interrogated, we find, in the significant meaning of the original name of the negro, the identical fact set forth, which the knife of the anatomist at the dissecting table has made appear; as if the revelations of anatomy, physiology and history, were a mere re-writing of what Moses wrote. In the Hebrew word "Canaan," the original name of the Ethiopian, the word *slave by nature*, or language to the same effect, is written by the inspired penman. Hence, there is no conflict between the revelations of the science of medicine, history, and the inductions drawn from the Baconian philosophy, and the authority of the Bible; one supports the other.

. . .

A knowledge of the great primary truth, that the negro is a slave by nature, and can never be happy, industrious, moral or religious, in any other condition than the one he was intended to fill, is of great importance to the theologian, the statesman, and to all those who are at heart seeking to promote his temporal and future welfare. This great truth, if better known and understood, would go far to prevent the East Indian Company and British government from indulging in any expectation of seeing their immense possessions in Asia enhanced in value, by the overthrow of slave labor in America, through the instrumentality of northern fanaticism; or of seeing the Union divided into two or more fragments, hostile to each other; or of gaining any advantages, that civil commotion on this side of the Atlantic would give to the tottering monarchies of Europe. With the subject under this aspect, the science of Medicine has nothing to do, further than to uncover its light, to show truth from error. . . .

Negro Consumption

Negro consumption is a disease almost unknown to medical men of the Northern States and Europe. A few Southern physicians have acquired some valuable information concerning it, from personal experience and observation; but this knowledge is scattered in fragments about, and has never been condensed in a form to make it of much practical utility. . . .

The popular opinion is, that negro consumption is caused by *dirteating*. The eating of dirt is not the cause, but only one of the effects—a mere symptom, which may or may not attend it. As in pica, there is often a depraved appetite for substances not nutritious, as earth, chalk, lime, etc.; but oftener, as in malacia, a depraved appetite, for nutritious substances to a greater degree, than for non-nutritious. In negro consumption, the patients are generally hearty eaters of all kinds of food; but there are exceptions. . . .

In order to be able to prevent or cure any malady, it is necessary to know its cause, and its seat. The seat of negro consumption is not in the lungs, stomach, liver or any organ of the body, but in the mind, and its cause is generally mismanagement or bad government on the part of the master, and superstition on the part of the negro. The patients themselves believe that they are poisoned; they are right, but it is not the body, but the mind that is poisoned. Negroes are very jealous and suspicions; hence, if they are slighted or imposed on in any way, or over-tasked, or do not get what they call their rights, they are apt to fall into a morbid state of mind, with sulkiness and dissatisfaction very plainly depicted in their countenances. It is bad government to let them remain in this sulky, dissatisfied mood, without inquiring into its causes, and removing them; otherwise, its long continuance leads to the disease under consideration. They fancy, that their fellow-servants are against them, that their master or overseer cares nothing for them, or is prejudiced against them, and that some enemy on the plantation or in the neighborhood has tricked them, that is, laid poison for them to walk over, or given it to them in their food or drinks. On almost every large plantation, there are one or more negroes, who are ambitious of being considered in the character of conjurers—in order to gain influence, and to make the others fear and obey them. The influence that these pretended conjurers exercise over their fellow servants, would not be credited by persons unacquainted with the superstitious mind of the negro. Nearly all, particularly those who have passed the age of puberty, are at times kept in constant dread and terror by the conjurers. These impostors, like all other impostors, take advantage of circumstances to swell their importance, and to inculcate a belief in their miraculous powers to bring good or evil upon those they like or dislike. It may be thought that the old superstition about conjuration has passed away with the old stock of native Africans; but it is too deeply radicated in the negro intellect to pass away: intelligent negroes believe in it, who are ashamed to acknowledge it. The effect of such a superstition—a firm belief that he is poisoned or conjured—upon the patient's mind, already in a morbid state, and his health affected from hard usage, over-tasking or exposure, want of wholesome food, good clothing, warm comfortable lodging, and the distressing idea, that he is an object of hatred or dislike, both to his master and fellow servants, and has no one to befriend him, tends directly to generate that erythism of mind, which is the essential cause of negro consumption. . . .

Drapetomania, or the Disease Causing Slaves to Run Away

Drapetomania is from [*drapeto,* the Greek word for] a runaway slave, and [*mania*], *mad or crazy.* It is unknown to our medical authorities, although its diagnostic symptoms, the absconding from service, is well known to our planters and overseers, as it was to the ancient Greeks, who expressed by the single word [*drapeto*] the fact of the absconding, and the relation that the fugitive held to the person he fled from. I have added to the word meaning runaway slave, another Greek term, to express the disease of the mind causing him to abscond. In noticing a disease not heretofore classed among the long list of maladies that man is subject to, it was necessary to have a new term to express it. The cause, in the most of cases, that induces the negro to run away from service, is as much a disease of the mind as any other species of mental alienation, and much more curable, as a general rule. With the advantages of proper medical advice, strictly followed, this troublesome practice that many negroes have of running away, can be almost entirely prevented, although the slaves be located on the borders of a free State, within a stone's throw of the abolitionists. I was born in Virginia, east of the Blue Ridge, where negroes are numerous, and studied medicine some years in Maryland, a slave State, separated from Pennsylvania, a free State, by Mason & Dixon's line—a mere air line, without wall or guard. I long ago observed that some persons, considered as very good, and others as very bad masters, often lost their negroes by their absconding from service; while the slaves of another class of persons, remarkable for order and good discipline, but not praised or blamed as either good or bad masters, never ran away, although no guard or forcible means were used to prevent them. The same management which prevented them from walking over a mere nominal, unguarded line, will prevent them from running away anywhere.

To ascertain the true method of governing negroes, so as to cure and prevent the disease under consideration, we must go back to the Pentateuch, and learn the true meaning of the untranslated term that represents the negro race. In the name there given to that race, is locked up the true art of governing negroes in such a manner that they cannot run away. The correct translation of that term declares the Creator's will in regard to the negro; it declares him to be the submissive knee-bender. In the anatomical conformation of his knees, we see *"genu flexit"* written in the physical structure of his knees, being more flexed or bent, than any other kind of man. If the white man attempts to oppose the Deity's will, by trying to make the negro anything else than *"the submissive knee-bender,"* (which the Almighty declared he should be,) by trying to raise him to a level with himself, or by putting himself on an equality with the negro; or if he abuses the power which God has given him over his fellow-man, by being cruel to him or punishing him in anger, or by neglecting to protect him from the wanton abuses of his fellow-servants and all others, or by denying him the usual comforts and necessaries of life, the negro will run away: but if he keeps him in the position that we learn from the Scriptures he was intended to occupy, that is, the position of submission, and if his master or overseer be kind and gracious in his bearing towards him, without condescension, and at the same time ministers to his physical wants and protects him from abuses, the negro is spellbound, and cannot runaway. *"He shall serve Japheth;* he shall be his servant of servants;"—on the conditions above mentioned—conditions that are clearly implied, though not directly expressed. According to my experience, the "genu flexit"—the awe and reverence, must be exacted from them, or they will despise their masters, become rude and ungovernable and run away. On Mason and Dixon's line, two classes of persons were apt to lose their negroes; those who made themselves too familiar with them, treating them as equals, and making little or no distinction in regard to color; and, on the other hand, those who treated them cruelly, denied them the common necessaries of life, neglected to protect them against the abuses of others, or frightened them by a blustering manner of approach, when about to punish them for misdemeanors. Before negroes run away, unless they are frightened or panic-struck, they become sulky and dissatisfied. The cause of this sulkiness and dissatisfaction should be inquired into and removed, or they are apt to run away or fall into the negro consumption. When sulky and dissatisfied without cause, the experience of those on the line and elsewhere was decidedly in favor of whipping them out of it, as a preventive measure against absconding or other bad conduct. It was called whipping the devil out of them.

If treated kindly, well fed and clothed, with fuel enough to keep a small fire burning all night, separated into families, each family having its own house—not permitted to run about at night, or to visit their neighbors, or to receive visits, or to use intoxicating liquors, and not overworked or exposed too much to the weather, they are very easily governed—more so than any other people in the world. When all this is done, if any one or more of them, at any time, are inclined to raise their heads to a level with their master or overseer, humanity and their own good require that they should be punished until they fall into that submissive state which it was intended for them to occupy in all after time, when their progenitor received the name of Canaan, or "submissive knee-bender." They have only to be kept in that state, and treated like children, with care, kindness, attention and humanity, to prevent and cure them from running away.

Dysesthesia Ethiopis, or Hebetude of Mind and Obtuse Sensibility of Body

A DISEASE PECULIAR TO NEGROES
CALLED BY OVERSEERS, "RASCALITY"

Dysaesthesia Aethiopis is a disease peculiar to negroes, affecting both mind and body, in a manner as well expressed by dysaesthesia, the name I have given it, as could be by a single term. There is both mind and sensibility, but both seem to be difficult to reach by impressions from without. There is partial insensibility of the skin, and so great a hebetude of the intellectual faculties as to be like a person half asleep, that is with difficulty aroused and kept awake. It differs from every other species of mental disease, as it is accompanied with physical signs or lesions of the body, discoverable to the medical observer, which are always present and sufficient to account for the symptoms. It is much more prevalent among free negroes living in clusters by themselves, than among slaves on our plantations, and attacks only such slaves as live like free negroes in regard to diet, drinks, exercise, etc. It is not my purpose to treat of the complaint as it prevails among free negroes, nearly all of whom are more or less afflicted with it, that have not got some white person to direct and to take care of them. To narrate its symptoms and effects among them would be to write a history of the ruins and dilapidation of Hayti and every spot of earth they have ever had uncontrolled possession over for any length of time. I propose only to describe its symptoms among slaves.

From the careless movements of the individuals affected with the complaint, they are apt to do much mischief, which appears as if intentional, but is mostly owing to the stupidness of mind and insensibility of the nerves induced by the disease. Thus, they break, waste and destroy everything they handle,—abuse horses and cattle,—tear, burn or rend their own clothing, and paying no attention to the rights of property, they steal other's to replace what they have destroyed.

They wander about at night, and keep in a half-nodding sleep during the day. They slight their work, — cut up corn, cane, cotton or tobacco when hoeing it, as if for pure mischief. They raise disturbances with their overseers and fellow servants without cause or motive, and seem to be insensible to pain when subjected to punishment. The fact of the existence of such a complaint, making man like an automaton or senseless machine, having the above or similar symptoms, can be clearly established by the most direct and positive testimony. That it should have escaped the attention of the medical profession, can only be accounted for because its attention has not been sufficiently directed to the maladies of the negro race. Otherwise, a complaint of so common occurrence on badly-governed plantations, and so universal among free negroes, or those who are not governed at all, — a disease radicated in physical lesions and having its peculiar and well-marked symptoms, and its curative indications, would not have escaped the notice of the profession. The northern physicians and people have noticed the symptoms, but not the disease from which they spring. They ignorantly attribute the symptoms to the debasing influence of slavery on the mind, without considering that those who have never been in slavery, or their fathers before them, are the most afflicted, and the latest from the slave-holding South the least. The disease is the natural offspring of negro liberty—the liberty to be idle, to wallow in filth, and to indulge in improper food and drinks.

In treating of the anatomy and physiology of the negro, I showed that his respiratory system was under the same physiological laws as that of an infant child of the white race; that a warm atmosphere, loaded with carbonic acid and aqueous vapor, was the most congenial to his lungs during sleep, as it is to the infant; that, to insure the respiration of such an atmosphere, he invariably, as if moved by instinct, shrouds his head and face in a blanket or some other covering, when disposing himself to sleep; that if sleeping by the fire in cold weather, he turns his head to it, instead of his feet, evidently to inhale warm air; that when not in active exercise, he always hovers over a fire in comparatively warm weather, as if he took a positive pleasure in inhaling hot air and smoke when his body is quiescent. The natural effect of this practice, it was shown, caused imperfect atmospherization or vitalization of the blood in the lungs, as occurs in infancy, and a hebetude or torpor of intellect—from blood not sufficiently vitalized being distributed to the brain; also, a slothfulness, torpor and disinclination to exercise, from the same cause—the want of blood sufficiently areated or vitalized in the circulating system. When left to himself, the negro indulges in his natural disposition to idleness and sloth, and does not take exercise enough to expand his lungs and to vitalize his blood, but dozes out a miserable existence in the midst of filth and uncleanliness, being too indolent and having too little energy of mind to provide for himself proper food and comfortable lodging and clothing. The consequence is, that the blood becomes so highly carbonized and deprived of oxygen, that it not only becomes unfit to stimulate the brain to energy, but unfit to stimulate the nerves of sensation distributed to the body. A torpor and insensibility pervades the system; the sentient nerves distributed to the skin lose their feeling to so great a degree, that he often burns his skin by the fire he hovers over, without knowing it, and frequently has large holes in his clothes, and the shoes on his feet burnt to a crisp, without having been conscious of when it was done. This is the disease called dysaesthesia—a Greek term expressing the dull or obtuse sensation that always attends the complaint. When aroused from his sloth by the stimulus of hunger, he takes anything he can lay his hands on, and tramples on the rights, as well as on the property of others, with perfect indifference as to consequences. When driven to labor by the compulsive power of the white man, he performs the task assigned him in a headlong, careless manner, treading down with his feet, or cutting with his hoe the plants he is put to cultivate—breaking the tools he works with, and spoiling everything he touches that can be injured by careless handling. Hence the overseers call it "rascality," supposing that the mischief is intentionally done. But there is no premeditated mischief in the case,—the mind is too torpid to meditate mischief, or even to be aroused by the angry passions to deeds of daring. Dysaesthesia, or hebetude of sensation of both mind and body, prevails to so great an extent, that when the unfortunate individual is subjected to punishment, he neither feels pain of any consequence, or shows any unusual resentment, more than by a stupid sulkiness. In some cases, anesthesia would be a more suitable name for it, as there appears to be an almost total loss of feeling. The term "rascality," given to this disease by overseers, is founded on an erroneous hypothesis and leads to an incorrect empirical treatment, which seldom or ever cures it.

The complaint is easily curable, if treated on sound physiological principles. The skin is dry, thick and harsh to the touch, and the liver inactive. The liver, skin and kidneys should be stimulated to activity, and be made assist in decarbonising the blood. The best means to stimulate the skin is, first, to have the patient well washed with warm water and soap; then, to anoint it all over with oil, and to slap the oil in with a broad leather strap; then to put the patient to some hard kind of work in the open air and sunshine, that will compel him to expand his lungs, as chopping wood, splitting rails or sawing with the cross-cut or whip saw. Any kind of labor will do that will cause full and free respiration in its performance, as lifting or carrying heavy weights, or brisk walking; the object being to expand the lungs by full and deep inspirations and expirations, thereby to vitalize the impure circulating blood by introducing oxygen and expelling carbon. This treatment should not be continued too long at a time, because where the circulating fluids are so impure as in this complaint, patients cannot stand protracted exercise without resting frequently and drinking freely of cold water or some cooling beverage, as lemonade, or alternated with pepper tea sweetened with molasses. In bad cases, the blood has always the appearance of blood in scurvy, and commonly there is a scorbutic affection to be seen on the gums. After resting until the palpitation of the heart caused by the exercise is allayed, the patient should eat some good wholesome food, well seasoned with spices and mixed with vegetables, as turnip or mustard salad, with vinegar. After a moderate meal, he should resume his work again, resting at intervals, and taking refreshments and supporting the perspiration by partaking freely of liquids. At night he should be lodged in a warm room with a small fire in it, and should have a clean bed, with sufficient blanket covering, and be washed clean before going to bed: in the morning, oiled, slapped and put to work as before. Such treatment will, in a short time, effect a cure in all cases which are not complicated with chronic visceral derangements. The effect of this or a like course of treatment is often like enchantment. No sooner does the blood feel the vivifying influences derived from its full and perfect atmospherization by exercise in the open air and in the sun, than the negro seems to be awakened to a new existence, and to look grateful and thankful to the white man whose compulsory power, by making him inhale vital air, has restored his sensation and dispelled the mist that clouded his intellect. His intelligence restored and his sensations awakened, he is no longer the *bipedum nequissimus,* or arrant rascal, he was supposed to be, but a good negro that can hoe or plow, and handle things with as much care as his other fellow-servants.

Contrary to the received opinion, a northern climate is the most favorable to the intellectual development of negroes, those of Missouri, Kentucky, and the colder parts of Virginia and Maryland, having much more mental energy, more bold and ungovernable than in the Southern lowlands; a dense atmosphere causing a better vitalization of their blood.

Although idleness is the most prolific cause of dysaesthesia, yet there are other ways that the blood gets deteriorated. I said before that negroes are like children, requiring government in everything. If not governed in their diet, they are apt to eat too much salt meat and not enough bread and vegetables, which practice generates a scorbutic state of the fluids and leads to the affection under consideration. This form of the complaint always shows itself in the gums, which become spongy and dark, and leave the teeth. Uncleanliness of skin and torpid liver also tend to produce it. A scurvy set of negroes means the same thing, in the South, as a disorderly, worthless set. That the blood, when rendered impure and carbonaceous from any cause, as from idleness, filthy habits, unwholesome food or alcoholic drinks, affects the mind, is not only known to physicians, but was known to the Bard of Avon when he penned the lines — "We are not ourselves when Nature, being oppressed, commands the mind to suffer with the body."

According to unalterable physiological laws, negroes, as a general rule, to which there are but few exceptions, can only have their intellectual faculties awakened in a sufficient degree to receive moral culture, and to profit by religious or other instruction, when under the compulsory authority of the white man; because, as a general rule, to which there are but few exceptions, they will not take sufficient exercise, when removed from the white man's authority, to vitalize and decarbonize their blood by the process of full and free respiration, that active exercise of some kind alone can effect. A northern climate remedies, in a considerable degree, their naturally indolent disposition; but the dense atmosphere of Boston or Canada can scarcely produce sufficient hematosis and vigor of mind to induce them to labor. From their natural indolence, unless under the stimulus of compulsion, they doze away their lives with the capacity of their lungs for atmospheric air only half expanded, from the want of exercise to superinduce full and deep respiration. The inevitable effect is, to prevent a sufficient atmospherization or vitalization of the blood, so essential to the expansion and the freedom of action of the intellectual faculties. The black blood distributed to the brain chains the mind to ignorance, superstition and barbarism, and bolts the door against civilization, moral culture and religious truth. The compulsory power of the white man, by making the slothful negro take active exercise, puts into active play the lungs, through whose agency the vitalized blood is sent to the brain, to give liberty to the mind, and to open the door to intellectual improvement. The very exercise, so beneficial to the negro, is expended in cultivating those burning fields in cotton, sugar, rice and tobacco, which, but for his labor, would, from the heat of the climate, go uncultivated, and their products lost to the world. Both parties are benefitted—the negro as well as his master—even more. But there is a third party benefitted—the world at large. The three millions of bales of cotton, made by negro labor, afford a cheap clothing for the civilized world. The laboring classes of all mankind, having less to pay for clothing, have more money to spend in educating their children, and in intellectual, moral and religious progress.

The wisdom, mercy and justice of the decree, that Canaan shall serve Japheth, is proved by the disease we have been considering, because it proves that his physical organization, and the laws of his nature, are in perfect unison with slavery, and in entire discordance with liberty—a discordance so great as to produce the loathsome disease that we have been considering, as one of its inevitable effects,— a disease that locks up the understanding, blunts the sensations and chains the mind to superstition, ignorance and barbarism. Slaves are not subject to this disease, unless they are permitted to live like free negroes, in idleness and filth—to eat improper food, or to indulge in spirituous liquors. It is not their masters' interest that they should do so; as they would not only be unprofitable, but as great a nuisance to the South, as the free negroes were found to be in London, whom the British government, more than half a century ago, colonized in Sierra Leone to get them out of the way. The mad fanaticism that British writers, lecturers and emissaries, and the East India Company, planted in our Northern States, after it was found by well-tried experiments, that free negroes in England, in Canada, in Sierra Leone and elsewhere, were a perfect nuisance, and would not work as free laborers, but would retrograde to barbarism, was not planted there in opposition to British policy. Whatever was the motive of Great Britain in sowing the whirlwind in our Northern States, it is now threatening the disruption of a mighty empire of the happiest, most progressive and Christian people, that ever inhabited the earth—and the only empire on the wide earth that England dreads as a rival, either in arts or in arms.

Our Declaration of Independence, which was drawn up at a time when negroes were scarcely considered as human beings, *"That all men are by nature free and equal,"* and only intended to apply to white men, is often quoted in support of the false dogma that all mankind possess the same mental, physiological and anatomical organization, and that the liberty, free institutions, and whatever else would be a blessing to one portion, would, under the same external circumstances, be to all, without regard to any original or internal differences, inherent in the organization. Although England preaches this doctrine, she practises in opposition to it every where. Instance, her treatment of the Gypsies in England, the Hindoos in India, the Hottentots at her Cape Colony, and the aboriginal inhabitants of New Holland. The dysaesthesia ethiopis adds another to the many ten thousand evidencies of the fallacy of the dogma that abolitionism is built on; for here, in a country where two races of men dwell together, both born on the same soil, breathing the same air, and surrounded by the same external agents—liberty, which is elevating the one race of people above all other nations, sinks the other into beastly sloth and torpidity; and the slavery, which the one would prefer death rather than endure, improves the other in body, mind and morals; thus proving the dogma false, and establishing the truth that there is a radical, internal, or physical difference between the two races, so great in kind, as to make what is wholesome and beneficial for the white man, as liberty, republican or free institutions, etc., not only unsuitable to the negro race, but actually poisonous to its happiness.

15

WILLIAM J. GRAYSON

The Hireling and the Slave

1854

William J. Grayson (1788–1863) was a South Carolina lawyer, politician, and man of letters. He opposed South Carolina's attempted nullification in the early 1830s and was a Unionist throughout his life, opposing secession in 1860. He supported the Confederacy, however, after secession occurred. Among his many accomplishments was his codification of the laws of South Carolina. He had a minor political career, serving in the

William J. Grayson, *The Hireling and the Slave, Chicora, and Other Poems* (Charleston, S.C.: McCarter, 1854).

*South Carolina House of Representatives and Senate and two terms
(1833–37) in the U.S. Congress. From 1841 to 1853, he served as col-
lector of the Port of Charleston. As a man of letters, Grayson published
two volumes of poetry, wrote a posthumously published autobiography
and a posthumously published biography of fellow Charleston attorney
James Louis Petigru.*

*Grayson defended slavery in a number of writings, but his most
important was "The Hireling and the Slave," a lengthy poem over fifty
pages long, containing about 1,500 lines. The burden of the poem is to
explain why slaves are better off than free workers. The poem attacks
industrial society, especially in Britain. Significantly, Grayson, a Unionist and a conservative, does not seek to fan the flames of sectionalism by
attacking the North or Northern industrial society.*

*He does, however, attack many prominent Northern politicians and
other opponents of slavery, including Senators Charles Sumner, William
H. Seward, and Salmon P. Chase, Congressman Joshua Giddings, and
abolitionists Gerrit Smith, William Lloyd Garrison, and the British abolitionist Thomas Clarkson. Grayson reserves his harshest comments
for Harriet Beecher Stowe, the author of* Uncle Tom's Cabin, *perhaps
because her book was in fact the most devastating attack on slavery in
the period. He also accuses abolitionists of opposing Scripture and
implies that slavery was ordained by God.*

Fallen from primeval innocence and ease,
When thornless fields employed him but to please,*
The laborer toils; and from his dripping brow
Moistens the length'ning furrows of the plow;
In vain he scorns or spurns his altered state,
Tries each poor shift, and strives to cheat his fate;
In vain new-shapes his name to shun the ill—
Slave, hireling, help—the curse pursues him still;
Changeless the doom remains, the mincing phrase
May mock high Heaven, but not reverse its ways.
How small the choice, from cradle to the grave,
Between the lot of hireling, help, or slave!
To each alike applies the stern decree
That man shall labor; whether bond or free,

*"Cursed is the ground for thy sake; * * * thorns and thistles shall it bring forth to
thee; * * * in the sweat of thy brow shalt thou eat bread."—*Genesis.*

For all that toil, the recompense we claim—
Food, fire, a home and clothing—is the same.
    The manumitted serfs of Europe find
Unchanged this sad estate of all mankind;
What blessing to the churl has freedom proved,
What want supplied, what task or toil removed?
Hard work and scanty wages still their lot,
In youth o'erlabored, and in age forgot,
The mocking boon of freedom they deplore,
In wants and labors never known before.
    Free but in name—the slaves of endless toil,
In Britain still they turn the stubborn soil,
Spread on each sea her sails for every mart,
Ply in her cities every useful art;
But vainly may the peasant toil and groan
To speed the plow in furrows not his own;
In vain the art is plied, the sail is spread,
The day's work offered for the daily bread;
With hopeless eye, the pauper hireling sees
The homeward sail swell proudly to the breeze,
Rich fabrics wrought by his unequaled hand,
Borne by each breeze to every distant land;
For him, no boon successful commerce yields,
For him no harvest crowns the joyous fields,
The streams of wealth that foster pomp and pride,
No food nor shelter for his wants provide;
He fails to win, by toil intensely hard,
The bare subsistence—labor's least reward.
    In squalid hut—a kennel for the poor,
Or noisome cellar, stretched upon the floor,
His clothing rags, of filthy straw his bed,
With offal from the gutter daily fed,
Thrust out from Nature's board, the hireling lies:
No place for him that common board supplies,
No neighbor helps, no charity attends,
No philanthropic sympathy befriends;
None heed the needy wretch's dying groan,
He starves unsuccor'd, perishes unknown.
    These are the miseries, such the wants, the cares,
The bliss that freedom for the serf prepares;
Vain is his skill in each familiar task,

Capricious Fashion shifts her Protean mask,
His ancient craft gives work and bread no more,
And Want and Death sit scowling at his door.
. . .
To gross excess and brutalizing strife,
The drunken hireling dedicates his life:
Starved else, by infamy's sad wages fed,
There women prostitute themselves for bread,
And mothers, rioting with savage glee,
For murder'd infants spend the funeral fee;
Childhood bestows no childish sports or toys,
Age neither reverence nor repose enjoys,
Labor with hunger wages ceaseless strife,
And want and suffering only end with life;
In crowded huts contagious ills prevail,
Dull typhus lurks, and deadlier plagues assail,
Gaunt Famine prowls around his pauper prey,
And daily sweeps his ghastly hosts away;
Unburied corpses taint the summer air,
And crime and outrage revel with despair.
. . .
Far from their humble homes and native land,
Forced by a landlord's pitiless command,
In uncongenial climes condemned to roam,
That sheep may batten in the peasant's home,
The pauper exiles, from the hill that yields
One parting look on their abandoned fields,
Behold with tears no manhood can restrain,
Their ancient hamlet level'd with the plain:
Then go in crowded ships new ills to find,
More hideous still than those they left behind;
Grim Chol'ra thins their ranks, ship-fevers sweep
Their livid tithes of victims to the deep;
The sad survivors, on a foreign shore,
The double loss of homes and friends deplore,
And beg a stranger's bounty to supply
The food and shelter that their homes deny.
Yet homebred misery, such as this, imparts
Nor grief nor care to philanthropic hearts;
The tear of sympathy forever flows,
Though not for Saxon or for Celtic woes;
Vainly the starving white, at every door,

Craves help or pity for the hireling poor;
But that the distant black may softlier fare,
Eat, sleep, and play, exempt from toil and care,
All England's meek philanthropists unite
With frantic eagerness, harangue and write;
By purchased tools diffuse distrust and hate,
Sow factious strife in each dependent state,
Cheat with delusive lies the public mind,
Invent the cruelties they fail to find,
Slander, in pious garb, with prayer and hymn,
And blast a people's fortune for a whim.

. . .

Companions of his toil, the axe to wield,
To guide the plow, and reap the teeming field,
A sable multitude unceasing pour
From Niger's banks and Congo's deadly shore;
No willing travelers they, that widely roam,
Allured by hope to seek a happier home,
But victims to the trader's thirst for gold,
Kidnapped by brothers, and by fathers sold,
The bondsman born, by native masters reared,
The captive band in recent battle spared;
For English merchants bought; across the main,
In British ships, they go for Britain's gain;
Forced on her subjects in dependent lands,
By cruel hearts and avaricious hands,
New tasks they learn, new masters they obey,
And bow submissive to the white man's sway.
    But Providence, by his o'erruling will,
Transmutes to lasting good the transient ill,
Makes crime itself the means of mercy prove,
And avarice minister to works of love.
In this new home, whate'er the negro's fate—
More bless'd his life than in his native state!
No mummeries dupe, no Fetich charms affright,
Nor rites obscene diffuse their moral blight;
Idolatries, more hateful than the grave,
With human sacrifice, no more enslave;
No savage rule its hecatomb supplies
Of slaves for slaughter when a master dies:
In sloth and error sunk for countless years
His race has lived, but light at last appears—

Celestial light: religion undefiled
Dawns in the heart of Congo's simple child;
Her glorious truths he hears with glad surprise,
And lifts his eye with rapture to the skies;
The noblest thoughts that erring mortals know,
Waked by her influence, in his bosom glow;
His nature owns the renovating sway,
And all the old barbarian melts away.
　　And now, with sturdy hand and cheerful heart,
He learns to master every useful art,
To forge the axe, to mould the rugged share,
The ship's brave keel for angry waves prepare:
The rising wall obeys his plastic will,
And the loom's fabric owns his ready skill.
　　Where once the Indian's keen, unerring aim,
With shafts of reed transfixed the forest game,
Where painted warriors late in ambush stood,
And midnight war-whoops shook the trembling wood,
The Negro wins, with well-directed toil,
Its various treasures from the virgin soil;
Swept by his axe the forests pass away,
The dense swamp opens to the light of day;
The deep morass of reeds and fetid mud,
Now dry, now covered by the rising flood,
In squares arranged by lines of bank and drain,
Smiles with rich harvests of the golden grain,
That, wrought from ooze by nature's curious art
To pearly whiteness, cheers the Negro's heart,
Smokes on the master's board in goodly show,
A mimic pyramid of seeming snow,
And borne by commerce to each distant shore,
Supplies the world with one enjoyment more.
　　On upland slopes, with jungle lately spread,
The lordly maize uplifts its tasseled head;
Broad, graceful leaves of waving green appear,
And shining threads adorn the swelling ear—
The matchless ear, whose milky stores impart
A feast that mocks the daintiest powers of art
To every taste; whose riper bounty yields
A grateful feast amid a thousand fields,
And sent, on mercy's errand, from the slave
To starving hirelings, saves them from the grave.

In broader limits, by the loftier maize,
The silk-like cotton all its wealth displays:
Through forked leaves, in endless rows unfold
Gay blossoms tinged with purple dyes and gold;
To suns autumnal bursting pods disclose
Their fleeces, spotless as descending snows;
These, a rich freight, a thousand ships receive,
A thousand looms with fairy fingers weave;
And hireling multitudes in other lands
Are blessed with raiment from the Negro's hands.
　　　　. . .

The weed's soft influence, too, his hands prepare,
That soothes the beggar's grief, the monarch's care,
Cheers the lone scholar at his midnight work,
Subdues alike the Russian and the Turk,
The saint beguiles, the heart of toil revives,
Ennui itself of half its gloom deprives,
In fragrant clouds involves the learned and great,
In golden boxes helps the toils of state,
And, with strange magic and mysterious charm,
Hunger can stay, and bores and duns disarm.
　　　　These precious products, in successive years,
Trained by a master's skill, the Negro rears;
New life he gives to Europe's busy marts,
To all the world new comforts and new arts;
Loom, spinner, merchant, from his hands derive
Their wealth, and myriads by his labor thrive;
While slothful millions, hopeless of relief,
The slaves of pagan priest and brutal chief,
Harassed by wars upon their native shore,
Still lead the savage life they led before.
　　　　Instructed thus, and in the only school
Barbarians ever know—a master's rule,
The Negro learns each civilizing art
That softens and subdues the savage heart,
Assumes the tone of those with whom he lives,
Acquires the habit that refinement gives,
And slowly learns, but surely, while a slave,
The lessons that his country never gave.
　　　　. . .

Hence is the Negro come, by God's command,
For wiser teaching to a foreign land;

If they who brought him were by Mammon driven,
Still have they served, blind instruments of Heaven;
And though the way be rough, the agent stern,
No better mode can human wits discern,
No happier system wealth or virtue find,
To tame and elevate the Negro mind:
Thus mortal purposes, whate'er their mood,
Are only means with Heaven for working good;
And wisest they who labor to fulfill,
With zeal and hope, the all-directing will,
And in each change that marks the fleeting year,
Submissive see God's guiding hand appear.
. . .

So here, though hid the end from mortal view,
Heaven's gracious purpose brings the Negro too;
He comes by God's decree, not chance nor fate,
Not force, nor fraud, nor grasping scheme of state,
As Joseph came to Pharaoh's storied land,
Not by a brother's wrath, but Heaven's command;
What though humaner Carlisle disapprove,
Profounder Brougham his vote of censure move,
And Clarkson's friends with modest ardor show
How much more wisely they could rule below,
Prove, with meek arrogance and lowly pride,
What ills they could remove, what bliss provide,
Forestall the Savior's mercy, and devise
A scheme to wipe all tears from mortal eyes;
Yet time shall vindicate Heaven's humbler plan,
"And justify the ways of God to man."
But if, though wise and good the purposed end,
Reproach and scorn the instrument attend;
If, when the final blessing is confess'd,
Still the vile slaver all the world detest;
Arraign the states that sent their ships of late
To barter beads and rum for human freight,
That claimed the right, by treaty, to provide
Slaves for themselves, and half the world beside,
And from the Hebrew learned the craft so well,
Their sable brothers to enslave and sell.
Shame and remorse o'erwhelmed the Hebrew race,
And penitence was stamped on every face;

But modern slavers, more sagacious grown,
In all the wrong, can see no part their own;
They drag the Negro from his native shore,
Make him a slave, and then his fate deplore;
Sell him in distant countries, and when sold,
Revile the buyers, but retain the gold:
Dext'rous to win, in time, by various ways,
Substantial profit and alluring praise,
By turns they grow rapacious and humane,
And seize alike the honor and the gain:
Had Joseph's brethren known this modern art,
And played with skill the philanthropic part,
How had bold Judah raved in freedom's cause,
How Levi cursed the foul Egyptian laws,
And Issachar, in speech or long report,
Brayed at the masters found in Pharaoh's court,
And taught the king himself the sin to hold
Enslaved the brother they had lately sold,
Proving that sins of traffic never lie
On knaves who sell, but on the dupes that buy.
    Such now the maxims of the purer school
Of ethic lore, where sons of slavers rule;
No more allowed the Negro to enslave,
They damn the master, and for freedom rave,
Strange modes of morals and of faith unfold,
Make newer gospels supersede the old,
Prove that ungodly Paul connived at sin,
And holier rites, like Mormon's priest, begin;
There, chief and teacher, Gerrit Smith appears,
There Tappan mourns, like Niobe, all tears,
Carnage and fire mad Garrison invokes,
And Hale, with better temper, smirks and jokes;
There Giddings, with the Negro mania bit,
Mouths, and mistakes his ribaldry for wit,
His fustian speeches into market brings,
And prints and peddles all the paltry things;
The pest and scorn of legislative halls,
No rule restrains him, no disgrace appalls;
Kicked from the House, the creature knows no pain,
But crawls, contented, to his seat again,
Wallows with joy in slander's slough once more,

And plays Thersites happier than before;
Prompt from his seat—when distant riots need
The Senate's aid—he flies with railway speed,
Harangues, brags, bullies, then resumes his chair,
And wears his trophies with a hero's air;
His colleagues scourge him; but he shrewdly shows
A profitable use for whips and blows—
His friends and voters mark the increasing score,
Count every lash, and honor him the more.
    There supple Sumner, with the Negro cause,
Plays the sly game for office and applause;
What boots it if the Negro sink or swim?
He wins the Senate—'tis enough for him.
What though he blast the fortunes of the state
With fierce dissension and enduring hate?
He makes his speech, his rhetoric displays,
Trims the neat trope, and points the sparkling phrase
With well-turned period, fosters civil strife,
And barters for a phrase a nation's life;
Sworn into office, his nice feelings loathe*
The dog-like faithfulness that keeps an oath;
For rules of right the silly crowd may bawl,
His loftier spirit scorns and spurns them all;
He heeds nor court's decree nor Gospel light,
What Sumner thinks is right alone is right;
On this sound maxim sires and sons proceed,
Changed in all else, but still in this agreed;
The sires all slavers, the humaner son
Curses the trade, and mourns the mischief done.
For gold they made the Negroes slaves, and he
For fame and office seeks to set them free;
Self still the end in which their creeds unite,
And that which serves the end is always right.
    There Greeley, grieving at a brother's woe,
Spits with impartial spite on friend and foe;
His Negro griefs and sympathies produce
No nobler fruits than malice and abuse;

---

*"Is thy servant a dog that he should do this thing?"—Mr. Sumner's answer, when asked whether he would obey the Constitution as interpreted by the authorities of the country.

To each fanatical delusion prone,
He damns all creeds and parties but his own,
Brawls, with hot zeal, for every fool and knave,
The foreign felon and the skulking slave;
Even Chaplin, sneaking from his jail, receives
The Tribune's sympathy for punished thieves.
And faction's fiercest rabble always find
A kindred nature in the Tribune's mind;
Ready each furious impulse to obey,
He raves and ravens like a beast of prey,
To bloody outrage stimulates his friends,
And fires the Capitol for party ends.
    There Seward smiles the sweet perennial smile,
Skilled in the tricks of subtlety and guile;
The slyest schemer that the world e'er saw;
Peddler of sentiment and patent law;
Ready for fee or faction to display
His skill in either, if the practice pay,
But void of all that makes the frank and brave,
And smooth, and soft, and crafty like the slave;
Soft as Couthon when, versed in civil strife,
He sent his daily victims to the knife,
Women proscribed with calm and gentle grace,
And murdered mildly with a smiling face:
Parental rule in youth he bravely spurned,
And higher law with boyish wit discerned;
A village teacher then, his style betrays
The pedant practice of those learned days,
When boys, not demagogues, obeyed his nod,
His higher law the tear-compelling rod;
While Georgia's guest, a pleasant life he led,
And Slavery fed him with her savory bread,
As now it helps him, in an ampler way,
With spells and charms that factious hordes obey.
    There Stowe, with prostituted pen, assails
One half her country in malignant tales;
Careless, like Trollope, whether truth she tells,
And anxious only how the libel sells,
To slander's mart she furnishes supplies,
And feeds its morbid appetite for lies
On fictions fashioned with malicious art,

The venal pencil, and malignant heart,
With fact distorted, inference unsound,
Creatures in fancy, not in nature found—
Chaste Quadroon virgins, saints of sable hue,
Martyrs, than zealous Paul more tried and true,
Demoniac masters, sentimental slaves,
Mulatto cavaliers, and Creole knaves—
Monsters each portrait drawn, each story told!
What then? The book may bring its weight in gold;
Enough! upon the crafty rule she leans,
That makes the purpose justify the means,
Concocts the venom, and, with eager gaze,
To Glasgow flies for patron, pence, and praise,
And for a slandered country finds rewards
In smiles or sneers of duchesses and lords.
      For profits and applauses poor as these,
To the false tale she adds its falser Keys*
Of gathered slanders—her ignoble aim,
With foes to traffic in her country's shame.
      Strange power of nature, from whose efforts flow
Such diverse forms as Nightingale and Stowe!
One glares a torch of discord; one a star
Of blessing shines amid the wrecks of war;
One prone to libel; one to deeds of love;
The vulture-spirit one, and one the dove;
In various joys their various natures deal,
One leaves her home to wound it, one to heal;
That to expose its sorrows, not deplore;
To help and cheer, this seeks a foreign shore.
                    · · ·
      Not such with Stowe, the wish or power to please,
She finds no joys in gentle deeds like these;
A moral scavenger, with greedy eye,
In social ills her coarser labors lie;
On fields where vice eludes the light of day,
She hunts up crimes as beagles hunt their prey;
Gleans every dirty nook—the felon's jail,

---

*Mrs. Stowe has published what she calls a Key to her tale. It is a compilation of all
the slanders and crimes among slaveholders; just as she would write a story denounc-
ing matrimony, and make a Key, from the courts or gossiping chronicles, of all the cruelties, murders, and adulteries of husbands and wives, representing the crimes as the
normal condition of the relation.

And hangman's mem'ry, for detraction's tale,
Snuffs up pollution with a pious air,
Collects a rumor here, a slander there;
With hatred's ardor gathers Newgate spoils,
And trades for gold the garbage of her toils.
· · ·
These use the Negro, a convenient tool,
That yields substantial gain or party rule,
Gives what without it they could never know,
To Chase distinction, courtly friends to Stowe,
To Parker, themes for miracles of rant,
And Beecher blesses with new gifts of cant.
The master's task has been the black to train,
To form his mind, his passions to restrain;
With anxious care and patience to impart
The knowledge that subdues the savage heart,
To give the Gospel lessons that control
The rudest breast, and renovate the soul—
Who does, or gives as much, of all who raise
Their sland'rous cry for foreign pence or praise;
Of all the knaves who clamor and declaim
For party power or philanthropic fame,
Or use the Negro's fancied wrongs and woes
As pretty themes for maudlin verse or prose?
Taught by the master's efforts, by his care
Fed, clothed, protected many a patient year,
From trivial numbers now to millions grown,
With all the white man's useful arts their own,
Industrious, docile, skilled in wood and field,
To guide the plow, the sturdy axe to wield,
The Negroes schooled by slavery embrace
The highest portion of the Negro race;
And none the savage native will compare,
Of barbarous Guinea, with its offspring here.
If bound to daily labor while he lives,
His is the daily bread that labor gives;
Guarded from want, from beggary secure,
He never feels what hireling crowds endure,
Nor knows, like them, in hopeless want to crave,
For wife and child, the comforts of the slave,
Or the sad thought that, when about to die,
He leaves them to the cold world's charity,

And sees them slowly seek the poor-house door—
The last, vile, hated refuge of the poor.
    Still Europe's saints, that mark the motes alone
In other's eyes, yet never see their own,
Grieve that the slave is never taught to write,
And reads no better than the hireling white;
Do their own plowmen no instruction lack,
Have whiter clowns more knowledge than the black?
Has the French peasant, or the German boor,
Of learning's treasure any larger store;
Have Ireland's millions, flying from the rule
Of those who censure, ever known a school?
A thousand years and Europe's wealth impart
No means to mend the hireling's head or heart;
They build no schools to teach the pauper white,
Their toiling millions neither read nor write;
Whence, then, the idle clamor when they rave
Of schools and teachers for the distant slave?
    And why the soft regret, the coarse attack,
If Justice punish the offending black?
Are whites not punished? When Utopian times
Shall drive from earth all miseries and crimes,
And teach the world the art to do without
The cat, the gauntlet, and the brutal knout,
Banish the halter, galley, jails, and chains,
And strip the law of penalties and pains;
Here, too, offense and wrong they may prevent,
And slaves, with hirelings, need no punishment:
Till then, what lash of slavery will compare
With the dread scourge that British soldiers bear?
What gentle rule, in Britain's Isle, prevails,
How rare her use of gibbets, stocks, and jails!
How much humaner than a master's whip,
Her penal colony and convict ship!
Whose code of law can darker pages show,
Where blood for smaller misdemeanors flow?
The trifling theft or trespass, that demands
For slaves light penance from a master's hands,
Where Europe's milder punishments are known,
Incurs the penalty of death alone.
    And yet the master's lighter rule insures

More order than the sternest code secures;
No mobs of factious workmen gather here,
No strikes we dread, no lawless riots fear;
Nuns, from their convent driven, at midnight fly,
Churches, in flames, ask vengeance from the sky,
Seditious schemes in bloody tumults end,
Parsons incite, and senators defend,
But not where slaves their easy labors ply,
Safe from the snare, beneath a master's eye;
In useful tasks engaged, employed their time,
Untempted by the demagogue to crime,
Secure they toil, uncursed their peaceful life,
With labor's hungry broils and wasteful strife.
No want to goad, no faction to deplore,
The slave escapes the perils of the poor.

16

GEORGE FITZHUGH

Sociology for the South
1854

and

Cannibals All!
1857

*George Fitzhugh (1804–1881) was a self-taught lawyer, an imaginative
social critic, and a self-styled sociologist. He was also one of the most creative proslavery theorists. In the 1850s, he was a regular contributor to*
De Bow's Review, *wrote editorials for the* Richmond Enquirer, *and published essays in other journals or as pamphlets. Never financially successful, he made his living writing, lecturing, and practicing a little law.*

George Fitzhugh, *Sociology for the South: Or the Failure of Free Society* (Richmond, Va.:
A. Morris, 1854); and *Cannibals All! Or Slaves without Masters* (Richmond, Va.: A. Morris, 1857).

George Fitzhugh in 1855.
The Granger Collection, New York.

*During President James Buchanan's administration, he held a minor
position in the office of the attorney general.*

In his two books, Sociology for the South: Or the Failure of Free
Society *(1854) and* Cannibals All! Or Slaves without Masters *(1857),
Fitzhugh argued that all societies had to have a lower class and a working class. He further argued that such people at the bottom of the social
ladder would suffer. The answer to this social fact, he argued, was
slavery. For Fitzhugh, slavery solved the problem of unemployment and*

labor exploitation. Since slaves were capital, they would always be fed, clothed, and housed, unlike free workers who could be turned out in an economic downturn to face starvation or worse.

Fitzhugh did not apologize for slavery; he gloried in it. Indeed, in a lecture tour of the North in 1856 and later in Cannibals All! *Fitzhugh followed his argument to its logical conclusion: that poor whites, as well as blacks, should be enslaved. He claimed to reject the racial defense of slavery, although his position seems somewhat insincere, as the excerpts on Negro slavery here illustrate. Furthermore, as one scholar notes, "His postbellum writings expressed a virulent racism."[1] By the late 1850s, Fitzhugh was intellectually at war with any free society. Because of his extreme views, including his rejection of free society and his advocacy of slavery even for whites, Fitzhugh had no great following in the South. Nevertheless, he was a powerful intellectual force who commanded respect.*

The chapters from Sociology for the South *and* Cannibals All! *reprinted here offer economic, racial, and biblical defenses of slavery. Fitzhugh also attacks the antislavery cause, in effect arguing that an abolition of slavery would destroy civilized society.*

Sociology for the South

Chapter V. Negro Slavery

We have already stated that we should not attempt to introduce any new theories of government and of society, but merely try to justify old ones, so far as we could deduce such theories from ancient and almost universal practices. Now it has been the practice in all countries and in all ages, in some degree, to accommodate the amount and character of government control to the wants, intelligence, and moral capacities of the nations or individuals to be governed. A highly moral and intellectual people, like the free citizens of ancient Athens, are best governed by a democracy. For a less moral and intellectual one, a limited and constitutional monarchy will answer. For a people either very ignorant or very wicked, nothing short of military despotism will suffice. So among individuals, the most moral and well-informed members of

---

[1] Drew Gilpin Faust, *Proslavery Thought in the Antebellum South, 1830–1860* (Baton Rouge: Louisiana State University Press, 1981), 273.

society require no other government than law. They are capable of reading and understanding the law, and have sufficient self-control and virtuous disposition to obey it. Children cannot be governed by mere law; first, because they do not understand it, and secondly, because they are so much under the influence of impulse, passion and appetite, that they want sufficient self-control to be deterred or governed by the distant and doubtful penalties of the law. They must be constantly controlled by parents or guardians, whose will and orders shall stand in the place of law for them. Very wicked men must be put into penitentiaries; lunatics into asylums, and the most wild of them into straight jackets, just as the most wicked of the sane are manacled with irons; and idiots must have committees to govern and take care of them. Now, it is clear the Athenian democracy would not suit a negro nation, nor will the government of mere law suffice for the individual negro. He is but a grown up child, and must be governed as a child, not as a lunatic or criminal. The master occupies towards him the place of parent or guardian. We shall not dwell on this view, for no one will differ with us who thinks as we do of the negro's capacity, and we might argue till dooms-day, in vain, with those who have a high opinion of the negro's moral and intellectual capacity.

Secondly. The negro is improvident; will not lay up in summer for the wants of winter; will not accumulate in youth for the exigencies of age. He would become an insufferable burden to society. Society has the right to prevent this, and can only do so by subjecting him to domestic slavery.

In the last place, the negro race is inferior to the white race, and living in their midst, they would be far outstripped or outwitted in the chase of free competition. Gradual but certain extermination would be their fate. We presume the maddest abolitionist does not think the negro's providence of habits and money-making capacity at all to compare to those of the whites. This defect of character would alone justify enslaving him, if he is to remain here. In Africa or the West Indies, he would become idolatrous, savage and cannibal, or be devoured by savages and cannibals. At the North he would freeze or starve.

We would remind those who deprecate and sympathize with negro slavery, that his slavery here relieves him from a far more cruel slavery in Africa, or from idolatry and cannibalism, and every brutal vice and crime that can disgrace humanity; and that it christianizes, protects, supports and civilizes him; that it governs him far better than free laborers at the North are governed. There, wife-murder has become a mere holiday pastime; and where so many wives are murdered, almost all must be brutally treated. Nay, more: men who kill their wives or treat them brutally, must be ready for all kinds of crime, and the calendar of crime at the North proves the inference to be correct. Negroes never kill their wives. If it be objected that legally they have no wives, then we reply, that in an experience of more than forty years, we never yet heard of a negro man killing a negro woman. Our negroes are not only better off as to physical comfort than free laborers, but their moral condition is better.

But abolish negro slavery, and how much of slavery still remains. Soldiers and sailors in Europe enlist for life; here, for five years. Are they not slaves who have not only sold their liberties, but their lives also? And they are worse treated than domestic slaves. No domestic affection and self-interest extend their aegis over them. No kind mistress, like a guardian angel, provides for them in health, tends them in sickness, and soothes their dying pillow. Wellington at Waterloo was a slave. He was bound to obey, or would, like admiral Byng, have been shot for gross misconduct, and might not, like a common laborer, quit his work at any moment. He had sold his liberty, and might not resign without the consent of his master, the king. The common laborer may quit his work at any moment, whatever his contract; declare that liberty is an inalienable right, and leave his employer to redress by a useless suit for damages. The highest and most honorable position on earth was that of the slave Wellington; the lowest, that of the free man who cleaned his boots and fed his hounds. The African cannibal, caught, christianized and enslaved, is as much elevated by slavery as was Wellington. The kind of slavery is adapted to the men enslaved. Wives and apprentices are slaves; not in theory only, but often in fact. Children are slaves to their parents, guardians and teachers. Imprisoned culprits are slaves. Lunatics and idiots are slaves also. Three-fourths of free society are slaves, no better treated, when their wants and capacities are estimated, than negro slaves. The masters in free society, or slave society, if they perform properly their duties, have more cares and less liberty than the slaves themselves. "In the sweat of thy face shalt thou earn thy bread!" made all men slaves, and such all *good men* continue to be.

Negro slavery would be changed immediately to some form of pconage, serfdom or villienage, if the negroes were sufficiently intelligent and provident to manage a farm. No one would have the labor and trouble of management, if his negroes would pay in hires and rents one-half what free tenants pay in rent in Europe. Every negro in the South would be soon liberated, if he would take liberty on the terms that white tenants hold it. The fact that he cannot enjoy liberty on such terms, seems conclusive that he is only fit to be a slave.

But for the assaults of the abolitionists, much would have been done ere this to regulate and improve Southern slavery. Our negro mechanics do not work so hard, have many more privileges and holidays, and are better fed and clothed than field hands, and are yet more valuable to their masters. The slaves of the South are cheated of their rights by the purchase of Northern manufactures which they could produce. Besides, if we would employ our slaves in the coarser processes of the mechanic arts and manufactures, such as brick making, getting and hewing timber for ships and houses, iron mining and smelting, coal mining, grading railroads and plank roads, in the manufacture of cotton, tobacco, &c., we would find a vent in new employments for their increase, more humane and more profitable than the vent afforded by new states and territories. The nice and finishing processes of manufactures and mechanics should be reserved for the whites, who only are fitted for them, and thus, by diversifying pursuits and cutting off dependence on the North, we might benefit and advance the interests of our whole population. Exclusive agriculture has depressed and impoverished the South. We will not here dilate on this topic, because we intend to make it the subject of a separate essay. Free trade doctrines, not slavery, have made the South agricultural and dependent, given her a sparse and ignorant population, ruined her cities, and expelled her people.

Would the abolitionists approve of a system of society that set white children free, and remitted them at the age of fourteen, males and females, to all the rights, both as to person and property, which belong to adults? Would it be criminal or praiseworthy to do so? Criminal, of course. Now, are the average of negroes equal in information, in native intelligence, in prudence or providence, to well-informed white children of fourteen? We who have lived with them for forty years, think not. The competition of the world would be too much for the children. They would be cheated out of their property and debased in their morals. Yet they would meet every where with sympathizing friends of their own color, ready to aid, advise and assist them. The negro would be exposed to the same competition and greater temptations, with no greater ability to contend with them, with these additional difficulties. He would be welcome nowhere; meet with thousands of enemies and no friends. If he went North, the white laborers would kick him and cuff him, and drive him out of employment. If he went to Africa, the savages would cook him and eat him. If he went to the West Indies, they would not let him in, or if they did, they would soon make of him a savage and idolater.

We have a further question to ask. If it be right and incumbent to subject children to the authority of parents and guardians, and idiots and lunatics to committees, would it not be equally right and incumbent to give the free negroes masters, until at least they arrive at years of discretion, which very few ever did or will attain? What is the difference between the authority of a parent and of a master? Neither pay wages, and each is entitled to the services of those subject to him. The father may not sell his child forever, but may hire him out till he is twenty-one. The free negro's master may also be restrained from selling. Let him stand in *loco parentis,* and call him papa instead of master. Look closely into slavery, and you will see nothing so hideous in it; or if you do, you will find plenty of it at home in its most hideous form.

The earliest civilization of which history gives account is that of Egypt. The negro was always in contact with that civilization. For four thousand years he has had opportunities of becoming civilized. Like the wild horse, he must be caught, tamed and domesticated. When his subjugation ceases he again runs wild, like the cattle on the Pampas of the South, or the horses on the prairies of the West. His condition in the West Indies proves this.

It is a common remark, that the grand and lasting architectural structures of antiquity were the results of slavery. The mighty and continued association of labor requisite to their construction, when mechanic art was so little advanced, and labor-saving processes unknown, could only have been brought about by a despotic authority, like that of the master over his slaves. It is, however, very remarkable, that whilst in taste and artistic skill the world seems to have been retrograding ever since the decay and abolition of feudalism, in mechanical invention and in great utilitarian operations requiring the wielding of immense capital and much labor, its progress has been unexampled. Is it because capital is more despotic in its authority over free laborers than Roman masters and feudal lords were over their slaves and vassals?

Free society has continued long enough to justify the attempt to generalize its phenomena, and calculate its moral and intellectual influences. It is obvious that, in whatever is purely utilitarian and material, it incites invention and stimulates industry. Benjamin Franklin, as a man and a philosopher, is the best exponent of the working of the system. His sentiments and his philosophy are low, selfish, atheistic and material. They tend directly to make man a mere "featherless biped," well-fed, well-clothed and comfortable, but regardless of his soul as "the beasts that perish."

Since the Reformation the world has as regularly been retrograding in whatever belongs to the departments of genius, taste and art, as it has been progressing in physical science and its application to mechanical construction. Medieval Italy rivalled if it did not surpass ancient Rome, in poetry, in sculpture, in painting, and many of the fine arts. Gothic architecture reared its monuments of skill and genius throughout Europe, till the 15th century; but Gothic architecture died with the Reformation. The age of Elizabeth was the Augustan age of England. The men who lived then acquired their sentiments in a world not yet deadened and vulgarized by puritanical cant and levelling demagoguism. Since then men have arisen who have been the fashion and the go for a season, but none have appeared whose names will descend to posterity. Liberty and equality made slower advances in France. The age of Louis XIV. was the culminating point of French genius and art. It then shed but a flickering and lurid light. Frenchmen are servile copyists of Roman art, and Rome had no art of her own. She borrowed from Greece; distorted and deteriorated what she borrowed; and France imitates and falls below Roman distortions. The genius of Spain disappeared with Cervantes; and now the world seems to regard nothing as desirable except what will make money and what costs money. There is not a poet, an orator, a sculptor, or painter in the world. The tedious elaboration necessary to all the productions of high art would be ridiculed in this money-making, utilitarian, charlatan age. Nothing now but what is gaudy and costly excites admiration. The public taste is debased.

But far the worst feature of modern civilization, which is the civilization of free society, remains to be exposed. Whilst labor-saving processes have probably lessened by one half, in the last century, the amount of work needed for comfortable support, the free laborer is compelled by capital and competition to work more than he ever did before, and is less comfortable. The organization of society cheats him of his earnings, and those earnings go to swell the vulgar pomp and pageantry of the ignorant millionaires, who are the only great of the present day. These reflections might seem, at first view, to have little connexion with negro slavery; but it is well for us of the South not to be deceived by the tinsel glare and glitter of free society, and to employ ourselves in doing our duty at home, and studying the past, rather than in insidious rivalry of the expensive pleasures and pursuits of men whose sentiments and whose aims are low, sensual and grovelling.

Human progress, consisting in moral and intellectual improvement, and there being no agreed and conventional standard weights or measures of moral and intellectual qualities and quantities, the question of progress can never be accurately decided. We maintain that man has not improved, because in all save the mechanic arts he reverts to the distant past for models to imitate, and he never imitates what he can excel.

We need never have white slaves in the South, because we have black ones. Our citizens, like those of Rome and Athens, are a privileged class. We should train and educate them to deserve the privileges and to perform the duties which society confers on them. Instead, by a low demagoguism depressing their self-respect by discourses on the equality of man, we had better excite their pride by reminding them that they do not fulfil the menial offices which white men do in other countries. Society does not feel the burden of providing for the few helpless paupers in the South. And we should recollect that here we have but half the people to educate, for half are negroes; whilst at the North the profess to educate all. It is in our power to spike this last gun of the abolitionists. We should educate all the poor. The abolitionists say that it is one of the necessary consequences of slavery that the poor are neglected. It was not so in Athens, and in Rome, and should not be so in the South. If we had less trade with and less dependence on the North, all our poor might be profitably and honorably employed in trades, professions and manufactures. Then we should have a rich and denser population. Yet we but marshal her in the way that she was going. The South is already aware of the necessity of a new policy, and has begun to act on it. Every day more and more is done for education, the mechanic arts, manufactures and internal improvements. We will soon be independent of the North.

We deem this peculiar question of negro slavery of very little importance. The issue is made throughout the world on the general subject of slavery in the abstract. The argument has commenced. One set of ideas will govern and control after awhile the civilized world. Slavery will every where be abolished, or every where be re-instituted. We think the opponents of practical, existing slavery, are estopped by their own admission; nay, that unconsciously, as socialists, they are the defenders and propagandists of slavery, and have furnished the only sound arguments on which its defence and justification can be rested. We have introduced the subject of negro slavery to afford us a better opportunity to disclaim the purpose of reducing the white man any where to the condition of negro slaves here. It would be very unwise and unscientific to govern white men as you would negroes. Every shade and variety of slavery has existed in the world. In some cases there has been much of legal regulation, much restraint of the master's authority; in others, none at all. The character of slavery necessary to protect the whites in Europe should be much milder than negro slavery, for slavery is only needed to protect the white man, whilst it is more necessary for the government of the negro even than for his protection. But even negro slavery should not be outlawed. We might and should have laws in Virginia, as in Louisiana, to make the master subject to presentment by the grand jury and to punishment, for any inhuman or improper treatment or neglect of his slave.

We abhor the doctrine of the "Types of Mankind;" first, because it is at war with scripture, which teaches us that the whole human race is descended from a common parentage; and, secondly, because it encourages and incites brutal masters to treat negroes, not as weak, ignorant and dependent brethren, but as wicked beasts, without the pale of humanity. The Southerner is the negro's friend, his only friend. Let no intermeddling abolitionist, no refined philosophy, dissolve this friendship.

Chapter XXIII. The Higher Law

In framing and revising the institutions and government of a nation, and in enacting its laws, sensible and prudent statesmen study carefully the will of God and designs of Providence, as revealed in Holy Writ, or as gathered from history and experience. "Truth is mighty, and will prevail," and laws in contravention of the great truths deducible from these sources, will become nugatory and inefficient. Yet whilst the law is on the statute book, every citizen is bound to respect and obey it, or else take the consequences of trespass, felony or treason. He may discuss the question, "Does the law coincide with the 'Higher Law'?" but he may not act on his conclusions if they be against the law.

Does slavery violate the Higher Law? Certainly not, if that Higher Law is to be found only in the Bible. Certainly not, if you throw aside the Bible, and infer what is right, proper, and natural, from the course of nature, the lessons of history, or the voice of experience. But consult the same sources for your Higher Law, and as certainly is free society a violation of the laws of Nature and the revealed will of God.

Chapter XXIV. Infidelity and Abolitionism

Every one who reads the newspapers must have observed that open-mouthed infidelity is never seen or heard in this country except in abolition meetings and conventions, and in women's rights conventicles. On such occasions some woman unsexes herself, and with Gorgon head and Harpy tongue pours out false and foul execrations against slavery and the Bible, aided by men with sharper tongues and duller courage than the women themselves. To this there is single exception. One pulpit in Boston is on the Sabbath made a rostrum whence an abolitionist fulminates contention and discord, and stirs up to bloodshed and murder.

Liberty, infidelity, and abolition, are three words conveying but one idea. Infidels who dispute the authority of God will not respect or obey the government of man. Abolitionists, who make war upon slavery, instituted by God and approved by Holy Writ, are in a fair way to denounce the Bible that stands in the way of the attainment of their purpose. Marriage is too much like slavery not to be involved in its fate; and the obedience of wives which the Bible inculcates, furnishes a new theme for infidelity in petticoats or in Bloomers to harp on. Slavery, marriage, religion, are the pillars of the social fabric. France felled them at a blow, and Paris and St. Domingo were crushed beneath the ruins of the edifice which they supported.

Frenchmen and Germans are generally infidels, agrarians and abolitionists. An Irish infidel, an Irish agrarian, or an Irish abolitionist, is scarcely to be found. No Irish woman ever disgraces her own sex, or affects the dress and manners of the opposite sex. The men of Erin are all brave, patriotic and religious; her women are

> "Chaste as the icicle
> That's curdled by the frost of purest snow,
> And hangs on Dian's temple."

This intimate connexion and dependence, of slavery, marriage and religion, we suggest as a subject for the investigation and reflection of the reader. If ever the abolitionists succeed in thoroughly imbuing the world with their doctrines and opinions, all religion, all government, all order, will be slowly but surely subverted and destroyed. Society can linger on for centuries without slavery; it cannot exist a day without religion. As an institution of government, religion is strictly within the scope of our work, and as such we treat of it.

For fear assaults upon us may weaken the force of our facts and arguments, we will take occasion more strictly to define our opinions as to government. We have ever, and still do belong to the Democratic party;—not, however, to the "let alone" and "largest liberty" wing of that party. We believe in the capacity of the people to govern, and would not deny them the opportunity to exercise that capacity. We think there is no danger from too much or too popular government, provided we avoid centralization, and distribute as much as possible to small localities powers of police and legislation. We would cherish and preserve all our *institutions* as they are, adding to them probably larger separate governmental powers to be vested in the people of each county. The cause of popular government is on the advance. The printing press, railroads, steamships and the telegraph afford opportunities for information, consultation and combination. But these agencies, which will make governments more popular, will at the same time render them more efficient, all-pervading, rigid and exact. Ancient Republicanism will supplant Laissez-faire Republicanism;—and ancient Republicanism we admire and prefer.

Cannibals All!

XXI. Negro Slavery

Until the lands of America are appropriated by a few, population becomes dense, competition among laborers active, employment uncertain, and wages low, the personal liberty of all the whites will continue to be a blessing. We have vast unsettled territories; population may cease to increase slowly, as in most countries, and many centuries may elapse before the question will be practically suggested, whether slavery to capital be preferable to slavery to human masters. But the negro has neither energy nor enterprise, and, even in our sparser population, finds, with his improvident habits, that his liberty is a curse to himself, and a greater curse to the society around him. These considerations, and others equally obvious, have induced the South to attempt to defend negro slavery as an exceptional institution, admitting, nay asserting, that slavery, in the general or in the abstract, is morally wrong, and against common right. With singular inconsistency, after making this admission, which admits away the authority of the Bible, of profane history, and of the almost universal practice of mankind— they turn round and attempt to bolster up the cause of negro slavery by these very exploded authorities. If we mean not to repudiate all divine, and almost all human authority in favor of slavery, we must vindicate that institution in the abstract.

To insist that a status of society, which has been almost universal, and which is expressly and continually justified by Holy Writ, is its natural, normal, and necessary status, under the ordinary circumstances, is on its face a plausible and probable proposition. To insist on less, is to yield our cause, and to give up our religion; for if white slavery be morally wrong, be a violation of natural rights, the Bible cannot be true. Human and divine authority do seem in the general to concur, in establishing the expediency of having masters and slaves of different races. The nominal servitude of the Jews to each other, in its temporary character, and no doubt in its mild character, more nearly resembled our wardship and apprenticeship, than ordinary domestic slavery. In very many nations of antiquity, and in some of modern times, the law has permitted the native citizens to become slaves to each other. But few take advantage of such laws; and the infrequency of the practice, establishes the general truth that master and slave should be of different national descent. In some respects, the wider the difference the better, as the slave will feel less mortified by his position. In other respects, it may be that too wide a difference hardens the hearts and brutalizes the feelings of both master and slave. The civilized man hates the savage, and the savage returns the hatred with interest. Hence, West India slavery of newly caught negroes is not a very humane, affectionate, or civilizing institution. Virginia negroes have become moral and intelligent. They love their master and his family, and the attachment is reciprocated. Still, we like the idle, but intelligent house-servants, better than the hard-used, but stupid outhands; and we like the mulatto better than the negro; yet the negro is generally more affectionate, contented and faithful.

The world at large looks on negro slavery as much the worst form of slavery; because it is only acquainted with West India slavery. Abolition never arose till negro slavery was instituted; and now abolition is only directed against negro slavery. There is no philanthropic crusade attempting to set free the white slaves of Eastern Europe and of Asia. The world, then, is prepared for the defence of slavery in the abstract—it is prejudiced only against negro slavery. These prejudices were in their origin well founded. The Slave Trade, the horrors of the Middle Passage, and West India slavery were enough to rouse the most torpid philanthropy.

But our Southern slavery has become a benign and protective institution, and our negroes are confessedly better off than any free laboring population in the world.

How can we contend that white slavery is wrong, whilst all the great body of free laborers are starving; and slaves, white or black, throughout the world, are enjoying comfort?

We write in the cause of Truth and Humanity, and will not play the advocate for master or for slave.

The aversion to negroes, the antipathy of race, is much greater at the North than at the South; and it is very probable that this antipathy to the person of the negro, is confounded with or generates hatred of the institution with which he is usually connected. Hatred to slavery is very generally little more than hatred of negroes.

There is one strong argument in favor of negro slavery over all other slavery: that he, being unfitted for the mechanic arts, for trade, and all skillful pursuits, leaves those pursuits to be carried on by the whites; and does not bring all industry into disrepute, as in Greece and Rome, where the slaves were not only the artists and mechanics, but also the merchants.

Whilst, as a general and abstract question, negro slavery has no other claims over other forms of slavery, except that from inferiority, or rather peculiarity, of race, almost all negroes require masters, whilst only the children, the women, the very weak, poor, and ignorant, &c., among the whites, need some protective and governing relation of this kind; yet as a subject of temporary, but worldwide importance, negro slavery has become the most necessary of all human institutions.

The African slave trade to America commenced three centuries and a half since. By the time of the American Revolution, the supply of slaves had exceeded the demand for slave labor, and the slaveholders, to get rid of a burden, and to prevent the increase of a nuisance, became violent opponents of the slave trade, and many of them abolitionists. New England, Bristol, and Liverpool, who reaped the profits of the trade, without suffering from the nuisance, stood out for a long time against its abolition. Finally, laws and treaties were made, and fleets fitted out to abolish it; and after a while, the slaves of most of South America, of the West Indies, and of Mexico were liberated. In the meantime, cotton, rice, sugar, coffee, tobacco, and other products of slave labor, came into universal use as necessaries of life. The population of Western Europe, sustained and stimulated by those products, was trebled, and that of the North increased tenfold. The products of slave labor became scarce and dear, and famines frequent. Now, it is obvious, that to emancipate all the negroes would be to starve Western Europe and our North. Not to extend and increase negro slavery, . . . with the extension and multiplication of free society, will produce much suffering. If all South America, Mexico, the West Indies, and our Union south of Mason and Dixon's line, of the Ohio and Missouri, were slaveholding, slave products would be abundant and cheap in free society; and their market for their merchandise, manufactures, commerce, &c., illimitable. Free white laborers might live in comfort and luxury on light work, but for the exacting and greedy landlords, bosses and other capitalists.

We must confess, that overstock the world as you will with comforts and with luxuries, we do not see how to make capital relax its monopoly—how to do aught but tantalize the hireling. Capital, irresponsible capital, begets, and ever will beget, the *immedicabile vulnus** of so-called Free Society. It invades every recess of domestic life, infects its food, its clothing, its drink, its very atmosphere, and pursues the hireling, from the hovel to the poor-house, the prison and the grave. Do what he will, go where he will, capital pursues and persecutes him. "Hæret lateri lethalis arundo!"†

Capital supports and protects the domestic slave; taxes, oppresses and persecutes the free laborer.

*"Irreparable injury."
†"The lethal arrow clings to her side." Virgil, *Aeneid*, IV, 73

17

JOSIAH C. NOTT

Instincts of Races

1866

Although slavery ended in 1865, the ideology of slavery lingered. Josiah C. Nott (1804–1873) was a well-known physician based in Mobile, Alabama. He published widely in medical journals and was in some ways a sophisticated scientist. He developed the theory that yellow fever was transmitted through an intermediate host. Dr. Walter Reed would later use Nott's work to solve how both yellow fever and malaria are

Josiah C. Nott, M.D., *Instincts of Races* (New Orleans: L. Graham, 1866).

spread. Nott was also a prominent ethnologist and racial theorist. He argued that blacks and whites were created separately and were in fact separate species. He set out most of his theories on the origins of the races in Types of Mankind, *published in 1854. His* Instincts of Races *illustrates how proslavery thought continued beyond emancipation. Here Nott argues that blacks can barely survive in freedom and are incapable of being productive or contributing to society as free people. He uses the examples of the British West Indies, Haiti, and Liberia, as well as data from the antebellum North, to support his conclusions that as a distinct race, blacks cannot thrive, or perhaps even survive, in freedom. In essence, Nott, the unreconstructed slaveowner, continues his antebellum theories to condemn emancipation and to set out what will ultimately become the justification for segregation and race discrimination in the last third of the nineteenth century. Ironically, Nott's work illustrates how the proslavery argument, which was ultimately based on racism, continued to shape American thought and society long after slavery itself ceased to exist.*

Man *(genus homo)*, has, by common consent, been placed by naturalists at the head of the animal kingdom, and although he has the means of protecting himself to a great extent, by clothing, fire, and houses, from extremes of heat and cold, he cannot abstract himself wholly from those climatic influences which modify the species of other genera. . . .

The natural history of *Man* has been the great stumbling-block to zoölogists—some contending that all the Races of Men, are but *varieties* springing from one original pair (Adam and Eve); while others contend that the Races are of diverse origin, and were created, like the species of other genera, in different divisions of the earth, forming parts of separate *Zoological Provinces.*

This subject is one of great interest both to the Naturalist and Theologian, but has little practical bearing on the points here to be discussed, and will therefore be left aside.

It is curious to see the perfect parallel which the genus *Canis* (Dog) runs with that of Man. The dawn of history finds the uttermost parts of the earth covered with different races of men, and every where, these human types have been associated with one or more races of dogs equally distinct from each other. . . .

It is now demonstrated from the monuments of Nineveh and Egypt, that the races of the genus *homo*, and those of the family of the

Canidae (Dogs), were as distinct in type 3500 years ago as they now are, and that no causes in operation from that date to the present, have been able to change one form into another. On those monuments, contemporary with Moses, and Joseph, and Abraham, are to be seen by thousands the faithful portraits of Egyptians, Berbers, Abyssinians, Nubians, Negroes, Arabs, Jews, Mongols and Assyrians, presenting the same lineaments which those races around the Mediterranean preserve to the present day. In like manner are preserved portraits of the Canines. The Mastiff is beautifully portrayed by Layard in his work on Nineveh. The Greyhound, Turnspit, Coachdog, Hound, other varieties of domestic dog, together with the Wolf, Jackal, Hyena and Fox on the monuments of Egypt. The Bulldog is well represented in Rome, and most of the dogs now known in Europe were familiar to Greeks and Romans. When America was discovered, the Indians were found in possession of several new races of dogs. The Dingo was found in Australia, and so with all newly discovered countries.

In Europe and Asia, as well as northern Africa, which were occupied by the highest races of men, the types of men, through incessant wars, commerce and migrations have been greatly blended and confused. So with their companions, the dogs—these have been intermixed, until no doubt many original types have been lost, and an endless variety of curs appear in their stead. . . .

It being conceded then that the Races of Men, and of Canines, if not distinct species, are at least *permanent varieties,* we propose next to inquire whether the *phisique* of each race has not a kindred *moral* inseparable from it; and whether the organic structure can be changed without altering its functions?

Is it not a law of nature, that every *permanent* animal form, call it by what name you like, carries with its physical type a *moral* of its own, which cannot be obliterated, changed, or transferred to another, so long as the *physique* stands? Can any reflecting man doubt that the instincts of the Bulldog, Greyhound, Pointer, or Hound, are inseparable from his anatomical structure; or believe that one can be educated to perform the duties of another? These races of dogs, all over the globe, where the climate permits them to live and prosper, so long as the *blood is kept pure,* remain substantially the same in *moral* and *physique.* A Bulldog is a Bulldog, a Greyhound a Greyhound, from generation to generation, and from the St. Lawrence to Cape Horn.

Why is it that dog-fanciers lay so much stress on *pure blood?* Does not an impure cross destroy the value of a stock, and its reliability for breeding purposes? An English breeder will not touch a horse or dog that has a drop of impure blood; because he knows that the stain cannot be washed out in many generations—the impure cross will crop out eight or ten generations after, or later, as many examples prove. So adhesive is the stain, that a mare of Lord Derby that had a colt by a Zebra, when bred afterwards for several successive years to thorough bred horses, had every colt more or less striped like the Zebra, which had been the father of the first colt only. The Greyhound has little sense of smell and pursues his game by sight and speed. The Hound on the contrary depends on smell and endurance. The Bulldog is useless for hunting purposes. The Pointer, Terrier, Shepherd's dog, each has its peculiar instincts and uses. These qualities are retained so long as the race is kept pure, and when two are crossed, an intermediate type is produced partaking of the *physique* and *moral* of both parents.

Do not the same general laws which govern the rest of the animal kingdom apply with equal force to Man? Has not the Almighty placed his stamp, intellectual and physical, upon the races of men just as strongly as he has upon the species or varieties of other genera? We have already stated, what the works of Champollion, Rosellini, Lepsius, and other hieroglyphic scholars, so fully prove, that the same races of men have been living around the Mediterranean for 3500 years. Since the literature of China and India have been laid open to us, we have the evidence that Mongol, Malay and Hindoo types are quite as old. America was found at its discovery covered with millions of red men of great antiquity. Australia and Oceanica have also their races of men and animals unlike all others. The *permanence* of these human types, I repeat, is no longer a point of dispute; so long as the physical causes which have for ages been acting on them, remain unchanged, they remain indelible.

It being conceded, then, that the *physique* of the Races of men is *permanent* through ages past and to come, the next question to be examined is the permanence of the *moral* which has accompanied each type in by-gone ages. If man is to be judged by analogies drawn from the animal kingdom, it would require little argument to settle the question in the affirmative. Every species, whether of the *Equidae*, the *Canidae*, the *Felines*, or other, has its own anatomical structure—its own physiological laws—its own instincts and mode of thought. The *moral* is quite as characteristic as the *physique*.

The Indo-European Races have, through wars, commerce, and migrations, been so blended, that old types have, to a great extent, been lost, and few *permanent varieties* can be identified in Europe, beyond Jews and Gipsies, and even these are far from being pure. When, however, we leave these migrating Races, the law of nature stands out in bold relief. Place beside each other an Arab, Egyptian, Anglo-Saxon, Negro, Hottentot, Mongul, Malay, Australian, and American Indian, and you have human types as old, as distinct, as permanent in *physique* and *moral,* as the canines and other species.

No one will deny that the animals nearest in the scale to man, as apes, dogs, and the elephant, are endowed with a degree of intelligence above mere instinct; nor is it less true that man to a great extent is a creature of *instinct.* If Races were guided by reason alone, each one would not possess the individuality which now characterizes it. The *instincts,* not only of Races, but of individuals, or, as a phrenologist would say, the *bumps,* drive reason aside or override it in the great majority of mankind. One man, generally, reasons well about the conduct of another, and can give very good advice, while violating the precepts he lays down. The first law of nature is *self-preservation,* which exerts a controlling influence all through life. Within an hour after a child is born, it instinctively sucks—it soon cries to make wants known. These and other animal instincts precede the first rudiments of mind, for whose action the senses have, as yet, furnished no materials. . . .

Suppose we should place a hundred children of each race, Anglo-Saxons, Monguls, Malays and Negroes, upon separate islands, and cause them to be reared, without any instruction, by deaf-mutes, to adult age, what would be the inevitable result? Does any one doubt, that like Greyhounds, Pointers, Bulldogs and Hounds, each would follow out its natural instincts? Each race would form its language, its mode of thought, and, in time, would work out a social organization peculiar to itself. Nay, more, what has been the result in our country of educating Whites, Blacks and Indians at the same schools? Have the instincts of the Indian or Negro been changed? The full blooded Indian has invariably wandered off to the forest and resumed the habits of his race. He is essentially a wild animal by nature, untamable, unimitative, uncivilizable. The Negro, on the contrary, is imitative, social, easily domesticated, and, as long as kept in subordination to a higher race, will ape to a certain extent its manners and customs. But the Negro rises only to a certain point of imitation—his intellect permits no approach to civilization but that of imitation, and, as soon as the race is thrown back upon itself and separated from the whites, as in the West Indies, it becomes savage.

The instincts of race are strongly illustrated in the Chinese. They have had their civil wars, and so called revolutions, for thousands of years, but these all result in mere change of rulers. A revolution there is like a pebble dropped in the ocean—not a dimple is left behind. The same form of government, the same mode of thought, the same social organization, has remained stationary for ages, while Europe has been changing like a chameleon, from the mongrel character of its population and progressive spirit. The semi-civilization of China and India and the savagism of the red men of America, have remained stereotyped for ages, while the Gipsies have been pitching their tents in the four quarters of the globe, resisting all climates, and all moral influences which philanthropy could bring to bear on them. No human power can change the fiat of the Almighty. He brought the races of men and animals into existence. He gave them moral and physical laws, and all the powers of the Freedmen's Bureau, or "gates of hell cannot prevail against them."

The Caucasian races have been the only truly progressive races of history. They have the largest heads, the highest instincts, the most comprehensive intellects have, in all ages, stood ahead of all others in civilization and have had no competitors in literature, art and science.

It would seem that "reason, the proud prerogative of man," is to a great extent subservient to the *instincts of races.* In all departments of knowledge into which *speculation* can enter, human reason runs wild. In religion, mental and moral philosophy, the science of government, law, political economy, etc., the attainment of absolute or fixed laws is hopeless. The world consequently makes comparatively little progress in morals, and vice simply changes its form. What is fashionable in one age, is not in another.

The only real progress made by mankind, is in the exact sciences, as Chemistry, Botany, Astronomy, Mathematics, Natural Philosophy, Mechanics, etc., which is almost Godlike, and in this the Negro, Indian, and other inferior races, *take no part whatever.* It is humiliating to look on the infirmities even of genius. Lord Bacon in morals was beneath contempt. Napoleon, Alexander, Caesar, Frederick the Great, were only great highway robbers, who trampled morals, religion and everything under foot to attain their ends.

How can any thoughtful American doubt the overruling influence of *instinct* in races? Can more conclusive facts be asked, than those presented to our view every day by the Whites, Negroes and Indians in our midst? . . .

To my mind, the foregoing conclusions with regard to the various instincts and intellectual characters of races are so self-evident, that I feel as if a labored argument on the subject would be an insult to the understanding of the reader. A few centuries, or even fifty years ago, before the various Freedmen's Bureaux had fairly commenced their destruction of Indians and Negroes, an array of facts and arguments might, with propriety, have been called for; but the colonial history of Spain, France and England, as well as the history of missions in Asia, Africa and Oceanica, tell the tale of Races.

The discussion, thus far, interests more particularly the naturalist and moral philosopher, but the practical end to which I have been aiming, is *the question of Negro labor at the South,* on which hangs the future prosperity of the Cotton States and the destiny of the Negro race. We see the remark quoted every day that history (of the white race) repeats itself, and there is no greater truism; but is the same law applicable to the Negro race? In my letter to General Howard, I asserted that *the Negro is, by instinct, opposed to agricultural labor, and will not till the soil for wages,* an assertion which is proven by the history of the race in and out of Africa.

The negro tribes have had undisturbed possession of the immense continent of Africa for thousands of years, except that portion north of the desert of Sahara—bordering the Nile and the Mediterranean; and yet the black population, geographers tell us, does not reach 100,000,000, while China and India with vastly less territory have respectively 400,000,000 and 200,000,000. Why this enormous difference? It is simply because the negro *is not* an *agricultural* race, while the Chinese and Hindoos *are* intensely agricultural. China and India are gardens from one extreme to the other, and all the food that can be made, *is* made out of the soil. There is reason to believe that those countries reached their maximum of population a thousand or two years ago, and could not increase because the soil could feed no more. In like manner, the black population of Africa probably reached its maximum quite as far back, not because the agricultural resources of the country were exhausted, but because the people will not cultivate cereals at all, and depend on the natural products of the country, such as yams, cocoa-nuts, plantains, bananas, etc. Nature provides on that continent food enough for seventy or eighty millions, and beyond this, there can be no more population, as there is no food for more.

So too, with the American Indian—he depended upon the scanty products of the chase, to the exclusion of agriculture, and had probably reached his maximum of population at the time the continent was discovered by Columbus.

North America in a few centuries will have a population of more than 1,000,000,000, and Africa might have the same, if the negro could be driven to agricultural labor.

The same inertness which characterizes the Negro physically characterizes him intellectually. No Negro ever invented an alphabet; and from the Great Desert to the Cape of Good Hope, no ruined temple, no crumbling monument, no work of art, no relic of science, no fragment of recorded history, point to any spot in this wide expanse as the cradle or grave of civilization.

The Negro has no excuse, but *that of race,* for the want of agriculture, art and science; for he has been, from the time of Moses to the present day, in constant intercourse with Egypt, the great granary of antiquity and fountain, from which the civilization of Palestine, Assyria, and Greece flowed. So much for the history of the Negro in his native land; let us now follow him into other countries.

When the late civil war broke out in the United States, there were 4,000,000 negroes in that country, about 500,000 of whom were free. The slave portion was not only the best cared for, most comfortable, contented, and increasing laboring population in the world, but was more intelligent, more moral, more christianized, more useful in the progress of civilization than this race had ever been in its native or in foreign lands, in freedom. These facts are fully borne out by all statistics, and will not be controverted by any unprejudiced mind.

What, on the other hand, was the condition of the 500,000 of the freedmen? The professional philanthropists had done everything in their power to educate, to humanize, to stimulate them to mental and physical activity, but all without result. No one can call the name of a full blooded negro in this country that has ever reached mediocrity in intellect—not one has made a discovery in science, an invention in the mechanic arts, written or spoken a line that has been preserved in print. Worse than all this, they have utterly abandoned all agricultural labor, for which they are well suited, and are either dying from the effects of indolence or occupied about towns as boot blacks, scavengers, waiters in hotels and steamboats, and other positions subordinate to the whites. I have never known a free negro family in the United States to settle on a farm and till the soil successfully from year to year. He will sometimes, driven by dire necessity, cultivate a little garden spot to avoid starvation, but his immediate wants are poorly supplied, and he never accumulates property by agriculture.

What has been the history of the colony of Liberia, on which so much sentiment, so much thought, so much energy, and so much money have been spent? Missionaries and school-masters have done their best; and at the end of half a century, the experiment has proved such a dead failure, that it is now talked of as a dream of misdirected philanthrophy. . . .

The limits of our essay will not permit additional examples or arguments on the *permanency* of human types; but it would be useless to attempt further argument with one who doubts, even after these few well authenticated facts. Nor, if it be admitted that the physical type, instincts, habits and intellect of the Negro have been the same for three thousand years, is it anything short of cruelty and folly for the Freedmen's Bureau to attempt to change this work of the Almighty. "Can the Ethiopian change his skin, or the leopard his spots," is the language of Scripture, and proclaims a physical law over which man has no control. . . .

The object has been to show from the physical and civil history of mankind, that the unadulterated Races, such as the Whites, the Negroes, the Mongols, and American Indians are *"Permanent Varieties,"* possessing moral and physical traits which are unchangeable from any known causes, so long as the race is kept pure, to say the least, during the lifetime of a nation—that each type has its peculiar instincts and adaptation, which cannot be obliterated by climate or Freedmen's Bureaux—and that governments can never legislate wisely, without giving due consideration to these important facts. . . .

The teachings of Ethnology have been fully vindicated in the history of the American Indians, and it requires no prophetic vision to see that our country is destined soon to complete the sad story of negro slavery and negro emancipation, so well elucidated by the experience of the West India Islands.

Dr. Franklin was the leader, backed by a number of the best and wisest men of Pennsylvania, of a benevolent association in Philadelphia, whose object was to *"form a plan for the promotion of industry, intelligence and morality among the free blacks."*

Its utter failure is shown in the report of another benevolent association, viz, the "Boston Prison-discipline Society," forty-seven years after, in its first annual report, in 1826, which shows by statistics, that from one-third to one-half of the convicts in the prisons at the North were free blacks and mulattoes, though the colored population formed but a small portion of the whole. This report says, "The first cause existing in society, of the frequency and increase of crime, is the *degraded character of the colored population.* The facts which are gathered from the Penitentiaries, show how great a proportion of the convicts are colored, even in those States where the colored population is small, and prove most strikingly the connection between ignorance and vice." The report might have added, that all efforts at educating the negroes to any useful extent, in Africa and America, had failed, and there has been no improvement in their prison or almshouse statistics from the time of the first emancipation set in Pennsylvania to the present day.

The Colonization Society, which was put in operation by some of our ablest and most patriotic men, is but an outgrowth of this emancipation failure.

It became evident that the idle and vicious negro population were becoming an incubus on our society, and that the attempt to improve their morals and habits of industry was hopeless. It was moreover evident that there was an antagonism of races unfriendly to the progress of the blacks while among us; and it was therefore thought best to send them back to Africa, where their native clime "liberty, equality and fraternity," together with the fostering care of philanthropic societies, missionaries, etc., would all combine to give them such advantages as no infant colony ever had before. But what has been the result? Let the utter failure of Liberia tell the tale. So signal had been the failure of abolitionism in benefiting either the blacks or the whites, that the progress of its party was stayed for a time, until, as Mr. Seward tells us, they at last had reared "a generation educated to hate slavery." They cried, but no one listened. They expostulated, but the public heeded them not. The freed negroes of the North were a standing monument to the folly of abolitionism. They had not progressed, or shown themselves active, enterprising members of society. They would black boots, whitewash, and do other menial offices, and they would hold conventions and pass ridiculous resolutions, but as *for clearing up lands and settling themselves in independent circumstances, they would not.* In 1852 Gerrit Smith, who has done more for freed blacks than any other man, for he gave all who would accept them, free homes on his lands, complained in a letter to Governor Hunt "that the most of them preferred *to rot, both physically and morally,* in cities, rather than become farmers or mechanics in the country." His own experiment with them resulted in signal failure. Even Horace Greel[e]y, in a moment of apparent forgetfulness, declared in the *Tribune,* September 22d, 1855, that "nine-tenths of the free blacks have no idea of setting themselves to work except as the hirelings or servitors of white men; no idea of building a church or other serious enterprise, except through beggary of the whites. *As a class, the blacks are indolent, improvident, servile and licentious.*"

The free colored population before the war were—in New England, 23,021; in New York, 50,000; in the little State of Maryland, 84,000!; in Pennsylvania, 46,000. Altogether the free colored population of the United States was about half a million; and how, let us ask, were they employed? No where regularly in agricultural labor! . . .

I might thus go on and fill a volume with such evidence from *antislavery authorities,* but it could add nothing to the strength of the argument, and I fear that I have already wearied the patience of the Medical reader, who does not look, in a Journal of Medical Science, for material of this description; but I could not otherwise illustrate the leading point in view, viz., *the instinctive disinclination of the negro to agricultural labor.*

In a preceding part of this article, I have given the faithful portraits of negroes from the ancient monuments of Egypt, dating back 1500 years B.C., and it would be an easy matter to add many more, with facts in abundance, to carry the existence of negro races one or two thousand years further back. The negro then has remained for at least 3500 years what God made him, and Exeter Halls and Freedmen's Bureaux cannot change his type. His black skin, woolly head, anatomical structure, small brain, inferior intellect, and *instinctive dislike to agricultural labor,* have characterized the race through this long lapse of time, and will continue to do so, until the Creator, in his wisdom, shall order otherwise.

I have none but the kindest feeling towards the Freedmen, and have perhaps done them as many real kindnesses as any member of the Freedmen's Bureau; but I shall continue to oppose all utopian ideas and schemes, which must end in anything but benefit to them.

A Slavery Chronology
(1619–1870)

1619 The first Africans come to the British colonies. Sold as indentured servants, some become free.

1660–1661 Virginia's assembly, the House of Burgesses, begins to pass laws regulating slavery.

1700 Samuel Sewell, a Massachusetts lawyer and judge, publishes *The Selling of Joseph,* the first American attack on slavery.

1701 John Saffin publishes *A True and Particular Narrative by Way of Vindication of the Author's Dealing with the Prosecution of His Negro Man Servant,* a defense of slavery and an answer to *The Selling of Joseph.*

1708 South Carolina colony has a slave majority population.

1712 A slave conspiracy is uncovered in New York City.

1739 The Stono Rebellion takes place in South Carolina.

1772 The Court of King's Bench in London rules in *Somerset v. Stewart* that a slave may not be held in England against his will.

1775 The American Revolution begins.

1776 The Declaration of Independence declares that "all men are created equal." The declaration does not deal with slavery directly but does contain a clause attacking the king for emancipating slaves and arming them to fight against the colonists.

1780 The Massachusetts constitution ends slavery in the state.

Pennsylvania passes the first "gradual emancipation statute." Under this law, no new slaves can be brought into the state, and the children of all existing slaves are free after serving an indenture.

1783 Jefferson writes *Notes on the State of Virginia* in which he implicitly defends slavery on racial grounds.

1784 Connecticut and Rhode Island pass gradual emancipation statutes.

1787 Delegates to the U.S. Constitutional Convention debate the relationship of slavery to the new system of government; South Carolina delegates defend slavery as justified by history, economics, and necessity.

1793 Congress passes the first fugitive slave law.

1799 New York passes a gradual emancipation statute.

1800 The Gabriel Prosser Rebellion is uncovered in Richmond, Virginia.

1803 The United States purchases Louisiana from France, setting the stage for future debates over slavery in the territories.

Ohio enters the Union as a free state.

1804 New Jersey passes a gradual emancipation statute.

The independent Republic of Haiti, the first nation in the New World governed by blacks, is established.

1808 The United States bans the importation of new slaves from Africa; the ban is inconsistently enforced until 1861.

1816 The American Colonization Society is established.

1817 New York passes a law ending all slavery in the state on July 4, 1827.

1819–1820 Debate over the admission of Missouri into the Union as a slave state sparks divisive debates in Congress over the value and importance of slavery.

1820 The United States defines the illegal importation of slaves from Africa as piracy.

Slavery is banned in territories north and west of Missouri under the Missouri Compromise.

1821 Missouri is admitted to the Union as a slave state.

1822 South Carolina discovers Denmark Vesey's plot to overthrow slavery in that state.

1823 South Carolina authorities persist in arresting and incarcerating free blacks who visit the state despite the assertion by a federal court asserting that this violates the Constitution. South Carolina authorities claim it is necessary to protect slavery in the state.

1831 Abolitionist William Lloyd Garrison begins to publish his newspaper, *The Liberator,* which marks the beginning of the abolitionist movement.

Nat Turner, a Virginia slave, leads the bloodiest slave rebellion in U.S. history.

1831–1832 The Virginia legislature debates and rejects a bill to consider the gradual abolition of slavery.

1832–1833 South Carolina's attempts to nullify a federal tariff lead to the national Nullification Crisis and are seen as a prelude for secession.

1835 The House of Representatives adopts the first "gag rule" to prevent the reading of antislavery petitions on floor of the House.

1837 John C. Calhoun asserts on the floor of the Senate that slavery is a "positive good."

1842 The Supreme Court, in *Prigg v. Pennsylvania,* upholds the federal fugitive slave law of 1793 and holds that no state can pass any laws to require a trial or other legal proceeding before the removal of an alleged fugitive slave.

1845 The United States annexes Texas and admits it to the Union.

1846 The United States declares war on Mexico. The war ends in 1848, with the United States acquiring vast territories in the West and Southwest, which leads to new debates over slavery in the territories.

1850 The Compromise of 1850 is passed. It allows slavery in new territories acquired from Mexico and creates a new, and much harsher, fugitive slave law.

1852 *Uncle Tom's Cabin* is published; it infuriates the South, where most states ban its sale.

1854 The Kansas-Nebraska Act repeals the ban on slavery in most of the Western territories. This proslavery victory in Congress leads to the creation of the Republican party in the North.

1855 David Christy publishes the proslavery volume *Cotton Is King.*

1857 Chief Justice Roger B. Taney writes the majority opinion in *Dred Scott v. Sandford,* holding that slavery is protected by the U.S. Constitution and that a ban on slavery in the territories is unconstitutional.

1858 James Henry Hammond gives the "mudsill speech" in the U.S. Senate.

President James Buchanan tries, and fails, to force Congress to admit Kansas as a slave state.

Abraham Lincoln and Stephen A. Douglas debate slavery and other issues during their U.S. Senate race in Illinois.

1859 Abolitionist John Brown leads a raid at Harpers Ferry, Virginia, in a failed attempt to ignite a slave rebellion in the United States.

1860 Lincoln is elected president after promising to stop the spread of slavery into the territories.

South Carolina adopts an ordinance of secession.

1861 The Confederate States of America is formed. Vice President Alexander Stephens declares that slavery is the "cornerstone" of the Confederacy.

1862 Lincoln issues a preliminary emancipation proclamation, and the United States begins to enroll blacks in the army.

1863 The Emancipation Proclamation is issued, setting the stage for the end of slavery.

1865   Congress passes the Thirteenth Amendment, ending slavery, and sends it to the states for ratification.

The Civil War ends.

The Thirteenth Amendment is ratified, ending slavery throughout the United States.

1865–1866   Most former slave states pass harsh "black codes" restricting the civil rights of ex-slaves, in effect implementing proslavery theory in the postslavery world.

1866   In response to the "black codes," Congress passes the Civil Rights Act of 1866 and the Fourteenth Amendment, which guarantees the rights of former slaves.

1868   The states ratify the Fourteenth Amendment, making all people, including former slaves, citizens of the United States and promising them "equal protection of the law."

1870   The states ratify the Fifteenth Amendment, which prohibits discrimination in voting on the basis of race or previous condition of servitude.

Questions for Consideration

1. Some scholars suggest that the excerpts from Thomas Jefferson are not "proslavery" but actually show his hostility to slavery. What do you think? Is it possible to offer a proslavery argument while at the same time disliking slavery and wishing it did not exist?

2. Why does John C. Calhoun argue that slavery is a "positive good"? Whom does he claim benefits from slavery?

3. Edmund Ruffin bases much of his proslavery argument on the difficulties encountered by free workers. Is his argument fair? Does the exploitation of free workers legitimize slavery?

4. Thomas R. R. Cobb seems to argue that slavery is legitimate because free blacks suffer. But we might assert that this is not a strong argument in favor of slavery but merely an argument in favor of better treatment of free blacks. How might Cobb respond to this assertion?

5. James Henry Hammond argues that blacks and slaves form a natural "mudsill" for his society. Does every society need a mudsill? Must there always be a social class on the bottom? If so, then is Hammond correct in implying that the lowest class in society *must* be suppressed?

6. Alexander Stephens declares that slavery is the "cornerstone" of the Confederacy. Do you think this statement undermines the credibility of the Confederacy or makes it stronger?

7. The religious defenders of slavery claimed that the Bible supports slavery, that God ordained slavery, and that God created Africans to be the slaves of whites. Are these arguments unreasonable? How would one counter them? How have such arguments affected our modern views of religion and race?

8. How did judges and legal theorists like Chief Justice Roger B. Taney, Thomas R. R. Cobb, and Chief Justice Thomas Ruffin of North Carolina use law and legal theory to defend slavery? Are there inconsistencies between the theory of law set out in *State v. Mann* and Cobb's notions of how the law of slavery should operate? While all three of these authors discuss law and the Constitution, what is at the heart of their defense of slavery?

9. Samuel A. Cartwright comes to us as a scientist, observing and reporting on what he has seen. How do you respond to his arguments? Apply what you know of modern scientific reasoning to his observations.

10. Samuel Cartwright, William J. Grayson, George Fitzhugh, and Josiah C. Nott all stress the importance of race for defending slavery. How do they differ in their approaches? Are they consistent with other writings in this volume? Would Thomas Jefferson's writings, for example, work with those of Nott? Is the speech by James Hammond or the lecture by Edmund Ruffin consistent with the work of Grayson or Fitzhugh? What counterarguments can you think of to these writings?

Selected Bibliography

Barnes, Gilbert Hobbs. *The Anti-Slavery Impulse, 1830–1844.* New York: Appleton-Century, 1933.

Craven, Avery O. *Edmund Ruffin, Southerner: A Study in Secession.* Baton Rouge: Louisiana State University Press, 1966.

Curtis, Michael Kent. *Free Speech, "The People's Darling Privilege": Struggles for Freedom of Expression in American History.* Durham, N.C.: Duke University Press, 2000.

Daley, John Patrick. *When Slavery Was Called Freedom: Evangelicalism, Pro-Slavery, and the Causes of the Civil War.* Lexington: University Press of Virginia, 2000.

Davis, David Brion. *The Problem of Slavery in the Age of Revolution, 1770–1823.* Ithaca, N.Y.: Cornell University Press, 1975.

Davis, David Brion. *The Problem of Slavery in Western Civilization.* Ithaca, N.Y.: Cornell University Press, 1964.

Donald, David. "The Proslavery Argument Reconsidered." *Journal of Southern History* 37 (Feb. 1971): 3–18.

Eaton, Clement. *The Mind of the Old South.* Baton Rouge: Louisiana State University Press, 1964.

Faust, Drew Gilpin. *The Ideology of Slavery.* Baton Rouge: Louisiana State University Press, 1981.

Faust, Drew Gilpin. *James Henry Hammond and the Old South: A Design for Mastery.* Baton Rouge: Louisiana State University Press, 1982.

Faust, Drew Gilpin. *A Sacred Circle: The Dilemma of the Intellectual in the Old South, 1840–1860.* Baltimore: Johns Hopkins University Press, 1977.

Fehrenbacher, Don E. *The Slaveholding Republic.* New York: Oxford University Press, 2001.

Finkelman, Paul, ed. *Proslavery Thought, Ideology, and Politics.* New York: Garland, 1989.

Finkelman, Paul. *Slavery and the Founders: Race and Liberty in the Age of Jefferson.* 2d. ed. Armonk, N.Y.: M. E. Sharpe, 2001.

Finkelman, Paul. "Thomas R. R. Cobb and the Law of Negro Slavery." *Roger Williams Law Review* 5 (1999): 75–115.

Franklin, John Hope. *The Militant South.* Cambridge, Mass.: Harvard University Press, 1956.

Freehling, Alison Goodyear. *Drift toward Dissolution: The Virginia Slavery Debate of 1831–32.* Baton Rouge: Louisiana State University Press, 1982.

Genovese, Eugene D. *The World the Slaveholders Made: Two Essays in Interpretation.* New York: Pantheon, 1969.

Greenberg, Kenneth. *Masters and Statesmen: The Political Culture of American Slavery.* Baltimore: Johns Hopkins University Press, 1985.

Horsman, Reginald. *Josiah C. Nott of Mobile: Southerner, Physician, and Racial Theorist.* Baton Rouge: Louisiana State University Press, 1987.

Jenkins, William Sumner. *The Pro-Slavery Argument in the Old South.* Chapel Hill: University of North Carolina Press, 1935.

Kolchin, Peter. "In Defense of Servitude: American Proslavery and Russian Proserfdom Arguments, 1760–1860." *American Historical Review* 85 (1980): 809–27.

McKitrick, Eric L. *Slavery Defended: The Views of the Old South.* Englewood Cliffs, N.J.: Prentice-Hall, 1963.

Miller, William Lee. *Arguing about Slavery.* New York: Knopf, 1996.

Nye, Russell B. *Fettered Freedom: Civil Liberties and the Slavery Controversy, 1830–1860.* East Lansing: Michigan State University Press, 1949.

Stanton, William. *The Leopard's Spots: Scientific Attitudes towards Race in America, 1815–1859.* Chicago: University of Chicago Press, 1960.

Takaki, Ronald A. *Pro-Slavery Crusade: The Agitation to Reopen the African Slave Trade.* New York: Free Press, 1971.

Tise, Larry. *Proslavery: A History of the Defense of Slavery in America, 1701–1840.* Athens: University of Georgia Press, 1987.

Index

abolitionism
  Calhoun's response to, 54–60
  Constitution and, 4
  Declaration of Independence and, 19–20
  as denunciation of religion, 197–98
  growth of abolition societies, 18
  plight of African Americans and, 192–93, 195–96, 210–11
Abraham (biblical patriarch), 66, 101, 108, 109–11, 124–27
Adams, John Quincy, 2
adultery
  Biblical definition of, 116–17
  slave marriage and, 116–21
African Americans. *See also* free blacks; race; racial inferiority arguments; slaves
  anatomy, 36–37, 158–63, 168
  appropriateness of slavery for, 86–88, 90–92, 156, 189–92, 198–201
  aptitude of, 163
  artistic abilities, 50–51
  benefits of northern climate for, 170–71
  benefits of slavery for, 147, 173–87, 188–89, 191, 199–201
  bravery of, 50
  characteristics of, 49–51, 75–76, 86–88, 147–56
  character strengths, 153–54
  childlike nature of, 160–61, 171, 190
  citizenship of, 133–42
  colonization outside the United States, 3, 21–22, 48–49, 192–93
  Constitution and, 133–42
  cultural achievements of, 160, 208
  Declaration of Independence and, 1, 19–20, 37–39, 136, 138
  diseases of, 36, 80, 148, 157, 163–73
  domestication of, 147, 154, 204–5
  education of, 105–7, 139
  exercise and mental capacity in, 160
  inability to sue in U.S. courts, 136
  as inferior race, 5, 20–21, 22, 36–37, 39–40

  instincts of, 205–11
  lasciviousness, 154
  mental capacity, 148–52, 159, 169–73, 191–92
  music and, 51, 159
  passivity of, 153–54
  physical adaptation to servitude, 148
  physical characteristics, 147–52
  population growth, 70–71, 154–55
  reasoning ability, 50
  religion of, 51
  sexual habits, 51
  skin color, 49, 147, 148
  sleep habits, 50
  vision, 159
African peoples
  barbarous tribes, 93
  cultural achievements of, 160
  disinclination toward agricultural work, 207, 208, 211
  governments of, 160
  mental capacity, 160
agricultural work
  agrarian society, 27
  disinclination of Africans toward, 207, 208, 211
  disinclination of American Indians toward, 207
American Indians
  artistic abilities, 50–51
  disinclination toward agricultural work, 207
  failure to prosper, 209
  instincts of, 205, 206
American Revolution
  ideological threat to slavery from, 15–16
  political threat to slavery from, 16–17
  racial equality and, 18–19
  slave enlistments, 16, 18
  social threat to slavery from, 17–18
animals
  dog breeds, 202–4
  slavery and, 145